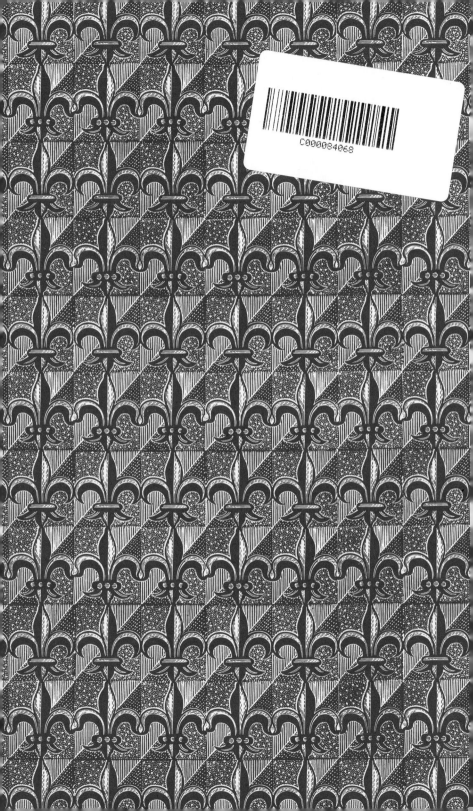

C000084068

Val Mauk,
Jan '84

THE SCHOLAR & THE GYPSY

Two Journeys to Turkey, Past and Present

James Howard-Johnston & Nigel Ryan

SINCLAIR-STEVENSON

TO
ANGELA HOWARD JOHNSTON
WHOSE IDEA IT WAS

First published in Great Britain by
Sinclair-Stevenson Limited
7/8 Kendrick Mews
London SW7 3HG England

Copyright © 1992 by James Howard-Johnston and Nigel Ryan

All rights reserved. Without limiting the rights under copyright reserved, no part
of this publication may be reproduced, stored in or introduced into a retrieval
system or transmitted, in any form or by any means (electronic, mechanical,
photocopying, recording or otherwise), without the prior written permission of
both the copyright owner and the above publisher of this book.

The right of James Howard-Johnston and Nigel Ryan to be identified as authors of
this work has been asserted by them in accordance with the Copyright, Designs
and Patents Act 1988.

British Library Cataloguing in Publication Data
A CIP catalogue record for this book is available from the British Library.

ISBN: 1 85619 133 8

Typeset by Rowland Phototypesetting Limited
Bury St Edmunds, Suffolk
Printed and bound in Great Britain by
Clays Ltd, St Ives plc

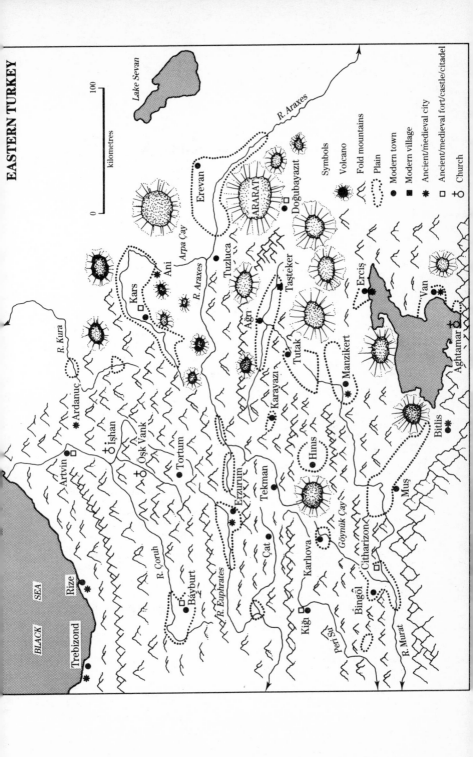

EASTERN TURKEY

Symbols

- ● Modern town
- ■ Modern village
- ✳ Ancient/medieval city
- □ Ancient/medieval fort/castle/citadel
- ☦ Church
- ✳ Volcano
- ⌇ Fold mountains
- ⬭ Plain

kilometres

0   100

Lake Sevan

R. Araxes

ARARAT

Doğubayazıt

Erevan

Arpa Çay

R. Araxes

Ani

Tuzluca

Kars

Ağrı

Tasteker

Erciş

Van

Tutak

Manzikert

Aghtamar

Karayazı

Bitlis

Ardanuç

İşhan

Osk Vank

Hınıs

Muş

Tortum

Artvin

Erzurum

Tekman

Çat

Cithanzon

R. Kura

R. Çoruh

Bayburt

R. Euphrates

Karlıova

Göynük Çay

Bingöl

Kiğı

Peri Su

R. Murat

BLACK
SEA

Trebizond

Rize

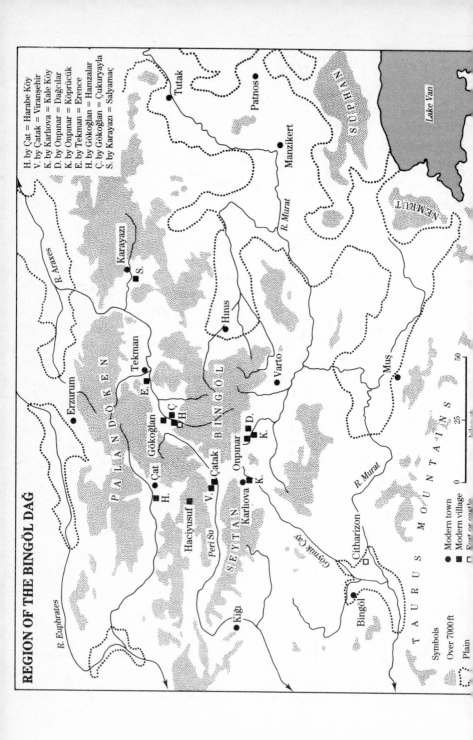

REGION OF THE BINGÖL DAĞ

H. by Çat = Harabe Köy
V. by Çatak = Viranşehir
K. by Karlıova = Kale Köy
D. by Onpınar = Dağcılar
K. by Onpınar = Köprücük
E. by Tekman = Erence
H. by Gökoğlan = Hamzalar
Ç. by Gökoğlan = Çukuryayla
S. by Karayazı = Salyamaç

Symbols

● Modern town
■ Modern village
□ Fort or castle

Over 7000 ft
Plain

0   25   50

Lake Van

SÜPHAN

NEMRUT

R. Araxes

R. Euphrates

PALANDÖKEN

Erzurum

Karayazı
S.

Tekman
E.

Çat
Gökoğlan
C
H
H.

BINGÖL

Haciyusuf

Peri Su
Çatak
V.
Onpınar
D.
K.
Karlıova
K.

ŞEYTAN

Kiğı

Bingöl

Citharizon

Göynük Çay

R. Murat

T A U R U S   M O U N T A I N S

Hınıs

Varto

Muş

Manzikert

Patnos

Tutak

R. Murat

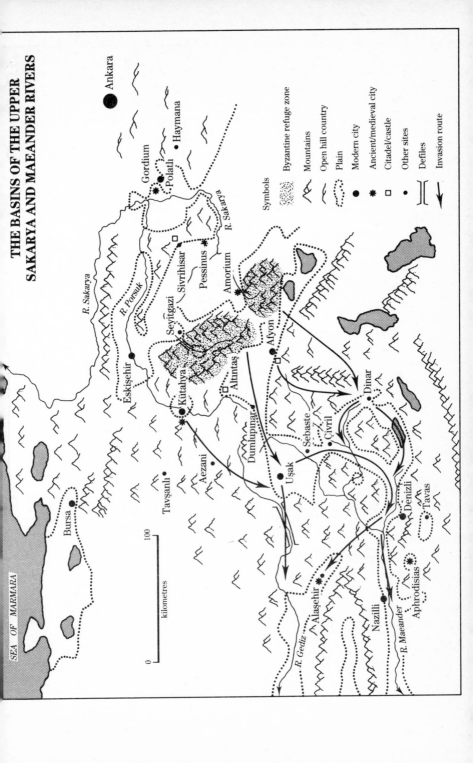

THE BASINS OF THE UPPER
SAKARYA AND MAEANDER RIVERS

Symbols

Byzantine refuge zone		
Mountains		
Open hill country		
Plain		
Modern city	●	
Ancient/medieval city	✳	
Citadel/castle	□	
Other sites	●	
Defiles		
Invasion route	→	

Ankara

Haymana

Gordium

Polatlı

Sivrihisar

Pessinus

R. Sakarya

Amorium

R. Sakarya

R. Porsuk

Seyitgazi

Eskişehir

Afyon

Kütahya

Altuntaş

Dinar

Dumlupınar

Sebaste

Çivril

Tavşanlı

Aezani

Uşak

Denizli

Tavas

Bursa

Nazilli

Alaşehir

Aphrodisias

R. Gediz

R. Maeander

SEA OF MARMARA

100

kilometres

0

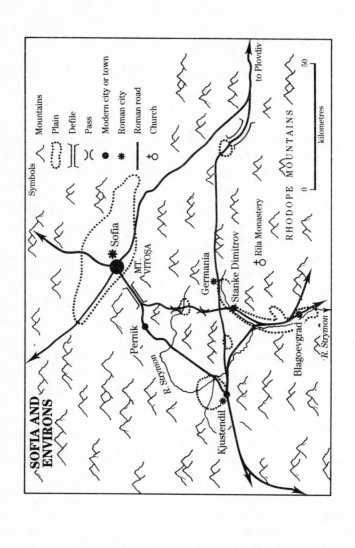

PREFACE

European travellers, foremost among them the English, have
been crisscrossing Turkey for several centuries. Their written
accounts form a sub-genre of European literature. Many of
them remain prime sources for the political and social conditions of the time, and for those many monuments which
have long since been digested by the local population and
transformed into houses, sheds and courtyard walls. The roll
call of names that have contributed to the sub-genre contains
some as exotic as the country they visited – among over 150
travellers who are listed as sources in a massive but highly
entertaining book on the Pontus are those of de Ferrières-
Sauveboeuf, Ouseley, von Klaproth, Hommaire de Hell and
Maw. There were, of course, many others who avoided the
rain-soaked northern shore of Anatolia and preferred to
range over the khaki-coloured uplands of the interior, reaching out into the southern mountains fissured by gigantic
canyons, or east into the volcanic landscape of Armenia.

Some were more loquacious than others. E. J. Davis, Angli-
can chaplain at Alexandria, wrote over 450 pages about the
three and a half months which he spent in the malarial plain
of Cilicia and the healthier Taurus highlands to the north in
1875. His is a marvellously informative and often evocative
account of natural scenery, classical monuments, contemporary social conditions, and the many vicissitudes and chance
encounters of travel. A generation earlier the young von
Moltke paid a much longer visit to the Ottoman high

command in the region of the Kurdish Taurus immediately to the east. His published letters about his experiences there are models of conciseness and lucidity. The ratio of words to time spent in eastern Turkey (at an average of twelve pages per month) is less than a tenth of Davis', but he manages to conjure up the places and people he saw, and to weave in observations on classical history no less effectively, while reserving considerable space for detailed accounts of military operations which he witnessed.

Modern travellers have introduced new strands into the sub-genre. There is that of the dreamy, bus-traveller who makes for a single destination in the east, but whose thoughts, as he does so, are so taken up by the experiences of past travellers that he fails to make many observations of his own. Or that of the erudite, intrepid, foot-slogging investigator of the wilder Kurdish country of the east, who has summarised the results of his researches over some twelve separate journeys in four weighty volumes, which between them cost not much less than £1,000.

Turkey, like the Arab lands, attracted adventurous spirits from the rapidly developing countries of Europe, because it was both exotic and accessible. Today it exercises as great a pull over the packaged tourists for rather different reasons – weather, price and the familiarity of the high-rise hotel. Old-style travellers with a genuine interest in the country, its past and its current Turkish and Kurdish populations must steer clear of the debased culture of the coastal strips in the west and south where their fellow-Europeans congregate in such large numbers. Elsewhere they can still find as varied a range of experiences as ever and can slip quickly across the occasional thoroughfares used by the supercharged coaches which transport the more discerning visitors to the main touristic sites of the interior.

Our two accounts add a new variant to the sub-genre. They have been written independently and are presented side by side to provide two contrasting points of view. The observations which they record often diverge and sometimes conflict. For however closely two travellers stick together, however alert they both are to the experiences which they share, differences of character and interest and patterns of thought will ensure that different selections of events are registered by each of them, that they are differently interpreted at the time, and that subsequently, as two minds get to work digesting the raw material, transforming it first into organised sets of memories and then into prose, markedly different accounts will be composed. That is certainly true of ours, which we have made no attempt to blend together.

Apart from the occasional factual discrepancy which we have not ironed out (mainly because we did not know which of us was right), our two versions of two successive journeys in different parts of Turkey, as well as a flying visit to Bulgaria on the eve of the collapse of the old order there, are far from indistinguishable. Nigel Ryan has reshaped the material into a more literary account. His is the more entertaining version, with its portrait (slightly touched up) of the Scholar at work. He has more to say about current events and allows emotion to tinge what he writes. I have stuck to the format of a journal, tried rigorously to exclude all emotion from the record of observations and lives in the past, conjuring history out of the fragmentary remains of late Roman and early medieval buildings. Nigel Ryan was, except for fleeting moments, extraordinarily relaxed and enjoyed himself to the full. I seldom succeeded in escaping completely from anxiety, if only about our future schedule, though there were occasions when I too was sucked into the present, overwhelmed by the atmosphere of a place or the hospitality of impoverished Kurdish hosts in the back of beyond.

We are confident that we have demonstrated in a minor way an obvious truth – that the lone eyewitness can never supply anything more than a partial view of reality, which will deviate further and further from it as the eyewitness recedes into the future. Only when the testimonies of a multitude of eyewitnesses are gathered and collated and rapidly fixed in writing, whether by a clutch of correspondents or an organised authority, is there any hope of achieving fullness and accuracy in reporting. This would not be worth saying, but for the strange fact that so many historians of the ancient world believe the contrary and find it hard to conceive of their classical predecessors relying on anything save what they term 'autopsy', i.e. the evidence of their own eyes and oral tradition.

We also have a few things to say about Turkey: first about an important phase in its history, extending from late antiquity to the high Middle Ages. Then an earlier epoch, when two heavily armed superpowers confronted one another in eastern Turkey on the eve of a final catastrophic conflict, will make an appearance in the following pages. So too will the Armenians in their early medieval heyday, the Byzantines as they fought a long guerrilla war for survival against the Arabs, and the Seljuk Turks whose conquest of Anatolia inaugurated a new age of economic and cultural development.

But we never ceased to be amazed and impressed by the country and the people we encountered. There are all sorts of minor absurdities, as well as the dark side of military rule in the east and the state's ceaseless attempts to obliterate Kurdish culture. But the energy and enterprise of the humblest of individuals, the pride and generosity of the countryman, the extraordinary surge of market forces and the success of the state in modernising the infrastructure of the whole country win the traveller's admiration. It is a country abuzz with life, where a man will travel 1,000 miles or more in search of work or profit. It is still a bastion of secularism, though under increasing attack from the Islamic revival. And it is one of the great powers of the Middle East, its population of well over fifty million easily outstripping that of any of its neighbours. These human resources, together with a military tradition which goes back to their steppe nomad origins and a geographical position which gives them control over the waters of the two great rivers of Iraq, will ensure that the Turks play an increasingly important part in the affairs of the region.

PART 1

TURKEY 1988

CHAPTER 1

A poultice of hot morning dust hung over Ankara's cracking concrete buildings as I arrived at the rendezvous. Ataturk's capital was already prostrated before the onslaught of another summer's day. Dressed in tweeds with black walking shoes, my travelling companion James Howard-Johnston was eating his breakfast in the hotel's dining room. He had a conspiratorial air. He came to the point at once:

'Have you brought the book?'

'Which book?'

'The one we discussed.'

'On Armenia? Certainly I have.' He winced and leaned forward.

'We don't use that word. You must get rid of it. I forgot to tell you.'

'It belongs to the London Library.'

'They will find it and assume we are terrorists.'

'Who will?'

'The Security Police. They will certainly pick up our trail.'

'I can leave it in the hotel.'

'As good as giving it to them. They'll search everything.'

It seemed ridiculous at first. After all, this was not Russia but Turkey, and our business was with the sixth century not the twentieth. The trouble, the Scholar explained, would be convincing the authorities. It was no joke. An academic colleague had recently been thrown into jail on the grounds that Byzantine research was a front for Armenian espionage. Following the attack on Ankara airport by Armenian terrorists in 1982, he had himself been forced by local police harassment to abandon research work in the area that was once Armenia. This prompted me to tell him of an exchange I had had at the Turkish Tourist Authority in London. I had told a lady assistant that I was planning an expedition with an Oxford historian to look for early Byzantine fortifications and wanted a good map of Turkish Armenia. I had been struck by the crispness of her response:

'There is no such area. It is called Eastern Turkey.' The Scholar turned pale.

'Did you give our names? They'll be on to us already. They have computers.' I said I had not, adding by way of lighter note:

'Just as well, I suppose, as my surname – Ryan – has a typical Armenian ending.' A look of frozen horror slowly transformed his features.

'Oh God,' he said.

It was a double initiation, into a dark corner of modern Turkish history, and a peculiar aspect of the Turkish character. The area that we were about to visit had been the scene of a massacre in 1915 after Ottoman Turkey had entered the Great War on the German side. On the pretext that they were fomenting trouble on the border with the Russian enemy, Turkey's Armenian population of a million people had been quietly exterminated. There was a deeper motive of long-standing racial and religious animosity towards a talented and doubtless troublesome Christian people who had settled in Turkey 1,500 years before the first Turks. The book I had brought – *Armenia: Story of a Nation* by Christopher Walker – described the orchestrated campaign of mass murder and deportation, and the plight of prosperous families turned overnight into destitute refugees, exposed to rape, kidnap, highway robbery and starvation. A few witnesses reached neighbouring countries like Syria. The body of evidence to support their story is overwhelming.

The official Turkish version of the massacre is that it never took place. Where others talk of genocide Turkish history books refer to the Resettlement Programme. To question it is taboo. The defence mechanism set off by this inconvenient episode has its roots in Turkish etiquette. To a people which

4

sets a high value on good manners, truth can be impolite.

By an irony of history Turkey's Russian neighbours paid a higher price for a more humane policy towards the Armenian population on their side of the border. By permitting a measure of autonomy they only succeeded in fanning the flames of separatism. Attempts by the Gorbachev regime to damp them down made matters worse, arousing the biblical wrath of a fierce race of early Christians more given to fighting than turning the other cheek, and even threatening the unity of the Soviet Union itself. The Turks were more astute: as any insurance agent knows, injury can be a more expensive claim to settle than death.

Meanwhile the ghosts of a million Armenians might yet come back to haunt Turkey if Europe were to demand a full confession of guilt, like the one extracted from Germany after the war, as a price for accepting it into the European Community. If so, how would Turks respond? What I was about to discover as I set out for these parts with the Scholar was that the Turkish mind-set was not a European one – far less so than Russia's – nor yet a wholly Asian one. It was Turkish, a fascinating blend of great talents and frightening defects, of sensibility, warmth and cruelty.

For glamour and mystery today's Trabzon compares with ancient Trebizond as Blackpool with Venice. The difference is that the first two are one and the same place. We awoke in the fabled city where the Argonauts stepped ashore, where Xenophon rested on his great march home, where Hadrian built a harbour, where Comnenus founded an empire that outlived Byzantium, to find ourselves in a dilapidated seaside resort in the off-season. From beyond the abandoned building site outside our hotel bedroom window the smell of mud reached us from the Black Sea. From the slowly descending lift we had ample time to take in the changing colour themes of each successive floor – aubergine, margarine, raspberry mousse – before joining a group of Dutch tourists eating their breakfast in silence in a room reminiscent of a wartime NAAFI.

5

A labyrinth of steep narrow streets led us down to a black patch of beach and the greying sea. A potholed dual carriageway ran along the front until it disappeared into a tunnel (dual carriageways are a symbol of urban prestige in Turkey). Beyond it was a fairground. A lone man in his sixties was riding on an old-fashioned roundabout to the sound of tinny music. Exuberant youths played a game of hand-operated table football. Small children gazed in rapture at shooting prizes beyond their reach. The driving belt on the big wheel had broken and suspended riders waited patiently while someone went to find a new one.

But if it was seedy, this was the seediness of poverty, not indifference: this region of Turkey had not yet imported decadence. My guidebook promised a recreation of the grandeur of ancient Trebizond in the partly restored church of Haghia Sophia on the outskirts of town. Here, it said, the great founding emperor himself may lie buried. Whether he does or does not, my eye sought in vain for grandeur among the damaged and rather crude frescoes until, directed by my scholar companion, it came to rest on the serene quartet of magnificent marble columns that form the basis of the church's cross-in-a-square plan.

Over lunch in a large empty restaurant with the television set turned on, the Scholar drew a map for me of the fortified enclosures on three different levels that guarded ancient Trebizond, making use of the natural defences provided by the steep ravines and the sea itself, and reinforced by massive walls, now reduced to ivy-covered remnants. Today Comnenus' palace is a broken ruin within the crumbling Byzantine citadel whose arches still tower above the modern town. The ancient churches stand in a wilderness set with white minarets, Rose Macauley's 'forlorn, lovely, ravished and apostate ghosts'. Some are wrecked, some have become grain stores, others mosques – all of which was only to be expected in a city that had been exclusively Moslem since the Greek population was expelled or slaughtered sixty years before in another unpublicised episode, officially called the 'Exchange of Minorities'.

That afternoon we set out south to cross the brooding

6

mountain barrier which traps the Black Sea towns against the shore giving them their subtropical climate. (My guidebook omitted to mention that it rains nearly every day of the year.) Heading up a deep cleft behind the town we entered a ravine of oppressive, dripping evergreens that reminded me of school walks. As we climbed the claustrophobia receded. The scenery underwent a dramatic change of scale. Precipices became steeper, gorges grander and more rugged. We were entering a world for giants.

After an hour we turned off the main road to visit the monastery at Sumela which clings by its fingertips to a vertical rock face many thousands of feet above the valley floor. It is approached for the last few hundred yards on foot along the edge of a heart-stopping precipice. Medieval masons carrying colossal blocks of stone had once made this same journey for the glory of God. So had Ron from Sheffield, only more recently and for his own glory: he had left his name and the date carved across the front of a fresco. We gazed at a grotto where medieval hermits, men of another clay, spent long cold winters, dependent on improbable pilgrims for their food. We were the last visitors of the day and we gave the caretaker a lift down the mountain. Good manners prevented him from letting his voice betray the smallest hint of urgency when he asked us, yet had we refused he would have had a two-hour walk. It was the first of many occasions that reminded me we were among a patrician race.

We came to a place where a recent landslide had buried a line of cars and a busload of tourists. We passed the spot where Xenophon's Ten Thousand, travelling in the opposite direction, caught sight of the sea and cried out in unison 'Thalassa! Thalassa!' Hereabouts, too, in 1855 the Turkish relief column that was to have raised the siege of the town of Kars by the Russians ran out of the will to continue, so that the British officers in charge of the defending garrison were forced to lay down their arms.

Soon the hairpin bends became more vertiginous and the road surface began to break up. We were an hour from the top of the pass when a night of blank ink fell on us. The Scholar was at the wheel; earlier signs had pointed to the highest standards of road safety. I had already noted the exemplary fastening of the seat belt when moving the car a matter of a few feet from one parking place to another, the foresight displayed in talk of filling up the petrol tank before it was half empty. There were special excursions each morning to check the oil (luckily the Scholar appeared not to know about tyre pressure). Here was a man to make sure his vehicle was left in gear, even on spirit-level flatness, lest the handbrake fail: whom the slightest incline would send off in search of a stone to place under the wheel. When it was my turn to drive I noticed that his voice rose a register as he inquired with agonised (if unfailing) politeness whether I had observed a forthcoming pothole: one man's pothole is another man's precipice. Better a nervous driver than a nervous passenger. I resolved that he should drive on through the night.

In the absence of a comprehensive railway system, Turkish lorry and bus traffic is heavy, night and day. As the eastern flank of Europe's defences – and the only place apart from a short stretch of Norway where the West directly confronted the Soviet Union – much money had been spent on communications in Cold War days. For the most part we found the roads surprisingly good. But there were gaps, and this stretch was one of them. As we climbed towards the watershed in the darkness the surface gave out. There were no parapets to mark the edge, and no signs to indicate where parts of it had collapsed into the blackness below. On one bend our headlights picked out a board of reflecting arrows, suitably sited but pointing in the wrong direction, towards and not away from eternity.

Lorry traffic grew denser. We caught up with a line of petrol tankers. Their drivers did not try to kill us, as they tend to in England when you wish to overtake, but instead affably waved us on into the blackness, emitting friendly blasts of their ocean-liner foghorns as we crept past. When we held back we were soon pressed from behind by another colossus and squeezed between the two until we summoned the courage to go forward. I think my companion was more afraid than I was; since he would certainly have been even more so as a passenger I was glad I had not insisted on sharing the task.

We stopped for the night at Torul, a village on the far side of the pass. To get our bearings we went out for a stroll. When we got back to the hotel the landlord was watching a television film of great violence with two dozen other men in a first-floor room. Their faces had the concentrated expression of children trying to learn something by heart. Every now and then there was a mutter of approval. After a moment I discovered that they were watching *Rambo II* dubbed into Turkish.

We awoke to find ourselves in another world. The balcony of our little room looked over a stream and towards a truly dizzying cliff face at the summit of which was a ruined fortress. This was the mountain down which we had zigzagged in the dark; the roar of straining lorries changing gear was borne to us on the fresh morning air. The country around us was at once drier now and more sparse. Gone were the oppressive evergreens and brooding clouds. We could see the start of the gorge where our road would shortly take us. Ahead were more swooping mountains.

The Scholar had spotted the fortress at once while my eyes took a little while to make it out. This brought home to me how ill-suited I was to help him in the task in hand, which he outlined over breakfast in the village *lokanta*, the all-day café–restaurant of traditional Turkey. In the sixth century, well before the birth of Mohammed, the Emperor Anastasius had set about reinforcing the borders of the Christian Byzantine Empire. In the east, where the Persians first swept through to conquer Greece, he built two large forts guarding the access to the valleys that run between the great east-west mountain ranges and lead to the Anatolian plain. It was the northernmost of these ranges that we had just crossed. Somewhere to the east of us in one of these valleys were the ruins of two mighty encampments: the more southern of the two was known as Citharizon. They had never been traced. Our mission was to find them.

The chronicler Procopius, a contemporary of Anastasius' great successor Justinian, had described the sites and the organisation and the building of the forts, in a six-volume account of the imperial building programme. The great work had been mastered by the Scholar and was now lodged verbatim, as far as I could tell, in his memory. Armed with knowledge of the characteristics and specifications of the forts he could now eye the terrain with an informed eye. The one above our window, for instance, was too far west and too small to be ours. Anastasius' had better access roads to supply or relieve it, and more elaborate provisions for withstanding a siege.

I asked why invading armies did not simply bypass the forts; the Scholar explained that they were centres from which Byzantine patrols would reconnoitre, and where powerful support forces were kept at the ready to deal with passing aggressors. Small forts like the local one would have been strongholds for lesser warlords to whom the region would pay money and goods for protection, and from whom greater princes would in turn exact dues.

As we bowled along the easterly road heading deep into Asia the Scholar told me how he had come to recognise his calling. As a child he had been interested in motor racing. He had subscribed to racing magazines, followed every race, learned about gear ratios and pistons and overhead valves, but never once felt the inclination to visit a racetrack or drive a racing car himself. After this he had decided that his talents lay in the realm of ideas.

The Scholar's vocabulary, interlarded with academic codewords, brought back to me a world briefly inhabited as an undergraduate. There were 'ascribing' and 'postulating' (i.e. guessing). There were 'arcane' (irrelevant) and 'embarrassing' (stupid). Research fell into several categories: 'rigorous' (reliable), 'modest' (unreliable), and 'distressingly modest', (the work of a rival). Then there was the academic death sentence reserved for an enemy's howler, passed down with raised eyebrows and a cry of triumph, in the single, terrible word: 'Wrong!'

But although he had turned his back on the world of action he had a well-developed practical streak. Procopius was not the only string to his bow. He had also brought to bear an ingenious new aid: German military maps. As allies and advisers to the Ottoman forces in the First World War, the Kaiser's strategists, like Anastasius before them, had grasped the strategic importance of eastern Turkey and, thorough in all things, they made sure they had good maps. These the Scholar had tracked down in the archives of the Bodleian Library in Oxford. Noticing that a number of different places all bore the same name; *harabe*, he looked the word up in a Turkish dictionary and found it to mean 'ruins'. A handful of *harabes* were located in areas compatible with the descriptions of Procopius. Armed with modern maps bearing a series of red crosses in the Scholar's neat handwriting, some of them well off the nearest road, we now set out. In the past archeology had little meaning for me; for one to whom Babylon had resembled a bombed-out brick factory, I was now strangely excited.

We were losing height now and heading east, towards the town of Erzurum, and the old north–south frontier between Roman Byzantium and Persia. Here our search would begin. As we descended the gorge the colours grew richer. Rust-red tinges betraying the presence of minerals flashed in the sunlight falling high above us on the rock face. The Scholar informed me there were no less than twenty words in Turkish for the varying shades of ochre. Once again the Scholar drove and, with his customary foresight, pressed the horn to warn a flock of birds of our approach. It rose from the road ahead, and settled elegantly again behind us like a black-and-white speckled carpet. Then we came to a chicken standing in the middle of the road. Hooting once more, the Scholar advanced. The bird stood its ground. Mindful of tales of the fate of travellers caught killing Turkish chickens, the Scholar braked and swerved. Still it did not move, but remained apparently oblivious of our existence as we passed by. I felt quietly pleased with the creature which, blind, deaf or mad, had chalked up a small triumph for anarchy.

At Bayburt we paused to look at the little town's magnificent medieval walls. We were accosted in the street by a smartly dressed boy, who replied to the Scholar's questions in elementary English which he was learning at school. Soon we were sitting in his father's tailor's shop drinking tea. The Scholar's wife, loyal but with limited knowledge of Turkey (of which until recently she had believed the capital to be Interpol), had told me that her husband had the advantage of being able to speak to Turks fluently. This was a relief to me, since I had a vocabulary of three or four words. It now became apparent that, though strictly accurate, her statement needed clarification. The Scholar indeed spoke fluently to Turks, but only partly in Turkish. He evidently belonged to the school holding that if you spoke clearly and speak up, foreigners will understand English. I was the principal beneficiary, finding his conversation relatively easy to follow. He had launched into a discussion of the relative costs of a Turkish and a Savile Row suit, touching on the workings of Value Added Tax. Eager to impress his father with his knowledge of English, the boy nodded knowingly. Warming to his subject the Scholar began waving his hands. Every now and then the boy said 'Really' in English and turned to say something in Turkish to his father, but with growing lack of conviction. Either misled by the gestures resembling those of a fisherman describing his catch, or misinformed by the son, the tailor clearly had got the impression that the Scholar wished to be measured for a suit. He rose, indicated his bales of cloth and said something to the Scholar. I thought it wise to warn him of my suspicion. The Scholar acted at once, raising a deprecating hand in a gesture of old-world courtesy.

'Unfortunately,' he said in English, 'we really must be on our way.' And with a flurry of exchanged addresses, we departed.

At Bayburt we crossed the Çoruh, the last of the rivers that empty their waters into the Black Sea. Soon we would be close to the source of the Euphrates, which begins its long journey through Syria and Iraq to the Persian Gulf in the hills to the north of Erzurum. After that we would come to the Araxes that carries the rains of Eastern Turkey along the border with the Soviet Union and then through Soviet Azerbaijan until it reaches the Caspian. We had turned our backs on the West.

Stopping at random in the dusty centre of Erzurum, the former capital of the Roman sector of Armenia, we walked into the first restaurant we saw. It had the tumbledown, defeated look that in Europe would be a conventional sign for really bad food. Our reward was one of the best meals I can remember, of *döner kebab* lamb cooked on a brazier, of *ayran* – a yoghourt drink that was to become indispensable to every meal – an aubergine confection known as the *imam bayıld* (as light and fresh as it was cloying and heavy the last time I had had it in London's smartest Greek restaurant), and a sweet pudding called *kataif*. It offered an object lesson to travellers in strange lands to suspend preconceived ideas: don't look at Asia with European eyes. I understood now why Turkish cuisine was mentioned in the same breath as French. It is not a skill learned by an élite, but part of a national culture practised at every level and has passed uninterrupted down the generations.

After lunch I proposed a visit to the social hub of life in most Turkish towns, the bus station. It was like ones I had already seen in Ankara, Konya and Izmir, and unlike any outside Turkey. More souk than transport terminal, the typical Turkish bus station operates on model market-force principles. It is divided into rival enterprises, each with a small kiosk where men tout tickets under bright, illuminated signs advertising destinations all over the country. Behind each kiosk is a restroom where the staff smoke and drink tea between departure times. One of the restrooms at Erzurum had a print of 'The Monarch of the Glen' on its wall. As departure time approaches animation reaches fever point.

Travel is extraordinarily cheap. That summer the 800–mile trip from Erzurum to Izmir cost the equivalent of roughly £8. At £1 for 100 miles, it is not surprising that travel is a national pastime. Turks – originally a Nomadic race, after all – appear to live in the grip of a ceaseless unrest. Travel is not so much

13

a journey as a way of life, nourished by a bus system reaching into every corner of the country. Printed timetables are unnecessary. Buses set off between most main centres regularly every hour on the hour or half hour. They also tend to operate with disconcerting punctuality. Such was the zeal of its driver that one I had taken recently left ten minutes early stranding several passengers. The buses themselves, made in Japan and Germany, and bearing names on their smart new livery like 'Superman Turbo' and 'Diesel Direct Injection,' thunder along the highways at sixty miles an hour, sometimes side by side. Most of them are comfortable and many equipped with air conditioning (a disadvantage in hot weather, since it tends to be turned off to save fuel and the windows are hermetically closed). Every hour or so eau de cologne is brought round to cool the passengers' hands and faces. On longer journeys there are stops at caravanserais – Turkey's answer to Trust House Forte's motorway pull-ins – where free tea is served with often delicious and extraordinarily cheap cafeteria meals. Meanwhile the bus, like its predecessor the camel, is watered and scrubbed down. No Turk would lavish such care on his house.

If Turkish bus stations (called *otogars*, presumably after the French '*auto*' and '*gare*') give the impression of a nation on the move, they also offer an unrivalled vantage point for observing local life. In Kayseri I witnessed a soccer hero being carried shoulder high on to a bus after a spontaneous display of dancing by his fans. At Nevşehir I had become absorbed by the spectacle of an old peasant man with benevolent blue eyes gazing impassively at a bus, the embodiment of rock-like patience; and at his side holding his hand a surprisingly fair-haired small boy, perhaps a grandson, crying with the full force of his lungs. I never knew the cause of the tears, only the sense of heart-break. The boy, too, was looking into the bus into which a woman – his mother? – and a young man – his elder brother off to do national service? – had disappeared. Every now and then he tugged at the horny old hand, as if by changing his position he could hope to ease his anguish. The pair did not move until the bus had vanished from view. The image of them haunted me insistently for several weeks. A shred for a novel, perhaps?

Erzurum's *otogar* did not let us down. Families with children and baskets sat propped against the wheels of their Superman, talking, waiting. The men carried plastic bags (suitcases seemed to run out somewhere east of Ankara). In the covered hall a Greek lady had spread a map on which Kurdish women were showing her where they lived. I had the impression that none of them, including the Greek lady, could understand the map, but this in no way impaired their enjoyment.

Set in a high plateau between higher mountain ranges Erzurum has the rough-and-ready look of a garrison town. It was fought over and held in turn by Armenians, Persians, Greeks, Romans, Arabs, Byzantines, Turks and Mongols, and three times – the last in 1916 – by Russians; but the Turks have obliterated nearly all traces of the other conquerors. In its centre we saw the first of the cone-shaped roofs atop the pillbox tombs characteristic of this part of Asia. (The Scholar told me there was Mongol influence in the style: I noticed it again in Georgian and Armenian churches we were to see later.) Under the portals of the early fourteenth-century *medrese* (theological school), my eye was caught by two Turkish sightseeing ladies who were clearly eating a snack underneath their *yashmaks* (veils).

In the ruins of another thirteenth-century *medrese* built into the city walls we were accosted by our second self-appointed guide of the day, who turned out to be from the same English class at Erzurum as the boy from Bayburt. He appeared delighted to learn that the Scholar came from Oxford.

'Is he very rich?' he asked me. I thought for a moment.

'He is very clever.'

The boy indicated the *medrese*'s medieval refectory and asked the Scholar if he had a dining room like it in his house.

'Much smaller,' said the Scholar. Our guide shook his head.

'Not so rich,' he said.

Leaving the plain of Erzurum we turned south down the line of the ancient frontier. Somewhere in the foothills of the formidable ranges and volcanoes ahead lay our objective. The first of the little red crosses marked on the Scholar's map indicated a spot just south of the village of Çat (which my guidebook's Turkish Primer Appendix had taught me to pronounce to rhyme with the English 'chat').

We reached Çat just before dark and took a room in the first of a number of minute hotels. It cost the equivalent of just under £1. In the main street the shops, including several blacksmiths, were still open for business, as were two mosques and a hall where a game like bingo was in progress. A flag flying outside a new building in a sidestreet with a wireless aerial on its roof indicated the presence of security forces. We were entering a sensitive zone.

I was becoming fond of my guidebook's foibles. Its Turkish Mini-Conversational Phrases Appendix devoted space to ordering meals (including 'Is the tripe soup old?'), motoring ('This car does not work. It needs sparking plugs, oil, petrol, tyres, brakes.'). There was a page of polite conversation about the health of Turks encountered. The shopping section included the word for gold (to become unexpectedly useful) and a sample phrase meaning: 'This carpet is very cheap', which seemed likely to be less useful than the opposite which, along with 'hayır', the word for 'no', did not figure.

Nor, more to the point at this juncture, was there a word for lavatory paper. The natural method of communication, in the absence of words, was by gesture. The possibility of misunderstanding that might arise in this particular instance in a strange Turkish village was already formidable enough. It was compounded by the relative rarity of the product. Turks use water, except where plumbing is westernised. Believing I had hit on a solution I started off along the little main street with pencil and sketchpad. At the first shop I was offered tea and on producing my drawing invited to purchase a tablecloth. Another showed me cigarette paper; a third a packet of paper table napkins, for which, under duress, I settled.

Dinner that night was not a success. Most *lokantas* cook at midday and serve the leftovers for dinner. At Çat's single *lokanta* these consisted of a chicken stew in which could be identified gizzard, windpipe, liver and claws. It was almost the only time we rose hungry from a Turkish table.

Breakfast looked like leftovers from the night before. However, disappointment in no way affected the good manners nor the good English of the Scholar, who completed an inspection of the kitchen by announcing with a courtly flourish: 'Quite delicious, I am sure, but I really believe it is more than I could possibly manage at this time of the morning, thank you very much. *Hayır*. No, thank you.'

I drove slowly while the Scholar kept watch for the tiny side road to the first red cross on his map. So far we had behaved as normal tourists. Turkish men regularly travel in pairs, so that in most places we visited the Scholar and I were accepted for what we were, as *arkadaş* – travelling companions. But now we were about to leave the beaten tourist track.

We came to the turning within a few hundred yards of where the Scholar had predicted, and bumped along a cart track following the contour of a hill. There, too, was the stream marked on the map. We left the car by a bridge and walked along the edge of a field where men were gathering the harvest. A heavily laden cart with solid wooden wheels passed us, drawn by a buffalo.

'*Gez*,' said the Scholar, waving cheerfully to the driver, a wizened, biblical figure.

'What is *gez*?' I inquired.

'It means "I am just taking a short walk".' At that moment a large guard-dog got to its feet where the harvesters were at work and started baying. The men looked up. '*Geziyorum*,' called the Scholar, waving again. 'Just going for a little stroll,' he added in English. The mastiff stopped baying and took a bound in our direction, snarling. 'They're quite friendly here,' said the Scholar, still waving and smiling. I noticed, however, that his step quickened perceptibly.

Soon we came to the lower slope of a hill girdled by what to my eye could have been either rock or masonry. The top of the hill commanded a view of the river and a cleft in the hills to the east. It was the sort of place we were looking for. The Scholar walked round the summit of the hill. There was no sign of man-made building. I kept my own counsel while he paced distances, gazed at the ground, sized up the configuration, studied the horizon, and finally decided to return to the car. We descended in silence, braving Cerberus once more. At the car the Scholar started: 'Where's the map? I must have left it on the hill.'

As we searched it struck me that its red crosses, whether construed as secret messages, meeting places or buried treasure, were every bit as incriminating as my banned history book. Added to this the Scholar had brought a Russian camera to complete our portfolio of impeccable KGB credentials.

I found the map not far from where we had begun our retreat from the guard-dog. As we set off again, a herd of goats ran across our path, in the charge of a boy of about nine years old – one of millions who seemed to supply the slave labour of eastern Turkey. The Scholar asked the name of the nearest village. The child flinched as we addressed him, as if expecting to be cuffed.

'Harabe,' he said.

'Ruins!' said the Scholar triumphantly. 'It's called Ruins!'

I asked cautiously: 'Does that mean this could be it?'

'Good heavens, no. It means the research work is sound.' The morning's work had been an object lesson in the distinction between journalism and scholarship.

The next red cross was a good hour's drive away. Arriving at a hilltop village, there was evidence of a small fort, but the site was too small to fit the description of Procopius. Before leaving I offered the village children a ride in the car: but the men soon pushed them out and got in instead. The children were resigned to the natural law, but I made one friend by insisting on taking a small boy in the front and making him help me change gear. He was transfixed with wonder, causing his nose to dribble on to the gear lever.

We lunched at Bingöl, a depressed-looking town noted for earthquakes. The local volcano bearing the same name stands at the junction of two great natural faults in the earth's surface: the upper extension of the Rift Valley that runs south to the Serengeti in southern Africa, and the east–west line of volcanoes that passes through Santorini in Greece to Ararat and Soviet Armenia. Under the circumstances it seemed unfair to blame the city planning authorities for not trying harder to please the eye. The town reminded me of the joke about a rundown place where the safest spot in an earthquake is said to be the hotel lift, the only object guaranteed to remain permanently stationary. But there was no question of a lift, stationary or otherwise, when we checked into our modest *otel*. We dumped our bags and went to explore.

Outside in the streets we were conscious of the presence of armed police: we even came across two women officers with pistol holsters, striding cheerfully by. It was hot and we decided to buy hats. Some boys following us in the street offered to sell us theirs, addressing us in pidgin German. One asked me if I came from Blackpool. Finally we found a pair of straw hats, the Scholar's far too small for his cranium.

In the afternoon we turned once more to Byzantine research. Heading for the next batch of the Scholar's neat red crosses we turned off the main road about ten miles east of Bingöl and drove along a track until we came to Yeni Köy – New Village – built to house Kurds made homeless by a recent earthquake. After fording a river, we came to a village path lined neatly on both sides with corrugated roofed houses, each with its own tiny walled courtyard in front.

An old Kurd greeted us with the natural warmth of his race. When we asked the way to Harabe Köy, he offered to guide us. It turned out to be a dozen miles away and there was no sign of a castle. The inhabitants told us of other ruins. There was a long discussion in which the Scholar nodded vigorously and made gestures of dawning comprehension. I asked him what was being said.

'Not the foggiest,' he replied.

A man drew an Armenian cross, which excited our interest, and led us down a precipice to a patch of ground that had once been tended: it turned out to be a disused cemetery. Light was failing as we set off for the next site, across fields

19

better suited to rough grazing than motoring. We stuck in mud, gave up and turned back. Our guide invited us to have tea in his garden, and we sat on chairs in a circle, served by his wife, a shy smiling woman with fine bones and weather-beaten face, dressed in the Kurdish manner in bright, contrasting primary colours.

We were joined by several villagers. A charming man in his sixties with sad eyes and moustache introduced himself as Sefket Durak. He had worked with an American company, spoke some English and chainsmoked. It is a common belief among Turkish peasants that when the Armenians departed they left buried gold behind, so the interest of our new acquaintances in archeology matched our own. Age had made Sefket more sceptical than the other inhabitants. With a world-weary shrug he said it was the dream of every ignorant Turk to find gold so as to go and work in Germany, amass a fortune and return to live forever in comfort. Evidently they had not heard the tales about the exploitation of Turkish *Gästarbeiter* in Germany. They were better off with dreams.

While we were talking we noticed two well-cut stones, each about one metre wide by half a metre high, lying beside the garden wall: on one was carved an Armenian cross similar to the ones we had seen earlier that afternoon. Sefket explained that the village had been built in part from masonry from a local site he described as a quarry – but the villagers had already searched it and there was no gold. We said that in spite of the lack of gold we would like to see the quarry. We would return early next day.

Soccer was a relatively new craze among Turks, but what they lacked in knowledge they made up in enthusiasm. On our stroll in the centre of town in search of dinner we spotted 'MANCESTER 3 UNITED 0' (*sic*) chalked on a wall. In the restaurant, opposite the monstrous modern block of the Security Directorate, ours were the only eyes not turned to the television set showing a match between teams from Istanbul and Vienna. From the silence around us greeting each

20

roar from the crowd we deduced that it was an away match and that the Turks were being trounced.

Being the place of his harassment on his previous trip, Bingöl had bad memories for the Scholar. These, combined with the overpowering presence of the Security Directorate made us uncomfortably conscious of the police activity on the street as we walked home. Passing a telephone box the Scholar decided to try to call to Oxford. While I was idling outside in the dark two policemen strolled by me, fingering their weapons. One said something into his portable walkie-talkie, but his voice was quickly drowned in a roar of voices from a nearby café. Evidently Turkey had scored. Outside our hotel we found a police car parked with two men in the front seat intently watching the entrance. With mounting unease we climbed the steps. In the dining room beside the lobby the hotel staff and guests were sitting in silence watching the soccer match. Then, as we looked out of the window, the explanation dawned on us. The television set was in direct line of sight from the front seat of the police car.

We reached Yeni Köy early for the rendezvous to find that a crowd had gathered round our guide's house, including a fat man wearing a woollen fez who looked remarkably like Peter Ustinov, and a shifty, unshaven Cassius figure with pebble-thick tinted glasses. The Scholar and I concluded that this would be the Secret Police representative. A certain formality had crept in. There was tea in the garden, then an interminable wait while more dignitaries arrived. Teenagers were climbing on top of one another to get a better view of us over the garden wall.

The sun was high when we finally set off, the grander members of the expedition in the car, others on foot. We crossed the ford, drove a few hundred feet across a field and stopped. It was clearly impassable. This seemed to come as a surprise to the villagers, who apparently assumed that such an unthinkable luxury as a car must be able to pass anywhere at least as easily as a humble horse and cart. We got out and walked.

Sweat poured from our foreheads as we climbed the steep slope on to a hill, similar to the one we had seen at Çat, only larger, and with a neck of land linking it to a ridge of hills to the south, thus perfectly matching the specifications of Procopius. The top was a flat surface 400 by 100 paces: it had a commanding view of the surrounding landscape, and unassailable precipices on three of its sides. Strewn round most of the circumference there was rubble, with occasional signs of masonry intact. It did not require the look of excitement on the Scholar's face to tell me that we had found one of Anastasius' forts.

I had never been present at a moment of great discovery. My previous experiences were all secondhand. I had been brought up on Tutankhamen (a distant uncle-archeologist was involved). With my contemporaries I had followed the exploits of Edmund Hillary and Neil Armstrong. But here was our very own discovery. I was in at the kill – and with the added luxury, unlike space travel or mountaineering, of a guaranteed return ticket. I was unashamedly thrilled.

The Scholar had every right to be. Excitement has different manifestations. In his case it appeared to bring out a need to communicate. Marching up and down and gesticulating he addressed whole sentences in English to the nearest bystander: 'This is extremely exciting' and 'This is far bigger than I had expected', and once: 'It is a great deal more important than any of us had hitherto anticipated'. Even at the moment of climax his syntax never faltered.

The villagers looked nonplussed.

Sefket said, 'I think your friend is very happy,' as if he thought him drunk. The man in pebbled glasses took him to one side. I heard the word '*altın*'. Sefket told me, 'He thinks your *arkadaş* has found gold.'

'As good as gold.'

'I think he must be taking a holiday today to celebrate.'

We spent an hour on the site, the villagers and I watching respectfully while the Scholar took photographs with his KGB camera, making measurements and drawings. We disturbed some indignant goats taking their siesta under the remnant of a well-built, three-course stone wall. The Scholar showed me where the grain and water would have been stored, and how reinforcements would have reached the camp – all evidence

22

that this was indeed the Citharizon described by Procopius. I picked up a stray piece of tiling for carbon dating in Oxford and was scolded by the Scholar for vandalism. When I pointed out that the entire site had been plundered to build the village he said nothing (nor did he seem to disapprove when I later produced the fragment in Oxford).

We returned to Yeni Köy, where the Scholar held court with his band of still mystified explorers over a tin of Dundee cake I had brought from London. (They did not seem to think much of it.)

Mulling over the day's events Sefket said, 'The castle is old. I think it is a hundred years old.'

'More than a thousand,' I said.

'The first part of the sixth century,' said the Scholar.

Sefket looked at us blankly, so I wrote the date '1988' on my pad and showed it to him, saying, 'Today.' Then I wrote '520' beneath it. But the Scholar was having none of this fudging.

'The precise date is unknown. It was founded somewhere in the mid–520s. Mid–520s,' he repeated, turning to Sefket and enunciating clearly. It was another triumph for scholarship over journalism.

We lingered for an hour, while the lady of the house rocked a whole sheep's skin slung from a tree to and fro to make curds. The Scholar told Sefket that the Kurdish people, like the Armenians, had been in Turkey far longer than the Turks, which seemed to surprise them. This led the conversation to politics and religion in Britain as well as in Turkey, and so to an inevitable topic.

'Tatcher?' said Sefket.

Not for the first time I noted that the more male-orientated the society the more the British Prime Minister seemed to be held in awe. The Scholar (a one-time Labour councillor) said he thought her a strong woman but did not support her. Sefket asked how this could be, since she was a member of the same church. The Scholar explained that voting does not follow a religious pattern in Britain and the Kurd shook his head in wonderment. The conversation turned back to gold and we took our leave.

23

Nothing could either mar or surpass the excitement of the discovery at Yeni Köy, so we coasted through the rest of the day, heading north again until we came to the little town of Tekman.

Tekman seemed sinister from the moment we drove up to its little roundabout. We were kept waiting for fifteen minutes at the first *otel* by an unsmiling proprietor before he slid a key across his desk and indicated the way upstairs with a jerk of his head. Upstairs proved to be a large, unlit room with several dirty beds and an evil-smelling privy. Honouring a silent vow to complain of nothing throughout the trip, I risked electrocution to exchange the shattered light bulb with another from the hall. It did not work either. Reluctantly the proprietor gave us some candles; but by now the Scholar had spotted another *otel* sign, and we were soon installed in marginally better quarters in a room giving on to the street at a point where two steaming manure lorries were parked for the night.

Whilst we were waiting to go out to dinner, a man who had been listening to us talking dragged a chair towards us across the floor blackened with peat.

'Clearly he understands English,' said the Scholar. He asked the man how far it was to Çukuryayla, the next village marked with a red cross. There was a long reply in Turkish. 'In other words, not in the immediate vicinity?' said the Scholar.

As we prepared for bed I asked the Scholar what plans he had to announce his find. He explained the need for an academic to have a learned paper published in his name. My last sight of him before I fell asleep was of a head still as a bust as he sat, bolt upright, writing up his notes by the light of the bare bulb suspended from our ceiling.

Then, in a rapid sequence, two things happened. The door burst open to let five men in, one of whom said: 'Passpo-orrt.' Among the faces I recognised the man whom we had asked the way to Çukuryayla. Next, all the lights went out. The Scholar was the first to recover his wits. Out of the darkness came his calm, authoritative voice:

'Good evening, gentlemen.'

24

There was a silence. I fumbled in the dark for the candles I had been given by the rejected hotel proprietor. Meanwhile someone found a match. Then the lights went on again.

'Passpo-orrt,' said the leader of the group. The Scholar now rose slowly to his feet and drew himself to his full height. With index finger extended towards the ceiling he addressed the intruders in ringing tones:

'Elsewhere that we have visited in Turkey – whether Ankara, Istanbul, Trabzon, Erzurum, even Bingöl – there has been no question whatever of surrendering documents' – the minatory finger was raised again – 'let alone the passport.'

There was another silence. I reached for my notebook to record the Scholar's oratory, Danton confronting the People's Court.

'Passpo-or-rt,' said the leader again.

'Are you suggesting . . . ?'

'Passpo-or-rt,' said the man. At this point the lights went out yet again. Yet again by the light of a match the Scholar remonstrated, but by now we had lost the advantage of surprise. The group absolutely wanted to take him off to the *jandarma* to have our passports inspected. It was a fine night. I felt an unaccountable serenity of spirit. Or perhaps I had learned a lesson from the driving. At all events, reasoning that the Scholar was more than a match for the local bureaucracy, I decided to let him handle the mission alone. Handing him my passport, I rolled over and was soon once more soundly asleep.

As far as I could judge he was back in about half an hour. He was exultant.

'It's a wonderful sky. You should look at the sky. You can watch stars you have never seen before.'

'What about the police?'

'The *jandarma* weren't interested.' It seemed that the townsfolk had observed our suspicious ways, our car with its Istanbul number plates which marked us out as foreigners, and had decided to report us. The *jandarma* – appointed as a matter of policy from other regions of the country – were more used to tourists and had simply shrugged their shoulders.

I hoped the incident would allay some of the Scholar's fears of being followed. So far at least no one had alerted the local police to watch for two Armenian agents disguised as Western tourists. But it still left unexplained the heavy army and police presence in the area. Eastern Turkey was beginning to take on the appearance of an occupied country, but we later learned it had nothing to do with Armenians. A little more than a hundred miles south of where we were, thousands of Kurdish refugees were at that moment streaming across the border from Iraq, fleeing from chemical weapons dropped on them by the Iraqi air force. Television later showed evidence of whole families hiding in mountain caves which had perished as the heavy, deadly fumes turned them into extermination chambers. The deaths were horrible.

It is the historic fate of minorities to be punished twice – once by being born without a freehold to their own home; and again by being persecuted when they demand their rights. Now it was the turn of the Kurds, deprived of a homeland by Turkey, Iraq and Iran, to suffer. Anxious to improve a dismal human rights' record (and thereby improve its chances of being accepted into the European Community), the Turkish government had let the refugees from Iraq in and housed them in camps. However, with the flood of civilians came members of a hardline nationalist group which refused to learn Turkish or compromise with the authorities over their demand for full recognition, as well as killing other Kurds who did.

The army and police were taking the threat seriously. Turks had reason to know that Kurds make good killers: they had used them a generation earlier to massacre the Armenians. Eventually the Turkish government hit on a simple way to finesse their dilemma by despatching the refugees across the border into Iran. There they would be welcomed by a regime that had long used its own Kurdish minority to stir up Iraqi Kurds against the Baghdad government. But these quietly murderous developments, all part of the small change of Middle Eastern politics, were unknown to us as we set off for the next little red cross on the map, only too happy to show Tekman a clean pair of heels.

We paused by the roadside, near a village where the dung for winter fuel was piled higher than the houses and the grain higher than either. We opened a mystery jar bought the night before and found it to contain strawberry jam free of pectin, delicious but volatile, that escaped on to the seat of the car and my trousers. We ate it with fresh bread. We continued westwards into the volcanic range of the Bingöl Dağ, following the river Araxes to its source. Soon we were back on another sector of the north–south line of the old Byzantine frontier, near where the second fort might be.

The villagers of Çukuryayla eagerly showed us to the house of a young man with strong jaw and white teeth who offered us tea in an elegant room with wooden casement windows and cushions and rugs on the floor. It reminded me of the once-prosperous farm houses of Afghanistan. There was a photograph on the wall of the owner in military uniform. Friendliness turned to curiosity, and curiosity to gold fever when we mentioned ruined forts. The young man wanted the Scholar's map with marks showing the buried treasure. The now-familiar symptoms made the Scholar uneasy. We thanked them and left.

We made several more stops on our way east to Van. One was at Salyamaç, to investigate reported ruins of a 'city' which turned out to be caves that had been thoroughly sacked, beyond which the villager accompanying us said there were other ruins. When his original estimate of 'only a few minutes' walk' turned into 'only a few more hours' we formally abandoned the search for forts. From now onwards we were simple tourists.

Our second stop was for tea at Tutak, on a junction of two roads, one running north-east to the Soviet Union and the other south towards Van. It proved to be a typical small Eastern Turkish town, basically conservative, paying lip service to progress. By now we knew the signs. At the approach to a Turkish town of any size the excellent state-funded highway widened into a stretch of dual carriageway ending in a roundabout (maybe two, funds permitting). At this point the tarmac would run out, together with the local funds for urban planning. At Tutak the main street was so pitted that it was

27

possible for only one car at a time to lurch and bump its way among its deep mud trenches. People stood talking in the middle of the street taking no notice as we threaded our way round them. We stopped for tea. The two buildings paid for by the state dominated the town: a new Emniyet (Security Directorate) and an imposing post office.

A platoon of young soldiers marched by with shaven heads and high swinging arms shouting the count of their steps: 'One! . . . Two! . . . Three! . . . Four! . . . ,' up to ten and starting again. Their marching song might be unimaginative, but they looked tough and disciplined. Most of the men around us wore hats. There was a roughly equal mixture of flatcap and fez (usually knitted wool) – regarded as symbols of the struggle within Turkey since the end of the Ottoman Empire, the flatcap for secular progress, the fez for pious tradition: Ataturk versus Allah, Army versus Church, West versus East. The fez had staged a comeback, echoing Moslem resurgence elsewhere, since Ataturk's Hat Law of 1925 banning it. My guidebook admirably summarised the very Turkish hat affair, explaining that Turks have always been sharp dressers, and hats have long played a role in affairs of state. In 1460 Mehmet the Conqueror enacted a law stipulating the colours of turbans at court: green for vizirs, red for chamberlains, white for muftis, red, yellow or black for everyone else except infidels, who were not allowed a turban at all. There was a shoe law, too, black for Greeks, blue for Jews, violet for Armenians. Ironically the fez despised by Ataturk had itself been introduced as a symbol of reform in the nineteenth century to replace the traditional turban. By the time the Scholar and I arrived on the scene things had moved on a stage. Moslem consciousness was on the increase: we came across signs of piety in the appearance of new mosques (often with corrugated iron minarets), and in the increasing number of restaurants which did not serve alcohol. But the hat war was confined to the east where Kurds traditionally wear flat-caps. In the west most Turks, like most European men, don't wear hats at all and the chief purchasers of the fez are tourists.

There was a commotion in the crowd as we rose to leave.

Three policeman were heading along the pavement towards a doorway, in the wake of a young man who was the centre of attention, neatly dressed with coat slung over his shoulders. All eyes were drawn to him. He looked disdainfully in our direction as he passed, and I assumed he was a leader of some sort of group. Then I noticed that he was wearing handcuffs. I thought of the young man again later when we drove by a barracks on a hillside surrounded by barbed wire and watchtowers – a terminal building with no runway – and recalled films of Turkish prison life. Probably the youthful prisoner had been dressed up for the occasion for the benefit of prying eyes. But whatever treatment he had received his pride had not been taken from him. We never knew his crime. Perhaps he was a thief. He did not look a terrorist. But then there is no reason why a terrorist should.

CHAPTER 2

The historian must be a ceaseless traveller. Every working day he rises, feeds, takes a bath for inspiration (if he has learned how a few precious moments of idle immersion can write whole chapters, thanks to the ambient heat which draws ideas up to the conscious surface of the mind), makes his way to office, study or library, and there prepares for the long trajectories through time and space to his subject. Those whose travels take them to the outer reaches of Europe in a relatively remote period encounter many more hazards than their colleagues whose interests are confined to the familiar, indeed rather parochial world of north-west Europe in the recent past. It is often hard to see anything when they arrive at their destinations, so scanty can the evidence be. A greater mental effort is required to escape from the gravitational field of their own culture and enter the strange *imaginaire* of a long-vanished people. Few individuals come into focus, so the history that is watched and later narrated is largely that of groups, of élites interacting with each other and with the mass of society within and across political frontiers. It is the history of actions and events rather than of private thoughts and declared aims. Still, great events, however dimly seen, deserve to be studied, both in their own right and because the past, especially that intermediary period between antiquity and the high Middle Ages which I visit day in day out, has shaped the cultures, institutions and self-perceptions of the present.

Armchair history is therefore a most demanding and debilitating activity. Travel within the present, however primitive the conditions (down to a point), provides welcome relief and eases the strain on the cerebellum. It is also absolutely essential in my case. The relative paucity of written evidence forces historians of the Near East and Eastern Europe in the early Middle Ages to turn their attention to the physical arenas within which states expanded or contracted and cultures advanced or regressed. Physical geography, the configuration of mountains and plains, of watered and arid lands, of coast and interior, shaped men's lives, determining routes and avenues of invasion, introducing natural though surmountable divides between peoples, and articulating economies around the large, often isolated pools of rich arable land scattered across the diverse countries of the region. The landscape is there, relatively unscarred by man away from the Mediterranean coast. It is a crucial part of the evidence which the historian must scrutinise with the utmost care. He must therefore travel with eyes open wide, ready to observe and register historically significant natural features. And, like any other tourist, he must visit such monuments as are still standing or have been revealed by excavation, to gauge for himself the economic and cultural ups and downs of his subjects.

Those were the general reasons why I wanted to go back to Turkey in the summer of 1988 and visit the far north-east. I had never been there. I had not seen Kars or Ani, two of the greatest cities of medieval Armenia, nor visited the magnificent domed churches of Tao, in the formidable mountains south of the lower course of the Çoruh river. No historian who purported to know something about Armenia in its heyday could claim respectability if he had not seen with his own eyes these great monuments built by members of the far-flung Bagratid princely dynasty, if he had not gazed with awe at the towering mass of Mount Ararat or made his way across the vast plain to its north, which straddles the Araxes river and the modern Turkish-Soviet frontier and has always formed the administrative heartland of Armenia.

But there was another, more particular and pressing reason. There were three places in what had once been western Armenia, which I was anxious to track down. They would be featuring prominently in the two books I was planning to write before too long. If only they could be pinned down on the map, I would acquire valuable solid points around which to reconstruct events involving them, events which had a considerable impact on the history of the whole of Armenia from the sixth to the eleventh centuries. Of course, the planned books might be nothing more than the latest instance of scholarly *oblomovka*, a not unpleasant condition in which enormous satisfaction can be gained from contemplating the scholar's future *oeuvre*. He can either devise a new projected work with each passing academic year or, if they become too many, can axe them one by one until a leaner, much more practicable programme is produced. Both processes, the addition and subtraction of projects, become achievements in their own right and provide encouragement to the scholar condemned as he is to a life of solitary mental travel and adventure. Still, I had to believe in the 1988 version of the programme and to prepare myself for the task.

The first of the books was to describe the collapse of the apparently stable balance of power between the Roman and Persian Empires. It brought the ancient phase of human history in western Eurasia to a bloody close in the early seventh century. The book would concentrate on the last rounds of escalating warfare which culminated in the ancient equivalent of a nuclear exchange (the ultimate weapon taking the form of Turkic nomad armies which each side called in from the north against the other).

Armenia was, as it had long been, one of the two main theatres of war then, and my first two unidentified and unlocated places had been key fortresses in the deep defensive zone on the Roman side of the frontier. It would be fascinating to find them and discover the exact position and size of each, the strength of their fortifications and their military functions. I knew their ancient names (Citharizon and Artaleson), roughly where to look (along the diagonal line of the Roman frontier running south-west from Theodosiopolis, modern Erzurum, towards the Taurus in the area of modern

32

Bingöl), and the approximate date of their construction (between AD 515 and 525 on my reckoning). It was evident from this skimpy information, culled mainly from the writings of the sixth-century historian Procopius, that they had been built to plug a gaping hole left in Roman frontier defences in south-west Armenia after a moratorium on the arms race had come into force in 441, and that they acted as secure bases for powerful regional armies and shifted the military balance in Armenia in the Romans' favour.

The third quarry was a medieval fortified town, founded by the Arabs after they had overrun Armenia in the seventh century. It was called Havjij and lay on the north-west side of a vast, flattened, extinct volcano, the Bingöl Dağ, which dominates the western half of Armenia, no less than Ararat dominates the eastern half. Its elevated mass pushes apart human settlements and forces long detours on all routes in the region. In winter it is a frozen wilderness of ice and drifting snow; in summer a paradise for shepherds who graze innumerable flocks of dark tan sheep and goats on the rich pastures of its flanks. Havjij, wherever it had stood, had guarded one of the approaches to Theodosiopolis, the main military base of the region under Arab rule as it had been under the Romans and as it still is for NATO. Havjij, therefore, attracted the attention of Byzantine military commanders in the 930s as they pushed out step by step into Armenia and increasingly concentrated their efforts on Theodosiopolis. By autumn 939 Havjij was in their hands. The noose was tightening and Theodosiopolis was doomed, despite some brilliant counterstrokes by a bold Arab emir.

Decades later, in 1000, Havjij would again be in the news when the Emperor Basil II went on a progress through his Armenian and Georgian territories with a formidable escort of 6,000 Russian troops. It was there that he received formal obeisance from two important client-princes. It was there too that his position and that of the Byzantines in the region were suddenly imperilled when a brawl between a Russian and a Georgian sparked off a full-scale riot in his army between the Russians and the locals.

33

So Havjij was going to play a part in the second of the projected books, dubbed *The Empire Strikes Back* by an old academic friend, the book which would detail the manoeuvres whereby the Byzantines sought to extract every possible advantage out of the slow break-up of the caliphate and their determined efforts to create a grand alliance with the Christians of Transcaucasia intended ultimately to eradicate Islam from the lowlands of the Near East. How eagerly awaited was the first glimpse of the doubtless plundered ruins of the town. They would provide a tangible index of the extent to which the vast transcontinental Islamic single market had hastened the economic development and urbanisation of remote highland regions, as well as being the setting for a few episodes recorded in the sparse surviving texts.

The search for Citharizon, Artaleson and Havjij began six years earlier in inauspicious circumstances and came to an unexpected and abrupt halt. The ultimate reason for this lay in events which took place as my then travelling companion and I were leaving Ankara on the road to Erzurum. Two Armenian terrorists attacked Ankara airport. They exploded a bomb in the crowded international departure lounge, then raked it with automatic fire, before one was seriously wounded and captured and the other took refuge with twenty-four hostages in the restaurant. There he was eventually shot dead after killing an American hostage. All told eight people were killed and seventy-two wounded. This horrific incident reactivated a deep-imbued collective paranoia throughout the lands of the east where the Armenian population had been either liquidated or driven out during the First World War. The paranoia gripped peasantry and officialdom alike.

A week later we were joined by a friend who spoke fluent Turkish. The three of us then moved into the search area. There was a glint of anxiety in our new companion's eyes, not unnaturally, as he had been travelling alone, by bus and on foot for many weeks. Our first evening out in the wilds, the Security Police called on us and saw the glint of anxiety. Immediately paranoia flared up inside them. We might be

Armenians. We might be another terrorist unit, with another terrible plan in mind. A day later, we were detained for questioning by the police in a yet remoter small town. Innocently we told them that we were aiming for Bingöl. BINGÖL? THE MINISTER OF THE INTERIOR IS DUE IN BINGÖL! That was it. We were given an armed escort and sent on to Bingöl. There we were met by all the top brass of the local security services on the bypass. They escorted us into the town, allocated us to a hotel and kept us under close surveillance. At night a searchlight was trained on our hotel window, a ferocious dog patrolled below and the muffled sounds of large men stirring in the neighbouring rooms could be heard. By day four men shadowed the three of us. We managed to half-convince the *vali*, the provincial governor, of our innocence, got his permission to visit the two most promising sites with a minder, but when we drew a blank, had to leave for the more touristic south-east. That was the end of the first search. Scholarship had scarcely advanced at all. It was most frustrating. The name Bingöl acquired rather unpleasant overtones.

1988 was to be the year of the return to Bingöl. A new intrepid travelling companion appeared in the form of Nigel Ryan. To him all of this would be child's play. He had crisscrossed the Middle East in his days as a Reuters correspondent. He had run television companies. He had been one of the first two journalists to venture into Afghanistan after the Soviet invasion. His talk would provide unceasing entertainment. He was the ideal *arkadaş*, the companion which every traveller is expected to have in Turkey. Apart from these admirable qualities, he could be introduced wherever we went as the second husband of the third wife of the first husband of my wife.

We arranged to meet in Ankara on 4 September. Nigel was going to spend much of August in the Aegean. To ease the transition from the luxury of a Patmos villa to roughing it on the roads of the east, he planned to take a few medium-length bus journeys in Anatolia, to visit the rock-cut churches of Cappadocia and the great Seljuk monuments of Konya, before our rendezvous. I would already be in Ankara, attending a conference on the eastern frontier of the Roman Empire.

1–3 September (Ankara)

Sessions were held in the British Council building. At one end was a low stage, behind which hung a screen and curtains. The lectern rose out of a structure which looked like an upended coffin. A wreath of funereal flowers, yellow, mauve and red, decorated it. Discreet neon lights illuminated the windowless space enclosed by walls of bare brick in which the audience sat. One expected to hear the murmur of an organ and watch the lectern right itself and move at a stately pace back towards the curtains.

The director of the proceedings sat to one side of the stage, a low gleam of anxiety occasionally visible in his eyes. Fearful of causing offence to the Turkish participants, he had begged us to avoid mentioning Armenia or Armenians – something not that easy to achieve, since one of the main sectors of the Romans' eastern frontier cut through Armenia. Most of us obliged, treating it as a game and enjoying devising our own circumlocutions. Mine were a stretched version of Transcaucasia, which was extended unnaturally to the south to reach the Taurus, a vague designation of territory north of the Taurus, and the equally convenient term, eastern approaches. Not once did the awful name surface in my lecture – not that our director could be sure of that beforehand. It might slip out despite the best intentions. It did every now and again in the course of the proceedings, and every time the director shuddered and the gleam brightened.

Then there was the odd participant who either could not or would not obey these rules of engagement. One, a young German scholar, viewed it as a matter of principle to keep the correct term in his lecture, but so thick was his accent as he read out an English translation of his paper that the names did not seem to strike home and the director breathed again. Another speaker had an insurmountable practical problem.

She was talking about the attitudes to foreigners from the east expressed or implied in Juvenal's satirical poems. Out of deference to the large Israeli contingent present, she excised almost all her planned discussion of Juvenal's derogatory references to Jews, leaving herself with no option but to focus upon his view of Armenians, who were of course not represented in the audience. She was English and her delivery was excellent. The director emerged ashen-faced after that session.

A British naval officer, who has managed to spent a lot of his career prowling the interior of Turkey looking for Roman remains, supplied us with snippets of news about the world outside. Ataturk's military cronies were being exhumed from their original burial places around his mausoleum, to make room for future presidents. That was the hot news on the first day. *Raki* was being recommended to drivers the next day, on the grounds that it was less intoxicating than beer. On the last day the translated corpses were once again the main topic. A full general had been re-interred in the new cemetery among the *lieutenant-generals*. His family was outraged and was lodging furious objections.

We were broiled in the streets as we made our way to and fro between the conference hotel and the British Council auditorium. Taxis which cost much less than buses in England zipped about, tooting for custom. Strange dummies filled the shop-windows. Some were completely bald, with fissures running down the backs of their skulls. Others were heavily and frighteningly made up. The smartest pretended to be robots or creatures from outer space, either with perspex featureless faces or flattened heads presenting mummy-like profiles. Elsewhere entirely invisible creatures seemed to be walking all over the bare walls and up a column in shoes of sombre colours. The main change since my last visit had been the sudden eruption of video shops everywhere in the city.

The conference ended with a great feast in an upmarket restaurant overlooking the polluted Gölbaşı Lake, some distance outside Ankara. Alcohol flowed freely. Animated talk rippled around the tables, as the whole conference with two exceptions (I being one of them) prepared for two weeks of academic tourism, visiting the scanty remnants of Roman installations and routes on the Euphrates frontier. The thought of this next phase in which they would all be packed into three buses in the heat of the summer, bumping from site to site, eating sometimes questionable food, sharing rooms at night, continuing the learned discussions of the formal sessions filled me with vicarious horror. Sub-groups would form, antagonisms would develop, some might become pariahs, the strong-willed would impose themselves on the weak, distinguished scholars might emerge broken characters.

I swallowed enormous slugs of *raki* neat and listened through an increasing muzziness to the strange tales of the naval traveller – about the mayhem caused after Prime Minister Ozal's finger was nicked by an assassin's bullet in a theatre as his bodyguards fired indiscriminately at the audience, about a colonel in the medical service whom he had met on one of his many forays into army messes, and who had offered to buy a kidney-donor in Turkey and bring him over to London so as to get the transplant which he needed.

September 4 (Ankara-Trebizond)

The *raki* wreaked its revenge from the small hours of the night. I staggered down for coffee at a late hour. Nigel appeared on schedule with his first, touristic travelling companion, Eleni. Eleni left the same day taking with her, much to my relief, the London Library copy of Christopher Walker's *Armenia: Story of a Nation*, which would have done us no good had it been found on us in the east.

We caught the evening flight to Trebizond. By the time we reached the vertiginous mountains behind the Black Sea coast darkness had fallen. We seemed to be turning the wrong way, into the mountains as we descended. There was a great deal of turbulence. The shortness of the runway was remembered. It was hard to concentrate on one's reading. Then suddenly we were down. A huge American car from

38

the fifties appeared and whisked us to our hotel. Within fifteen minutes of landing we had booked in and were sitting in a small restaurant on the main square stuffing ourselves with roast chicken. Nigel remarked cryptically on the many resemblances of Turkey to Spain.

September 5 (Trebizond-Torul)

I woke to see Nigel reading an extract from my learned friend Bryer's massive book on Trebizond and the Pontus. He found it rather tough going. But the water was hot. The bath had a plug. So we had the last baths for several days to come. We descended through the carefully varied colour schemes of the different floors to breakfast.

We collected our car from Avis and set off on a brief tour of the capital of the pocket-empire of the Komnenians. Crammed into a narrow mountainous zone between the sea and the Turkish-controlled open country in the interior, it maintained an isolated, often precarious existence from 1204 to 1461. We lunched in a rooftop restaurant overlooking the main square. The naval traveller had announced that all good provincial restaurants were to be found in such positions. This one was very disappointing, save for the view of life below. The most arresting sight was that of a wife, swathed in black, soundlessly following her husband on a crowded pavement. She kept exactly three paces behind him, never allowing anyone to step between them, moving to right or left in his exact track as he cut a sinuous course through the passers-by.

In the early afternoon we set off for Erzurum, 320 kilometres away. Ten kilometres out a bus swept past and the windscreen shattered. I drove cautiously back, peering through a small clear patch in the web of cracks. We had coffee in the main square while Avis took charge of the repairs. The sun was now out. A fountain played. A Dutch girl asked if she could sit at our table, then knitted something out of a metallic dark blue wool. She liked travelling, she said. She had been to India, Indonesia, Thailand . . . India was her favourite place. She was now 'shaving' money to go to Japan. We listened politely and bought her some coffee. Loudspeakers blared away. Nigel began talking about his relatives by marriage. I remembered my wife and rang her. One jeton got me unlimited time and won my undying affection for the telephone system which had recently extended itself throughout the country. Back at the table the Dutch girl's two male friends had returned. They bought us coffee. A fly began to sting my ankles.

An hour had gone by, but the car was not ready. We went down to the seashore, crossing the dualled bypass to reach the smallest, most decrepit funfair imaginable. Half an hour later we were back at Avis. Our car reappeared and we set off again.

It was a long journey. Darkness fell long before we reached the main pass on the road to the interior, the Zigana. When at last we did so, a youth flagged us down and invited us into his café. There were several on either side of the road, each with two whole sheep's carcasses hanging outside. Inside ours swarthy truckdrivers, with a healthy growth of stubble, sat around the stove. Everything was dark brown, faces, chairs, tables, walls. The television news was on, mainly tableaux of officialdom, with the juniors watching their boss as he lounged on a sofa and addressed the camera. We ate grilled steak and bread with a murderous-looking carving knife.

We drove on through the night to Torul, Nigel worrying about the precipices on one side of the road. Gentlemanly truckdrivers let us pass. Torul is a small mountain town, straddling a rushing river at the bottom of a steep-sided valley. The left bank was full of life at 10.00 pm. The cafés were packed with men playing backgammon and dominoes. The shops were open. Nigel bought a cake which tasted like castle pudding. Clerks were working frantically in the back room of the bank amid ancient calculating machines. Everything was staider on the other side of the river, apart from our hotel, the New Hotel, the best of the three in town, where a silent throng of men was watching *Rambo II*. A small library had its television framed by bookcases. A kettle steamed in a kitchen at the back. A few men looked silently at the television. Two policemen and four soldiers materialised as we made our way back to the New Hotel. Nigel then watched the audience watching *Rambo II*. There was no sadistic gleam in their eyes, he reported, just puzzled interest.

September 6 (Torul–Çat)

I slept badly and got up an hour or so before the *arkadaş* woke from his deep sleep. I looked out at the cliff opposite on top of which sits Torul castle, while we ate a breakfast of soup, bread and tea. A detail of soldiers came by at the double, rifles all over the place.

We set off for Erzurum at nine. We were waved through a military roadblock, but a chicken stood its ground and forced us to make a detour. First stop was Bayburt which is dominated by a Seljuk castle. The town lies in a broad basin drained by the headwaters of the Çoruh river which flows into the Black Sea far to the east at the frontier with the Soviet Union. Large, Cheviot-like hills, burned to every conceivable shade of ochre, dominate the surrounding country.

The fourteen-year-old son of a prosperous tailor talked to us in halting English and invited us into his father's shop for tea. We sat on upholstered chairs, contemplating others covered in red velvet, too sumptuous to be sat on, which were arranged along the opposite wall. The tailor sold suits for 200,000 Turkish lire or £80. The son went to boarding school in Erzurum.

The shops in Bayburt, as everywhere else in the east, were crammed with produce and manufactured goods. Women wore brown *yashmaks* with blue stars and blue edging, made of coarse wool. A raw-wool shop displayed its stock of brown and white wool in huge, bulging sacks.

Nigel drove from Bayburt to Erzurum. He had an uncanny knack of going into potholes, at one point barely resisting the lure of a great cleft on the edge of the road. Surmounting

41

the high, steep saddle of the Kop Geçidi, we looked over a vast tract of open country, the great plain of the upper Euphrates running away without apparent limit to the east towards the watershed with the Araxes. Viewed from below at closer range, the Euphrates carries a meagre flow of water at this early stage in its long curving descent to the Persian Gulf. Beside it, we caught a first glimpse of those honey encampments which, in the course of our travels, were to become a familiar feature of the landscape (especially in the wildest and remotest regions), hives painted a Cambridge blue, a tent, a hut apparently clad with plastic and two heavily protected figures opening the hives. The plain seemed to be deserted (it was midday) except for a large herd of cattle grazing on the right bank of the river.

God smiled on us at Erzurum. We parked outside a good restaurant, walked in and were fed piping-hot shish in a flash. We gorged ourselves. Nigel likened himself to an elderly spinster discovering sex in Venice. Properly fuelled, we set out to see the sights of Erzurum.

They are medieval and Moslem. Most of the massive defences of the Roman city, doubtless much modified by Byzantines, Arabs, Byzantines again, Seljuk Turks, Mongols and Ottoman Turks, which comprised a double circuit of walls with sixty-two towers, were demolished in the second half of the nineteenth century. For they were superseded then by a modern defensive system which guarded the suburbs around the core of the old city and was extended outwards to cover the main approaches to the city. Only a few remnants of the old inner wall still stand. One section with two towers was converted to form the east side of a magnificent *medrese* or theological school built by the Seljuk Turks in the brief period when they occupied the city, between 1230 and 1242. Another section with two more towers, both with the characteristic prow shape of late Roman work, begins a few metres to the north and runs towards a rather unimpressive citadel.

We hardly spared a glance for these. Our eyes were fixed on the Seljuk *medrese*, the Çifte Minare Medresesi, which has been restored and opened to the public. The portal in the main northern façade has magnificently carved bands of floral decoration on its stonework. These frame a deeply recessed doorway and are flanked by two massive buttresses which support fluted brick minarets. Inside, on either side of the central courtyard, there are two-storey arcades fronting the twenty-eight cells where the pupils of the establishment were taught in style. The windows and doorways are framed with a great variety of stonecarving. A boy, who turned out to be a friend of the Bayburt tailor's son, showed us round and practised his rather better English on us.

The other notable monument is at the opposite, west end of the city. It is the Yakutiye Medresesi, which was built by the Mongols in 1310 in emulation of the *medrese* put up by their Seljuk predecessors. It was closed, but, to judge by its portal, which protrudes from the western façade, the Mongols won this artistic competition easily. The general impression is that of a huge, vertical carpet design impressed on the stone surface of the portal. The carving is shallower than the Seljuk but much more inventive and intricate. It combines the severity of a complex geometrical design (eleven-point stars composed of continuous zigzags which fill the inner of the two main bands of decoration) with the fluidity of two superimposed but independent floral patterns (which, when combined, allow the shape of a bird to materialise at regular intervals on the surface of the outer of the two main bands). The minarets (one of which has fallen) also pull rank: they are placed at the corners, so as to frame the whole building, and are more elaborately decorated with coloured tiles.

Of the mosques of Erzurum we only visited one, the Lala Paşa Camii, founded in the mid-sixteenth century. It is a rather nondescript Ottoman building, next door to the Mongol *medrese*. Inside, the faithful sat bent and silent. The sacristan looked dauntingly impassive. A massive chandelier hung overhead. All the time a grandfather clock was ticking away. Its pendulum swung back and forth, measuring western months and western time, and a little illuminated galleon rocked to and fro with each swing.

Our final visit was to the *otogar*, the bus station. No one,

43

Nigel said, understood Turkey if he had not seen the families crowding the concourse, the agents of the different companies competing ferociously for custom, and the extraordinarily dignified attempts to control the universal grief at parting as the travellers prepared to climb into the gleaming, turbo-charged coaches which would sweep them off to distant destinations. Nigel took photographs of the wide cross section of society visible there. Then we set off through the new housing estates under construction around the old city. One of them, off the Trebizond road, consisted of identical, mass-produced blocks, each with a concrete framework and brick infill and each, for some reason, raised up on concrete stilts. At a garage an attendant filled our tank to overflowing. His mate, glowing cigarette in mouth, came along with a cloth to wipe the car down. I kept him away.

Our route was south-west, roughly along the line of the old eastern frontier of the Roman Empire. The search for lost fortresses was beginning, the first quarry being early sixth-century Artaleson which I believed was to be found roughly half way between Erzurum and the Bingöl plain on the Murat Su. A likely spot lay in the valley of the Tuzla Çay, a southern tributary of the Euphrates which feeds off the mountains immediately south of Erzurum and then runs west to join the main river. Its valley looked relatively open on the maps I had consulted, German ones produced in the run-up to the First World War. So it could have done with a Roman fortress, and a tempting hill, on the south bank of the river, above a village called Harabe – Ruins – cried out for investigation.

We aimed for Çat, the main town of the Tuzla Çay valley. The road skirted the western end of the formidable Palandöken range which shuts off the Erzurum plain from the south. It rode over low hills and lush upland plateaux. The grass was still green at the end of summer and nature provided standing pools of water to slake the thirst of numerous large flocks of mainly brown sheep grazing there. It was a paradise of cool, well-watered pasture, a true *yayla*, high ground with summer pastures, which also supported herds of brown cattle and a number of honey encampments. The

44

slanting light of the evening sun picked out the relief of the Tuzla Çay valley as we threaded our way down between now rather sombre-coloured hills, circumventing the gorge cut by the streams draining the high pastures behind. The German army surveyors had done their job well. Çat did indeed stand in broad open country.

It is not a large place, announcing its population as 3,000 (all towns with an administrative function declare two basic facts about themselves to travellers, their population and their height above sea level). Çat's height is such that it is bitterly cold for eight months a year. We were arriving at the tail end of the summer interlude. Shops were stuffed with fruit and vegetables. As dusk deepened, cattle, many of them with elegant, dark shadowing on their brown flanks, made their way along the main street. Overhead flocks of birds swooped down on what was clearly also their district capital. The noise grew steadily louder as more and more of them settled on rooftops and trees.

A former *Gastarbeiter* invited us into his shop. He had been back some time and his German had deteriorated to the level of unintelligibility. Besides the shop he owned a hotel and café. Nigel said that meant he was a capitalist, a remark greeted with much amusement. We installed ourselves in his hotel and then, to escape his son's determined attempts to exercise *his* English on us, strolled down the main street between concrete shop-units, each lit by a single neon bulb. The cattle pushed their way in at a gentle pace. The occasional soldier walked by. Songs blared from radios until the call to prayer from the mosques induced instant silence.

Dinner in the only *lokanta* open was expensive and disgusting. The first offering, which we rejected, consisted of chicken gizzards and innards.

September 7 (Çat-Bingöl)

We both woke early. Nigel had dreamt as usual. Princess Margaret told him that all men everywhere should love each

45

other – at which he switched off the dream and found himself in Hollywood having his hair cut. Before long, having drunk tea in the capitalist's café, we drove off to visit Harabe village. The Çat *jandarma* was drilling as we left.

My heart rose as we approached the hill above Harabe Köy which I had seen on the German army map. Seen from the south, several markings showed up clearly on its side in the light of the early-morning sun. Admittedly there were disturbing gaps between them and they seemed to run at more than one level, but they might still be the grass-covered remnants of a Roman fortress' inner and outer walls. We pulled off the road and walked up a track. Villagers were raking hay in a field below.

Hope began to fade as we climbed. The markings looked more and more like long-abandoned terracing. Still on we went, if only to see the view from the top. A lone figure came towards us. He showed not the least surprise at foreigners taking a walk there. There were indeed no sherds or brick or tile fragments or cut stones visible on the surface when we reached the low embankments, nor was there any trace of an embankment on the steeper northern side which descended to the Tuzla Çay. Worse still, a higher hill immediately upstream obscured the view to the east, the direction from which an enemy attack was to be expected in late antiquity. We had very definitely drawn a blank.

So we drove on. A long side valley, sloping so gently that the stream which had made it seemed to be flowing in the wrong direction, led south to a range of formidable mountains, stained red, brown and green by rich mineral deposits. Beyond lay the broad, undulating valley of the Peri Su, another potential east-west invasion route which Artaleson might have been guarding. However, we did not stop to talk and look, since I had already visited the most likely site six years earlier and everyone had said that there were no ruined castles or other ancient sites in the vicinity. So we sped across it, eyes dazzled by the sunlight reflected off the brand new corrugated iron roofs of standard-issue post-earthquake houses, arranged in neat grid patterns on bare hillsides; then

46

over an easy saddle, through rich, sodden pastures into the rather bleak, relatively unexploited plain of Karlıova.

This pass is an important one. It is the only break in a series of mountain ranges which run west from the massif of the Bingöl Dağ and form an otherwise almost impenetrable natural rampart barring movement by organised bodies of men north–south or *vice versa*. Immediately to the west they rise steadily and the relief becomes more and more difficult. Then they acquire the apt name of the Mountains of Satan. Six years earlier, in the company of two friends and a shifty police spy, I had gazed at them from an eminence above the small town of Kiğı. The three innocent foreigners had all been awestruck at the sight of rank after rank of rearing grey peaks, bunched tightly together, which filled the northern horizon, and had marvelled at the Peri Su which somehow manages to cut a tortuous channel through them. Further west the mountains fuse together and rise still higher as the Munzur Dağ. At their western end, the Euphrates performs the Herculean feat of carving out deep canyons to force its way south towards Malatya and the Taurus mountains. It is only when one reaches its west bank that once again there are feasible routes running north-south.

So Karlıova and the settlements nearby stand in a position of great strategic importance. For the only militarily useful north-south route between the Bingöl Dağ and the Euphrates debouches on to its plain. There it intersects with one of two lateral invasion routes which entered Roman territory between the Bingöl Dağ and the Taurus. This latter route runs from the plain of Varto, and, grazing the southern face of the Bingöl Dağ, crosses a manageable pass to the Karlıova plain from where it can enter the relatively open hill country to the west. So Artaleson really ought to have been built in the general area of Karlıova.

Our destination was a village some two kilometres away, on the bank of the upper Göynük Çay, a stream which runs south-west to join the Murat Su in the Bingöl plain. Its name, Kale Köy – Castle Village – made it worth investigating, and ruins had indeed been noted there by the Russian forces which had outmanoeuvred and defeated the Turks in the

Göynük valley in August 1916. First, though, a pause in Karlıova, a market town which was bustling with life. Bright-liveried minibuses, with 'DIESEL DIRECT INJECTION' written in large letters on their sides, were coming and going, ferrying villagers to and from the town. Men stood about chatting, on the pavements and in the main road. A wind had risen and was blowing along the streets. We had some tea, coffee being hard to come by in these remote country districts. Nigel went in search of a knife. He brought back a fearsome, razor-sharp weapon with a wooden handle, wrapped in a bit of old newspaper. In future days it was always puncturing the thin plastic bags, resembling vast, pale grey condoms, which the shops supply. Eastern Turkey is full of men carrying provisions in bulging condoms.

Kale Köy was almost as disappointing as the hill above Harabe Köy. Again there was the initial foolish optimism, aroused this time by two solidly built houses which protruded from the line of their neighbours and looked, from a distance, like the converted stumps of square towers. Close to they were simply houses, built of surprisingly large rough-hewn stones. All vestiges of the castle had vanished: not a trace of a square-cut Roman block of stone in any house wall; no grass-covered swellings in the ground which might be the remnants of its foundations; only sherds of smooth red ware and fragments of bricks strewn in considerable quantities on the ground. The villagers, however, were well aware that their houses stood on the site of a castle and said that there had once been a church. One, a young man, muttered *sotto voce* that it was Roman or *Armenian*.

The site, a low, narrow hill, some 300 metres north to south, looks out north and west over the Karlıova plain, but higher hills on the opposite bank of the river interpose themselves between the site and the approaches to the Karlıova plain from the east. Its natural defences are weak and its position is far from commanding. There was no trace of Roman masonry. There was therefore no question of its being Artaleson. We had failed again in the hunt for our first quarry.

We turned now to track our second, Citharizon, dating

48

from the same period as Artaleson and designed to stop up the main invasion route through southern Armenia, which follows the general line of the Murat Su. After crossing a broad swathe of open, undulating uplands (which stretch west, without visible interruption, to the valley of the lower Peri Su), we entered a thick belt of mountains which confines the Murat Su to its east-west alignment on the northern edge of the massive Taurus range; this then combines forces with the Euphrates far to the west and dares strike south against the whole grain of the Taurus. The Göynük Su has cut a broad trench through and provides a relatively easy route to the plain of Bingöl.

Unhappy memories stirred as we approached Bingöl. Two donkeys fighting in a ditch could be taken as a bad omen. Yet, when we arrived it seemed a cheerful place. A restaurant with a small area screened off where women could be brought produced a decent lunch. The hotel where every movement of mine and my earlier companions had been watched in 1982 seemed to have been demolished. The barber's shop where we had smartened up in preparation for an audience with the *vali* (governor) had vanished. But the Security building was still the most imposing structure and the two-storey bazaar was still there.

Not many people were about early in the afternoon of a hot day. We wandered into the bazaar, vaguely looking for Panama hats to protect our cerebella from the blazing sun. The furniture section on the lower floor was swathed in gloom. Large, brown-black wardrobes and chests of drawers loomed in the dim light, all of the utmost flimsiness. In the brightness upstairs, to our amazement, one shop had two piles of straw hats. They were made for rather smaller crowns, but we took the two largest which could just be given some purchase on the head. Outside the wind immediately whipped them off and blew them across the street. So Nigel devised Ryan's Knot, tying a loop in one end of the string which was intended to go under the chin but seemed designed for extraordinarily flattened skulls, and attaching it to the second button of the shirt. The hat was thus retained like a monocle, sometimes perched on the head, sometimes dangling from the upper body.

We left Bingöl for the next search area, in the south-east segment of its plain where several *harabes* were a powerful lure and any rational Roman military engineer would have placed a fortress with Citharizon's strategic functions. As we did so, we nearly careered off the twin carriageway boulevard by which any self-respecting large Turkish town is approached when we saw two policewomen strolling along, as if it were the most natural thing in the world for two women with revolver holsters swinging at their hips to walk along unveiled and in shortish skirts.

The sketchmap of the Bingöl area which I had drawn hastily in Ankara failed to get us to Harabe Köy. Instead we arrived at Yeni Köy – New Village. This was indeed new, one of several settlements in the neighbourhood, built to receive refugees from hill villages eight hours' walk away which were devastated in the great earthquake of 1976. Each family has a regulation-issue house with a corrugated iron roof, but each has added a courtyard on the street side, which makes Yeni Köy, in spite of its newness and the dead straight line of its street, seem more habitable than most villages. An old man with watering eyes, wearing grey Turkish trousers, grey waistcoat with a watch chain and a woollen, fez-like hat came out and offered to guide us to Harabe Köy. It was quite close, he said.

The villagers at Harabe Köy knew of no ancient site either in the village or on Harabe Hill above it. There was only an ill-kept, unenclosed cemetery below the village, to which the young men led us – ostensibly to show us a tomb with an Arabic inscription and another with a cross incised, but in reality in the hope that we might lead them to gold. They drifted away after we returned to the village. The older men and children gathered round. Stools were produced for the guests. Tea materialised, the glasses being cleaned with boiling water, which was carefully poured from glass to glass by our host. Our guide explained who we were, adding as he turned to us that he knew of an ancient castle near *his* village. The *muhtar*, the village headman, appeared in a clean white shirt, squatted down beside us, avoided meeting our eyes and began asking questions about us.

Our guide offered to take us to his site. So we took leave of our Harabe host and set off down a rough track. This petered out and we drove diagonally across a field to another faint track. This deteriorated rapidly and we came to a halt in a muddy, rutted section. We managed to extricate ourselves, Nigel and our guide pushing while I drove. Our guide seemed unconcerned at the thick coating of mud on his black-leather slip-on shoes. When we got back to the first track, our guide pointed west and spoke in a loud voice. Evidently he looked on the car as a wonder-working conveyance which could make its way over trackless fields to whatever destination he pointed out. Nigel, more intrepid than I, was all for carrying on. So we turned due west and drove along the high bank of the Murat Su.

Ridge upon ridge of the Taurus rose to the south-west, veiled in evening mist. Silhouettes of figures riding donkeys could be seen in the distance, moving over the level fields ahead of us. Once again our guide directed us inland, this time along a rock-strewn track. How far away was it? I asked after a short while. Only four kilometres, was the reply. But the sun was low in the sky and we decided to make straight for Yeni Köy. We returned to the river bank and followed it until we came to a sharp drop, and saw the plain continue below at a lower level. Dik Köy, the village next to Yeni Köy, was immediately below us, the cattle moving towards it as dusk drew on. A track led down and was easily negotiated.

Within a few minutes we were back in Yeni Köy and our guide became our host. He invited us into the courtyard next to his house, had stools brought out and ordered his wife to make tea. Several of the village's older men joined us. One of them had worked for an American firm in Diyarbakır and spoke English. A charming, gentle man, with drooping eyes and moustache, he had a wry sense of humour. He quietly dismissed the villager's perennial dream of finding gold as fantasy. He told us that our host had fathered ten children, observing that, as there was no work to do by day, they worked hard at night. He wore brown tweed trousers and a

51

jersey. The others included an old smoker with a racking, cancerous cough, and a fine-looking figure with a distinguished grey moustache and grey hair, the image of a nineteenth-century Kurdish brigand leader, save for the jeans and short-sleeved mauve sweater which he wore. He gazed at us intently. Another had a mouth emptied of all but two teeth. Yet more villagers looked in through the gateway or over the wall.

Darkness fell. Tea was drunk from glasses, each carefully cleaned by our host. Suddenly he pointed out the blocks of stone on which several of the company were sitting, their backs leaning against the wall on the street side, saying they came from the ancient castle nearby. Genuine, soundly based hope now stirred. For they were well-cut, rectangular blocks, the typical building material used by Roman army engineers in the sixth century. One of them had a cross carved on it. Although I had been convinced that Citharizon was to be found somewhere near the south-east corner of the Bingöl plain and would have been bitterly disappointed if we had failed to find it, this was an exciting moment. There was now no doubt that it was nearby.

We arranged to come again the following morning and went to find beds for the night in Bingöl. After dinner, where once again the arkadaş' appetite far outstripped mine, we walked around the town. Old fears began to revive. A police car was parked by our hotel, in such a position as to give the two officers inside a good view of all movements in and out of the lobby. Two other officers stood near us, on a street corner, as we tried in vain to call England from a telephone box. But they made no attempt to apprehend us, and soon Nigel realised that the others in the car were not watching the comings and goings in the hotel lobby but a televised broadcast of a European football match involving a Turkish team. That was what most of male Bingöl was doing at that hour.

Not that Bingöl assumed a really ordinary character for us. Huge but psychologically broken dogs were scavenging for food in the streets. Small boys were enjoying teasing them.

52

A large concrete building under construction was being given a thorough wash by a man with a hosepipe.

We left them to it and prepared ourselves for sleep, by washing ourselves in the only available place, the loo.

September 8 (Bingöl-Tekman)

The barking of three of the scavenging dogs woke me at five. They seemed to be standing in for the *muezzin*. A donkey soon joined in. I envied the *arkadaş* who once again was sleeping like a log, presumably dreaming. Eventually he woke up and we sped back to Yeni Köy.

We waited a while before our host came out into the street and invited us in for tea. Some familiar and some new faces appeared. The English-speaker was there once again. The brigand leader looked as distinguished as ever but now had bloodshot eyes. They seemed closer set than on the previous evening and he had lost a lot of his presence. He asked, earnestly, almost pleadingly, to be taken to England. Among the new faces was one wearing pebble-lensed glasses whom I took to be the village intellectual. He was unshaven and put no hat on his short, frizzy, greying hair. We sat in the shade of a tree. A young daughter of the household pushed a large leather receptacle made out of the skin of a whole sheep to and fro to solidify a yoghourt-related substance inside. Her mother stood contemplating her and the guests with a calm, impassive air. Nigel remarked that she was very handsome.

The best table was produced – with legs and frame painted a shiny gold and a top of plastic imitation wood – and the best chairs, two of them, with silver-coloured legs and frames and brown patterned seats. We talked. Time passed. Our host's wife relieved her daughter and began pushing the sheepskin with powerful movements. The substance within rushed around rhythmically, emitting a deep splatting sound as it hit each end.

The sun was blazing down by the time we reached the site, which lies about a kilometre north of the village. It occupies a low hill which has the general shape of a boomerang. A stream has cut its way around the northern, convex side, leaving a steep slope there which modest fortifications would have made virtually unassailable. We approached from the south, where the climb, though still demanding, is less formidable and trees provide some cover. This is the concave side of the hill, again not too difficult to defend since a garrison could direct a murderous, enfilading fire from both ends against attackers. No standing remains were visible as we climbed but faith in our guide was undiminished.

The force of the sun drove some of our party back downhill to the shade of the trees which we had passed, within a few minutes of our reaching the top. But they had all accompanied us across to the northern side where one section of wall with a small postern gate still stood. Some of the facing of large, rectangular, well-cut stones, arranged in regular courses, was preserved and left us in no doubt that we were looking at Roman workmanship. It was a standard which had not been matched beforehand in this region and which would only be surpassed in the high medieval heyday of Armenian military architecture.

Nigel insisted on taking a posed photograph of the Scholar pointing at his discovery, surrounded by the natives. I was rather surprised to feel no sudden agitation of the emotions or racing of the pulse. The evidence, from texts and the testimony of the Yeni Köy villagers the previous evening, had been so strong that the physical remains *in situ* did not make much impact. So I simulated a smile of excited triumph to please the *arkadaş*.

We spent all too short a time inside the fortress. I scrambled about, taking photographs and scrawling notes about the scanty remains which we saw. The fortress, I reckoned, occupied an area of roughly 300 by eighty metres, and was only vulnerable at the south-east end where it was joined by a narrow saddle to the higher level of the plain over which we had been driving on the previous day. The most powerful defences were concentrated there, including a large semicircular bastion and a somewhat smaller square tower. They probably flanked and guarded the main gate. Not that there was much to go on, just the foundations of the towers which gave an idea of their shape and a few fragments of low walling, much of it robbed of its outer facing. Indeed the whole fortress was melting rapidly away. The inhabitants of the new villages around it had been busy digging up and carting away the well-cut blocks of stone to beautify their bleak, box-like government-issue houses. They had made a pretty good job of it, especially at the western end of the hill, where deep trenches had been dug to extract all the foundations. At the time of our visit the only substantial remains left above ground were the ruined bases of three towers and two sections of circuit wall. Their chances of survival for more than a few months were poor.

It was therefore quite impossible to trace the overall design or gauge the effectiveness of the fortifications put up in the early sixth century. We could not tell whether Procopius was right to praise the work of the Roman military engineers (a profession to which, I think, Procopius himself belonged) who were serving the imperial regime (with which Procopius was anxious to ingratiate himself). We could only judge whether or not they had chosen a good site for the fortress. The unequivocal answer was that they had. The natural strength of its position was such that they merely had to make minor improvements to God's handiwork to make it virtually impregnable, and it was well placed to perform two valuable strategic functions.

It commanded, from the highest section at its south-east end, a view of almost 180 degrees north to south. The field of vision from the lower west end was restricted by higher ground to north and south, but it covered the whole central sector of the Bingöl plain which would have had to be crossed by any force approaching or leaving the strategically important pass which connected south-west Armenia with the rich grainlands of the upper Tigris basin across the Taurus. A garrison based there would therefore have been able to monitor movements along both the main routes which intersected in the Bingöl plain, to deter an enemy from using either unless he came in great force, and to inhibit foraging and raiding if he did.

Besides these two strategic functions, Citharizon also had the political one of imposing Roman authority directly on the frontier region between the Bingöl Dağ and the Taurus (along with the associated fortress of Artaleson to the north). Doubtless the full array of walls and towers of different shapes, all built to the same high specifications, was intended to impress the local Armenian provincials as well as the Persian enemy with the power and majesty of Roman rule. The fortress would have been visible from afar, and by its mere presence would have contributed to the process of Romanisation which was being set in train in this remote region at this very late stage in Roman imperial history.

In the event, Citharizon seems to have performed quite well. Very few enemy forces are known to have ventured past it in the course of the great power conflicts which became more frequent and longer-drawn-out over the century following its construction. A large force of Huns from the Caucasus allied to the Persians was clearly nervous of its garrison as it emerged from the Taurus pass on its way home from raiding the upper Tigris basin in the winter of 531–2. A detachment was sent, not to make a serious assault, but to keep the defenders busy while the main body slipped north across the plain. Many years later, in 578, another army, Persian this time, commanded by the great general Tam Khusro, passed by on the way to raid the region around Amida (modern Diyarbakır) south of the Taurus, after an earlier feint by a second Persian army in the south had drawn a Roman field army, commanded by the future Emperor Maurice, away from its camp near Citharizon. Citharizon itself was left untouched.

It only fell into Persian hands once, in the first phase of the last and greatest war of late antiquity, when, in 607, the Persians had destroyed the Roman field army in Armenia in a series of crushing victories and were advancing west without encountering organised resistance outside the isolated military bases. It was probably only recovered by the Romans in the late 630s when the Persian Empire began to fall apart under the triple pressure of defeat (after the miraculous recovery of the Romans in the last phase of the war), war weariness and the apparently remorseless advance of the Arabs. A bishop was installed, but he did not rank high in the Orthodox hierarchy. He turned up at a council held in Constantinople in 691–2 and was the very last of the delegates to sign the minutes. Thereafter Citharizon disappeared from view, as the plain of Bingöl was relegated to the margins of early medieval Armenian history, an underpopulated marchland between the Arab emirate of the lower Murat Su valley to the west and the Armenian principality of Taron, centred on the plain of Muş to the east.

Our brains began to addle in the noonday heat. Everything visible to the archeologically inexpert eye had been noted down. Our companions were clearly eager to return to the village and entertain us in more comfortable surroundings. And we had a lot of driving to do if we were to stick to our plan and start the search for our third quarry, Havjij, the following day. So we went back to Yeni Köy and to our host's by now familiar courtyard. The midday wind started up on schedule and cooled us down, as we drank long glasses of *ayran*. Nigel brought out his treasured tin of the Earl of Denbigh's cake, a rich fruit cake, and offered it to our host. Though he and his friends evidently did not think much of it, they were pleased by the gesture.

The conversation turned to politics. The villagers were Kurds, like most inhabitants of eastern Turkey south of the line of the Euphrates valley. Ozal, then Prime Minister of Turkey, did not have their support because he was the friend of 'cheap' (i.e. chief) men. The conversation touched on the Kurdish question. We watched our words, until the historian in me could not resist telling them that they had been in Turkey for a millennium and a half longer than the Turks. There was a visible swelling of Kurdish pride. They asked about the price of things in England and marvelled at the astronomical figures which we mentioned. Our host brought out a long-defunct Japanese camera, in the hope that the foreigners could magically make it work again (without film, battery or overhaul). Regretfully we explained our powerlessness, then bade them all adieu, assuring them that we would send copies of the photographs which Nigel had taken with his automatic, hyper-modern apparatus.

Our direction now was first east, over low passes, covered with a stubble of dwarf oak, which allow easy communication between the Bingöl and Muş plains. Roughly half way, a long, narrow, flat-bottomed fissure in the hills provides rich grazing for sheep, goats, horses, cattle and buffalo. We stopped for lunch at Solhan, another bustling market town, at its eastern end. Enormous quantities of fruit and vegetables were on sale, spilling out onto the road. An old gentleman, wearing the beard of a *haji* (a Moslem who has made a pilgrimage to Mecca) and the most elegant hat I had ever seen in Turkey (light green and white, with yellow embroidery), walked past at a slow, dignified pace, a lethal, curved dagger at his side in its sheath. A fire engine was parked in front of the town hall. I watched open-mouthed as Nigel ate course after course, in a determined attempt to satisfy an appetite inflamed by memories of hunger in Afghanistan.

Soon we were crossing the northern edge of the plain of Muş which runs away south-east as far as the eye can see, towards the immense frozen lava flow which pens in Lake Van on this side, and turned north, along the route which skirts the east side of the Bingöl Dağ. It seemed to me to pose hazards which were neither greater nor lesser than those on the Çat–Bingöl route, the most difficult section being the crossing of the Akdoğan range which abuts on to the east flank of the Bingöl Dağ and marches to the north of the Murat Su valley as far as the plain of Manzikert. North of the Akdoğan Dağ lies the undulating plain of Hınıs, over which lowers the sinister dark mass of the great flattened volcano.

Hınıs with its apparently fertile plain puzzles me. It had the potential to act as the focus of a local principality, with the added bonus of powerful natural defences on all sides, yet it seems to have suffered from historical stagefright. Certainly it played no part in the events of the periods which interest me, merely providing a through-passage for the forces of outside military powers as they moved north or south between the main east–west invasion avenues running along the upper courses of the Murat Su and the Araxes.

Its economic role was probably always more important, as long as conditions were stable enough to allow long distance trade and the sheep which had grazed on the *yaylas* of the Bingöl Dağ through the summer months could be driven off to meet the demand generated by the large population centres south of the Taurus. Around the turn of the century Hınıs was the chief sheep market for the eastern half of the Bingöl Dağ. As autumn approached, merchants came from the great cities of Syria, notably Damascus, installed themselves in relative comfort at Erzurum, used agents at Hınıs to buy sheep and then arranged to have the flocks driven by their own shepherds across the mountains, sometimes after the first snowfalls, to Diyarbakır and thence to the cities of Syria.

Easily surmounted grassy hills separate the plain from the uppermost reaches of the Araxes. The river draws most of its early waters from the northern half of the Bingöl Dağ, around which it curves in a great arc. I had envisaged it struggling to force a passage, cutting narrow valleys and deep canyons for much of its course. This is very far from the truth, insofar as one can judge from those sections of the river visible to the passing traveller. Although it is not a grand river so near its sources, it moves in a calm, authoritative way through a largely open landscape. It navigates its way around low hills and, in between, meanders through extensive water meadows (the most impressive are west of the junction of the Tekman road with the main road north to Erzurum and south of Gökoğlan). Sheep, goats and cattle graze there in large numbers. They are also well peopled, the men scything hay, the women milking the sheep and goats, and carrying churns back to their camp, children and unoccupied adults on the move. Animals and human beings, especially the women wearing the bright colours which mark them off from Turkish country women, offset the predominating greens and ochres, and give a *pointilliste* appearance to the landscape. Ever-present, though, on the horizon is the sombre rim of the Bingöl Dağ, reminding those luxuriating in these unmatched *yaylas* in the clear, dry, warmth of a summer's day of the existence of less hospitable worlds and seasons.

We reached Tekman before nightfall. The *arkadaş* was initially impressed. A small roundabout at a junction on its outskirts and the paving of the main street were doubtless there to achieve precisely such an effect (the outback equivalent of a dualled boulevard). It also had the other distinguishing feature of a local administrative centre: a few four– or five-storeyed concrete blocks of flats and offices, painted cream with one broad vertical brown stripe on each side, clustered together on the edge of the town. It claimed to be roughly the same size as Çat, but lacked many of the latter's amenities. There was no sign of a mosque. The shops were fewer in number, worse stocked, and relied on steel grilles for protection at night. Geese patrolled the streets.

An ex–*Gastarbeiter* owned the first hotel we saw. He invited us into his shop next door and offered us tea. One of his daughters carried on sweeping the floor. Another brought the tea, jogged Nigel's elbow and laughed when the tea spilt. It grew darker. The light was not switched on. The *arkadaş'* profile was outlined against the dimming sky outside, spectacles on nose, hair springing up from the scalp. Momentarily it was transformed into that of a previous *arkadaş*, the second, with whom I had explored the Taurus and the south-east in 1974. This fleeting, phantom companionship from the past gave a pleasurable feeling of added security. The hotel owner forgot about us, and became absorbed in selling groceries and talking to his customers.

We asked to see our room. He took us up the outside stairs, shoes crunching on broken glass. The interior stank. There was a broken bulb in a broken socket in the ceiling. So we turned tail and went in search of a rival establishment. There was one further down the main street, owned by a long-faced, lugubrious character. The smell was less intense and the light worked. So we took a room for the princely sum of sixty pence per head per night. Nigel gave a brief lecture on the eradication of cholera in London, a task long impeded by the natural, though erroneous assumption that a disease and an associated offensive smell were causally connected. He then washed himself down in the loo.

We tracked down a *lokanta* with its kitchen in the basement, which fed us on grilled steaks. Sated, Nigel made for bed back in the hotel, clad as usual in his long, bright blue, tubular nightshirt which reaches the ankles. After a page of *The Towers of Trebizond* he fell into a deep sleep. I examined my notes on Citharizon and started turning them into something more connected and intelligible . . .

There was an urgent knocking on the door. Our lugubrious host opened it, anxiety flaring in his eyes. There were other figures visible behind him. He said something which I did not understand. Then the electricity failed. Our host's face was, I knew, less than a foot from mine, but had entirely vanished in the perfect darkness. Eventually someone lit a candle and I gathered that the *jandarma* wanted to keep our passports overnight, being suspicious of the foreigners who were driving a Turkish car. As we wanted to be off at the crack of dawn, I refused to hand them over and insisted that we call on them instead.

The *jandarma* base, protected by a perimeter fence of barbed wire, was near the roundabout. The hotel keeper and I made our way through the darkened town. Torches were shone in our faces by the sentries. They asked our business, then sent for an officer. When he appeared, the officer, dishevelled and sleepy, was not much interested in our business. He heard out the hotel keeper, whom he clearly thought had been overzealous, cast a cursory glance at the passports and dismissed us. Back in the hotel, Nigel was lying in bed, awake and feeling 'serene'.

The electricity never returned. Lorries, loaded with manure, were parked along the main street. The manure dripped steadily through the night. Some of them gunned their engines in the small hours and were gone.

September 9 (Tekman–Van)

No *muezzin* called at dawn; there was only the distant howling of dogs. We were up early and after downing some tea in our host's café, its floor black with dirt, set off for Gökoğlan some forty kilometres away, the last place marked on our map before the wilds. The *jandarma* were drilling in water-meadows outside the town. The Bingöl Dağ, with patches of snow clinging to it, spread low across the southern horizon.

Just possibly our third quarry was to be found at the foot of the north-west flank of the great mountain or on the watershed between the Araxes and the Peri Su which rises a little to the west. I had been told that an intrepid traveller had once caught a glimpse of a castle on a journey between the two rivers, and there were one or two places marked on the far from accurate German army maps of this region with enticing names. Would one of these turn out to be the castle of Havjij, built by the Arabs to guard the south-west approach to Erzurum, probably in the ninth-century heyday of their rule in Armenia? Would there be traces of the town which grew up there and which later, under Byzantine rule, became an important administrative centre? Doubts had already surfaced as we contemplated the open uplands of the Araxes which must be extraordinarily bleak in winter, with the winds sweeping unopposed across hills and water-meadows, driving the snow before them. It was hard to envisage either an Arab garrison or the usual apparatus of Byzantine provincial government installing itself here. They would have needed all the protection afforded by the most luxurious of northern furs to survive, protection which the Byzantines, unlike the Arabs, forewent from a traditional abhorrence of this typically barbarian garb.

Ten kilometres on we halted for a breakfast of bread and very liquid strawberry jam, bought the previous evening by the *arkadaş*. The razor-sharp knife from Karlıova went to work, slicing through the bread. The jam flowed. He ate voraciously. The knife, unattended, punctured the newspaper protecting his lap. The jam flowed on over jeans and car seat. But there was no pause in the ingestion until the demands of appetite had been met in full.

Eventually we continued on our way, Nigel having made momentous but not entirely successful efforts to remove the adhesive jam. The hillsides were bespattered with small delicate flowers, each with ten azure-blue petals. A desert rat (so identified by Nigel) stood on guard as we sped by. A bird with a bright blue sheen on its wings flew lazily away. Large villages, set far apart, lined the course of the Araxes and its tributaries. Plentiful stocks of fuel and fodder had been laid in for the winter. Beside each house, dung pats were piled up in tall cones. Huge haystacks were grouped together, often well away from the village, perhaps on the far side of a shallow valley, and formed an inanimate suburb which was much better constructed than the main village. We swept past them, failing to notice that one, though just as dilapidated as the others, was rather larger and had one concrete administrative building. That was Gökoğlan, where we had intended to ask about castles and ruins in the area.

The road came to an end at Çukuryayla. A young man rushed out to welcome us and led us to his father's house. Within a minute of arriving we were being shown up the wooden stairway, the women of the household scurrying away on the ground floor, and into the carpeted reception room. We sat on cushions which were arranged against the walls. A low casement window punctured the thick outer wall. The family's precious possessions were displayed on shelves on the opposite wall: a broken wall clock and two sets of cooking pots with flowered patterns on their sides. Tea, bread of two sorts, butter and cheese were produced. Our host, a small bearded man, very weather-beaten, with a large hooked nose and smiling eyes, sat close to me. His son, who had swept us in, to seize the honour of entertaining the strangers for his family, made conversation. A younger brother who had injured his leg limped in, stayed a while, limped out and later returned. Three other villagers appeared. One of them had worked as a *Gastarbeiter* in Libya. His hooded eyes gave him a slightly sinister look. He wore a light blue jacket and matching fez. There being no German-speakers among them, we had to rely on my halting Turkish, sign language and drawing. The elder son did his best to help me understand, by repeating key words loudly.

We gathered that there were ancient remains nearby, including tombs which had been robbed (we were shown two complete ancient pots which they had found), a stone with an incised cross, and three sites which they called 'castles'. Were the doubts then foolish? Should we stay for most of the day and visit the 'castles', which might well turn out to be no more than heaps of stones excavated from tombs or vestiges of an abandoned village? At this point the former Libyan *Gastarbeiter* began pressing us as to exactly how much it had cost to hire the car. Then he wanted to be shown English money (and, thus, to see inside our wallets). Another of the company, a short young man from Elazığ, began examining my map and the tell-tale red crosses marked on it (indicating possible positions for our three quarries) with considerable interest. It was thoroughly pusillanimous of us and showed little faith in the traditions of Kurdish hospitality, but, at my suggestion, we rose, thanked our host warmly, took photographs of the company and left. We knew we were fifty or sixty kilometres from the nearest government outpost (at Tekman) and there had been nothing to indicate that any of the sites referred to had walls or towers or were built of cut stones or brick. The prospects of success were poor and we were reluctant to abandon other elements of our planned itinerary.

We retraced our steps, past Gökoğlan and Tekman to the junction with the main Hınıs–Erzurum road, then struck east over hills and valleys rich in pasture to the small town of Karayazı. This was the most rundown place we saw in the course of our travels. Its plain is a desolate rock-strewn expanse of largely uncultivated land. No figures were visible apart from a sixteen-strong detail of post office workers who were trying to fix telegraph poles more securely in the ground. There was no bustle in the main street, which was flanked by raised pavements, as if whatever passed through was to be repelled from the buildings of the town. Many of these were blocks of flats, their concrete walls stained, their iron balconies rusting. Instead of the brightly-painted, ultra-modern midi- and mini-buses which normally throng such places, there was the hulk, clearly incapable of motion, of an aged, rusting red bus. There was no *lokanta* to be seen, only a one-storeyed hotel without any sign of life which called itself the Ozar Palas but looked like a decayed hovel. The only decent building was the mosque which, an inscription declared, had been put up in 1982.

We took one look at Karayazı and decided to forego lunch. Instead we went a short distance back on our tracks, across a low range of rocky hills, to the village of Salyamaç. I had promised a colleague in England, an adventurous traveller who had given up after a spell in jail on his last trip to eastern Turkey, to visit a so-called city said to be not far from the village. A smartly turned-out young man in flimsy slip-on shoes came out to meet us and offered to take us there. We walked up a side-valley cut by a small stream which we crossed several times. Ox-drawn wagons with huge loads of hay came slowly and silently the other way. Others returned empty to fetch more. Three riders, on fine-looking mounts, husband, wife and child, trotted past. The 'city' was four kilometres from the village and turned out to be a string of chambers cut into the low cliffs on either side of the valley. One was a chapel with two bays and an apse, which had once had a mosaic floor (long since destroyed in the search for buried gold). It was part of a two-storey complex.

Our guide told us of a 'castle' and a church which were not far away. So we returned to the car and followed his directions. He took us to a point near three low hills which rise out of the Karayazı plain, close to its western edge, and command a good view. The church had once stood on the highest of the three, he told us, but, when we reached the top, the masonry had all been removed and all that was to be seen were piles of rough stones. Our guide pointed out the site of the castle on the flat summit of the lowest of the hills, told us that it had been picked clean of stones, and thus discouraged us from climbing up to it too.

We dropped him back at Salyamaç, thanked him warmly (again no question of his accepting any payment), and started on the next lap of our journey which would take us out of the remote world of the Bingöl Dağ and the neighbouring ranges into richer and more accessible country. First, though, we had to struggle along sixty kilometres of dirt-track road over broken, difficult country. The *arkadaş* impressed me with his ability to talk, baring bits of the soul in the process, and drive with faultless skill. The hills which seemed to rise and fall without end passed by almost unnoticed as different scenes were conjured up by him. Finally the hills dropped miraculously away and we entered the plain of the upper Murat Su which runs south from the small town of Tutak.

Tutak is a more cheerful place than Karayazı, but the military and *jandarma* were much in evidence. A unit of the latter came past at the double, chanting imaginatively 'ONE–TWO–THREE–FOUR . . .' A young Kurd was frog-marched past in handcuffs.

The teahouse was half-tent, half-building which seemed to be in the process of being demolished. It was packed and buzzing with talk. We sat, watched and drank tea until worry flashed over Nigel's face. He rushed off and rummaged in the car, with increasing urgency, to find a large notebook containing his observations on Turkey. At last it was discovered and calm returned to the *arkadaş*.

The last stage of the day's drive took us south along the eastern edge of two huge alluvial plains with level surfaces through which the Murat Su flows at leisure. It slips between two mountains, aligned as usual east–west, which divide the plains. The northern plain, that of Tutak, has not yet made much of a mark on history. Not so the southern one which runs from Patnos in the east, a town now enveloped by army and *jandarma* camps, to Manzikert in the west.

The battle which sealed Byzantium's fate was fought near Manzikert in August 1071. The Seljuk Sultan, Alp Arslan, proved a master of strategic deception. His opponent, the Emperor Romanos Diogenes, was misled into believing that the Turkish army had retreated east from Syria in considerable disorder. He seized the opportunity to march south from Erzurum, intending to occupy Manzikert and Ahlat, which, between them, commanded the plains of the upper Murat Su and the route leading south-west to the Bitlis pass and beyond to the basin of the upper Tigris. His advance south which took him through the Hınıs plain was slow, encumbered as he was with a huge train of wagons and livestock. Still, confident that he faced no serious threat as he approached Manzikert, he sent ahead a large detachment with some of his best troops to soften up Ahlat. The capitulation of Manzikert without a fight gave the impression that everything was going smoothly.

Alp Arslan had succeeded in drawing him south, in dividing his army and in inducing over-confidence. He himself had meanwhile been taking his army on a long, looping march, crossing the mountains of Kurdistan from northern Iraq, then moving rapidly west from Azerbaijan to Lake Van. Concealed by the towering mass of Süphan and its surrounding lava flows, he advanced along the north shore of the lake and seized control of the Manzikert–Ahlat route. He now attacked the Byzantine force outside Ahlat and drove it west. The main army under Romanos was kept busy with a day-long skirmish which inflicted considerable damage and sapped its morale. Soon (the sources differ as to whether or not there was an interlude of two days) Romanos, aware now of the identity of his adversary, began a cautious advance south towards the western foothills of Süphan, over the only sector of the plain around Manzikert which was not covered with extruded lumps of lava and was therefore suitable for a cavalry engagement. The Turks now used the classic tactics of the steppe nomad, irritating the Byzantines by their arrow fire, inducing increasing disorder in their formations by feigned retreats, sudden counterattacks and ambushes. As the day neared its end and disarray grew in the Byzantine ranks, they attacked in force, sliced the Byzantine army into its four component parts (centre, two wings and rearguard) and concentrated on the annihilation of the centre commanded by the Emperor. The Emperor was among the survivors taken prisoner.

The civil war in the Byzantine Empire which followed allowed the Turks to consolidate their hold on Armenia and to prepare for the invasion of Anatolia, which now lay exposed to attack along the easiest approaches, those often-mentioned routes along the Murat Su, the open uplands to the north and the Euphrates valley. Within ten years, the wilder nomad tribesmen of the Turkish world and their Seljuk political masters would have reached the shores of the

67

Marmara and the Aegean, and it would take sustained effort over a generation and a half, after the First Crusade halted the Turkish expansion, for Byzantium to recover the periphery of Anatolia.

The battlefield, indeed the whole Patnos–Manzikert plain, is dominated by Süphan, the most elegant of the volcanoes of Armenia. Only the topmost part of the cone is missing. The mountain soars up to a little over 4,000 metres from the frozen rivers of lava which it spewed out to east and west, and which now form smooth high ridges, penning in Lake Van.

We were racing south, while there was still daylight, but the eyes of driver as well as passenger kept being drawn away from the road by that majestic mountain. Night was falling as we crossed over one of its giant shoulders and came down to Lake Van. Before long we were in the city of Van, too down-at-heel to be admitted to the smart hotels which have mushroomed to meet the demand from the tourists who sweep over the mountains, lava flows and flat alluvial plains of what was once Armenia in air-conditioned, turbo-charged coaches. We ended up in a hotel of decaying grandeur, dating from an earlier age and now shunned by well-heeled foreigners.

CHAPTER 3

We reached Van in the dark and resolved to treat ourselves to comfort. Looking up my list of good hotels ('first class' meaning least good, 'second class' better and so on progressing upwards) we found that Van possessed two third-class hotels. In the heavy gilded lobby of the Grand Urartu Oteli men in braided uniforms stared into space. The reception clerk was writing a note. We asked for a room. He finished his writing and said 'Full up' without glancing at us. I thought of small villages where humble *otels* made it their business to find accommodation for a traveller when they had no room themselves. The Grand Urartu Hotel, designed to deal in block bookings with international agencies, felt no such obligation.

We fared no better at the other third-class hotel and settled instead for two nights in an old-fashioned rooming house from which the previous occupant, a lady who apparently used it for entertainment, had to be ousted to make way for us. The beds were unmade and the ashtrays full, but there was a balcony – to me always an irresistible attraction – looking on to the street, complete with table and chairs, a light with coloured plastic shade and a curtained window into the bedroom. After our treatment at the Grand the smell of drains was somehow comforting.

From our balcony we watched an open lorry drive slowly by sounding its horn with a load of young men shouting slogans. One beat a drum. The others waved sticks and banners. The noise was tremendous. Returning from dinner, we saw it again and paused to watch at a shop selling post-cards and carpets.

A youth came up: 'Hello – *danke* – are you from Blackpool?' It did not need a Sherlock Holmes to deduce that package tourism had reached Van.

Nothing lives in or on Lake Van. Too salty for fish, devoid of birds to prey on them, it is an azure expanse of lifeless water six times the size of Lake Geneva, ringed by snow-capped mountains, with the haunting melancholy of a beauti-ful dead woman. On a small off-shore island half an hour's drive from the town of Van stands one of the wonders of the world. The Armenian church of Aghtamar was built, with an accompanying imperial palace, in the tenth century by King Gagik II Artsruni, whose dominions stretched north to the Araxes and deep into Persia to the east. It was lovingly tended for the millennium in which it was the seat of Armenian bishops; desecrated during the terrible Armenian massacre of 1915; allowed to go to ruin during the next fifty years; and finally 'rediscovered' in recent years as a tourist attraction. Aghtamar is described on postcards we bought in Van simply as 'Van Church': there is no mention of its pedigree.

The Church of the Holy Cross is reached by a twenty-minute boat ride during which its ravaged beauty slowly reveals itself to the approaching eye. Grass grows through cracks between its sand-coloured stones. Tufts of moss show in the conical roof. Two breeze-block army posts, fortuitously hidden from the sea, stand cheek-by-jowl with the sacred precinct, presumably to deter Armenian terrorists. Yet noth-ing can dim Aghtamar's glory. The church stands on a lime-stone crag facing the mountains to the south, rising visibly above its adversities. The quality of the masonry alone bears the thumbprint of a superior civilisation that dominated the region for a thousand years. Aghtamar is a voice crying in the wilderness.

The outer walls of the church are alive with charming and often witty carvings of Old Testament stories. Lions, foxes, dogs, hares, gazelles and a horse pursue one another in bas relief round the eaves. Below them a frieze known as the

70

Vine Scroll celebrates day-to-day events in the lives of birds, beasts and men. On one wall King Gagik presents a model of the church to Christ; on another Jonah enters the gaping jaws of a particularly merry whale; David slays Goliath; Samson is getting ready to despatch a Philistine; and Adam and Eve, heavy-bellied from the feasts of Eden, prepare to tackle the fruit course. The Scholar, whose aesthetic sense sets him apart from most other academics I know, pointed out many of the details to me. He had an eye for eccentricity: the patron Saint Sargis' horse which was the only one out of step in a cavalcade; an anachronistic Mongol horseman in the middle of an otherwise biblical scene; and a local variant of the story of the fiery furnace in which the flameproof trio were endowed with women's breasts. Inside the church the frescoes seemed sadly faded, but the scope and scale of the themes still conveyed the grandeur of its founder's vision. By comparison with Aghtamar contemporary Norman architecture in Britain seemed like the work of crude peasantry. By any standards Aghtamar is breathtaking.

Of the royal palace nothing remains. Looking for it, all we came across was a group of Swedish tourists eating a barbecue lunch among the tombstones. On one stood an empty Coca-Cola bottle. We waited in the sun by Aghtamar's little jetty while the Swedes had a dip in the lake's sticky brine, and shared their boat back to the mainland with an outgoing shift of sentries.

Waiting for sleep that night I had the opportunity to study yet another frieze. The Scholar had settled down at the desk on the balcony to write up his day's notes. Projected by the balcony light on to the net curtains of the bedroom window his profile loomed immediately above my head in the form of a gigantically enlarged silhouette. For minutes at a stretch it remained motionless. The masterful gaze dominated both bedroom and balcony. The bulging cranium and awesome brow knotted in thought bore down as if to quell any detail

71

that might be so foolish as to attempt an escape. It was like the Wizard of Oz.

Twice in the night I was disturbed by a crashing sound. Looking up I saw that the silhouette had moved and the Scholar was now drinking from what appeared to be a ten-gallon bottle of water. I had already been struck by the unusual pattern of his water consumption, in gargantuan sessions between long intervals, as if he were accustomed to equipping himself for crossing deserts. Each morning we bought two two-litre bottles which he would consume largely unaided in sessions accounting for up to a litre a time. Now I had the opportunity to observe the phenomenon in magnified close-up. The colossal Adam's apple worked steadily against the blind as draught succeeded draught. There was a pause followed by a great sigh. Then the operation resumed.

It was our last morning in Van. We were having breakfast served by a slothful, overweight youth in a café housed in an office block beside the Security Directorate, where the sign 'EMNIYET' stretched across the front in Orwellian capitals. I was recounting a perplexing dream starring Princess Margaret and a Hollywood hairdresser when a car drew up. Two policemen sprang out, followed by yet another man in hand-cuffs, again with a coat slung over his shoulders. The trio quickly disappeared into the building, but not before I had time to notice the distinctive Kurdish features.

I did not immediately associate the young man in my mind with the recent general outbreak of Kurdish unrest, still knowing nothing of the genocidal activities of the Iraqis that had set it off. Instead he became part of a plot taking on a life of its own inside my head, in which outside events were stage props. There is a manacled prisoner whose crime we don't know. No more does he. He is accused of treachery; his treachery is the result of a divided loyalty. Like the man who is both Kurd and Turk he is destined to betray one of his loyalties. Deeper still, he is morally damaged goods; he has been dishonoured by his past, used as a tool in someone's

72

else's game which he did not understand – just as Kurds were used to kill Armenians against the expectation of being given land.

The idea of programmed treachery took hold. I envisaged one of the characters committing an act of treachery against the others, without knowing why, through a secret loyalty to a tyrannical force. He would be a prisoner, like the young Kurd, but of his past, and like him destined to be punished twice, once in the original wrong done to him, then repeatedly for the rest of his life.

From Van we headed north again, towards the point on the map where the Soviet Union, Iran and Turkey met. At Erciş we paused to see what traces remained of a medieval town said to have been inundated by a sudden rise in the Van's water level. We found only a great salt flat, a distant mausoleum in the now-familiar pillbox shape of a cone standing on a drum, and a burial ground where one gravestone, mixing Christian and Moslem calendars, recorded the remarkable lifespan: 1335–1982. We had no time to look for three nearby sites of the Urartu kingdom dating back to 800 BC. In a *lokanta* at Patnos we ate like kings for less than fifty pence a head.

Thirty miles on we came to the great Silk Road, and turned east towards the Iranian border and Doğubayazıt. We drove through a long grey moonscape of rock – grey-blue, grey-red, grey-green and then just grey. In the evening light horizons appeared on either side and began to advance towards us, until we were flanked by an escort of mountains. Then, slightly to the north, there came into view the formidable and unmistakable outline of Mount Ararat, the symbol of Armenia. The great snowcapped volcano a thousand feet higher than Mont Blanc, legendary resting place of Noah's Ark and centre from which mankind set out once again to populate the earth, resembled an enormous and rather threatening steam jam pudding. Ararat had no clearly defined peak, but the eye was drawn by its commanding presence. Given to apocalyptic eruptions, its rounded shoulders seemed to be hunched for another onset. We stopped the car and watched the mountain turn dark violet in the night sky.

Doğubayazıt had the vitality of a frontier town with the raw, freebooting air of private enterprise. Its streets were troughs of hard mud. Its shops were filled with food, clothes and Turkish souvenirs. The whole town had recently become a duty-free emporium for Iranian tourists pouring over the newly reopened frontier twenty minutes away. After Iran's recent upheavals it seemed surprising to see them behaving just like middle-class tourists the world over. They were everywhere, richer than most Turks we had met. For the most part they wore Western clothes, drove Western cars and had the universal look of prosperous families on holiday. As we walked about, begging boys pulled at our sleeves. Irritated after a while, we began to fend them off. As one departed rebuffed I noticed that he was dragging his feet, apparently affected with a motor disease. Stricken with remorse I gave the equivalent of eighty pence to the next one, a child of perhaps five. Taking my offering in his hand he held it up shouting 'Ho! Ho!' in triumph. The Scholar, who had views about indiscriminate charity, looked at me reprovingly. Still chortling the boy marched off.

Our hotel, formerly the Ararat, had been renamed the Isfahan. In the carpark two attendants vied for the privilege of washing (more accurately 'watching') our car. The hotel had its own adaptations of modern life: a lift with a light which remained illuminated until you got in; then it went out, and you travelled in darkness. In the bedroom there was piping hot water, but no cold; a sign advertising a 'Save Water' campaign, but no plug in the basin. Drawn to the television set in the lobby by a familiar theme tune I found an Iranian woman wearing a silk *yashmak* watching an episode of 'Yes, Prime Minister' dubbed into Turkish. Sadly I had no means of knowing what she made of it since all I could see of her face was a pair of black eyes. Somewhere in the darkness outside our hotel a dog howled all night. In the morning as we left a heavy mist hid Ararat from view.

Like Ozymandias, King of Kings, the ghostlike palace of Ishak Pasha stands in the desert, or rather on its edge, on the road to the Iranian frontier a few miles from Doğubayazıt. An Ottoman folly of the eighteenth century, it was built on the proceeds of trade from the Silk Road which it overlooks. Like Randolph Hearst's megalomaniac pile in California, it has something borrowed from every epoch and so belongs to none – Seljuk doorway, Mongol mausoleum, Ottoman state rooms with carving that seemed crude after Aghtamar. It is a monument to elegant indolence, a ruin celebrating imperial decay. Above all it is a spectacular sight best seen from afar. We left it to the cold dank mist and an Iranian couple busily photographing one other.

Northbound now, our road took us over a pass skirting the hidden colossus of Ararat. As we reached the mountain's shoulder, its smaller twin, Aragats, came into view sixty miles away inside the Soviet Union. The extraordinary elevation of mountains above plain – the higher peak stands over 4,000 metres above the Araxes valley floor – greatly added to their magnificence. Somewhere in the mist below us was the Soviet city of Erevan: near it, the epicentre of the earthquake due to hit Armenia in a few weeks' time. From our vantage point the manmade border in the middle of the ancient kingdom appeared to be not just an affront to Armenians, but an act defying nature. Partition, as Solomon knew, is a poor way to resolve human affairs. He had been proved right in Armenia.

Approaching the Soviet border we came to Iğdır, a bustling market town that reminded me of a very early movie, with horsedrawn traffic including a once-smart brougham with painted panels, men on bicycles laden with farm produce. A knot of children played with hoops made from rusted wheel rims. (Why don't European children still play with hoops?) It was still morning as we drove by, but we could sense the animation of the market place.

A few miles away across the border the rival system would be at work. The scene would be a very different one, with farmers in collectives shipping their produce to Moscow for centralised distribution. But the Soviet Union might have been on another planet. The border had been closed for seventy years and nobody we spoke to had any inkling of the land beyond.

Soon our road converged with the frontier and ran along the gorge carrying the Araxes in the opposite direction towards the Caspian Sea. On the far bank where the Soviet Union began we could see no sign of life apart from the occasional large, low, concrete farm building. It did not look much fun.

At the little border town of Tuzluca where we stopped for tea a thirteen-year-old boy in a smart black leather jacket came up and addressed us in English in tones of great formality and gravity. To our astonishment, but not at all to his, he was the third member of the Erzurum English class that we were to meet. Like the boy from Erzurum itself he had a poor opinion of the academic skills of the Bayburt tailor's son.

'He is not a good student,' he stated solemnly. 'He does not learn good English. He does not work well.' I had begun to feel a new respect for this secret rebel who had seemed so docile in his dealings with us. Our new friend was a greengrocer's son. At the family store a human chain of workers was unloading melons from a lorry. The boy presented one to me with a bow. I took his photograph and offered to send it. He turned to the Scholar and said he would greatly prefer to open a correspondence with him, and asked him to return all his letters with grammatical errors corrected. He gave us his name and address, shook hands, bowed again and walked off. Pausing, he turned, smiled stiffly and said, rolling his 'r', 'You will not forr-get me . . . ?'

At the outskirts of the town we turned on to a road that would take us north again along the Soviet border. We passed an unoccupied Turkish watchtower, then others manned by bored sentries. As we headed for the fortified town of Kars the mountains melted away behind us and the scenery turned greener.

The plain of Kars had already captured my imagination thanks to the small amount of background reading I had done. Here nature, legend and history were heightened. From springs near here flowed three great rivers. We had already seen Ararat, pondered on the adventures of Noah, looked in vain for the Ark of the Covenant . . . Somewhere to our west Islamic legend placed the Garden of Eden, supposedly on a mountain top (so I had read) between Kars and Erzurum. In short, we were not far, to the not too rigorously academic mind, from the source of the human race.

The Scholar explained that we were entering an alluvial plain. Geography-blind, I listened to his discourse on rough grazing and dry farming, on the advantages and drawbacks of volcanic soil. I was introduced to the phenomenon of tectonic movement; and even discovered for the first time what tundra was. Unlike me, the Scholar could relate history to geography. He knew what terrain was suitable for defence and what for sustenance. For him the lie of the land was a key piece in the jigsaw of this extraordinary region over which wandering tribes had fought since the beginning of time; whereas in my mind there lingered a schoolboy image of a hole in the ground somewhere in central Asia out of which men like Genghis Khan and Tamberlain erupted at intervals with oven-ready hordes of Mongols and Cossacks to overrun the world.

A lapidary clarity lent wings to his presentation and his mesmerising grasp of detail gave it the ring of conviction (although I noted with small satisfaction that on one occasion a river had the impertinence to be flowing in the opposite direction to the one he had announced). At my request the Scholar now undertook the challenge of preparing for me a map in which there would be nothing incomprehensible to a child of twelve (the age at which I had abandoned geography in despair).

CHAPTER 4: HISTORICAL EXCURSUS

Henceforth we would be traversing at greater speed the more open lands of central Armenia, east of the entanglement of mountains which centres on the Bingöl Dağ. We would be visiting the capitals of the two premier Christian principalities of Armenia in the tenth century, as well as two of the magnificent domed churches which were created by extraordinary feats of patronage in the most out-of-the-way places on the fringes of Georgia.

The most imposing natural features of Armenia are the volcanoes, which have exercised a pervasive, though indirect influence over its history. The huge flows of lava extruded by them form bare, semi-desert zones which, together with the older fold mountains running across the landscape, separate and isolate the cultivable areas. They played an important part in fostering the particularism of localities which was a fundamental feature of Armenian life. Agriculture flourished most and settlements were densest in the river valleys which skirt them, wherever the action of wind, snow and rain over the millennia brought down and spread out a rich volcanic alluvium scoured off the frozen lava flows. The level, fertile plains thus created formed the natural economic and political centres of the region. The volcanoes were therefore ultimately responsible for much of the friable character of Armenia, a land of violent contrasts, which is in effect a mosaic of mountains, lava flows and rich alluvial basins, a land where movement is difficult outside the natural corridors carved by the rivers.

The great faults in the earth's crust which intersect beneath Armenia and were responsible in relatively recent geological times for the extrusion of the volcanoes made a more immediate and dramatic impact. The periodic earthquakes which they caused were devastating in their effects, both material and psychological. They reminded, as they still remind, the Armenians of their weakness and vulnerability in the face of nature, as well as the great powers of the surrounding world, and instilled in them a conception of God far more akin to the irascible deity of the Old Testament, alert to human wrongdoing and quick to punish it, than to the softer-hearted, sympathetic image projected in the New Testament.

The climate, with its sharp contrast between long, harsh winters and shorter, luxuriant summers has exercised an even more profound influence than the volcanoes. The principal responsibility for the social and political fractiousness of Armenia lay with winter. Communications became hazardous, often impossible. Localities were isolated from each other, families confined to their own houses within localities. In the longer term winter ensured that the basic social, economic and political unit was small (a geographer, writing in the seventh century, enumerated around 200 of these basic districts) and that families with claims to pre-eminence had to struggle unceasingly to maintain, let alone extend their sphere of authority.

The fold mountains are the final geographical feature of importance. Besides contributing to the fragmentation of the region and imposing a simpler, mainly pastoral way of life on their local inhabitants, their principal role was to help the Armenians in the darkest days of foreign oppression. For certain extensive and tangled gatherings of mountains, notably those adjoining the south-east corner of the Black Sea and the highlands of modern Kurdistan south-east of Lake Van, could be turned into large natural fastnesses at times of crisis. Nobles and their retinues could establish secure bases from which to continue the struggle against the outside power when the battle had been lost on the plains. There warfare naturally assumed a guerrilla character and the invader faced a virtually impossible task in attempting to impose his authority permanently, unless he was able to persevere for several generations. Without these formidable highland redoubts, it is doubtful whether the Armenians could have preserved their cultural independence and political identity in late antiquity and the early Middle Ages.

But in one vital respect the fold mountains failed the Armenians and the other peoples of Transcaucasia. While they gave them succour at times of oppression, they did not defend them against invasion from east or west. High mountain ranges, aligned roughly east–west, provided defensible northern and southern frontiers for Transcaucasia as a whole, the Caucasus in the north, and the line of the Zagros and Taurus in the south. But the ranges in between, which are likewise aligned east–west, left clear avenues for predatory foreign powers to use. These inviting routes, over the open plains of ancient Caucasian Albania (now Soviet Azerbaijan) on either side of the Kura river led to the rich heart of Armenia in the middle Araxes valley and the exposed plains of eastern Georgia. Eastern and central Transcaucasia was so vulnerable to attack from the east that it was bound to be drawn for most of its history into political structures centred in Iran. The narrower western section, squeezed between the Black Sea and the Taurus was equally accessible, with three invasion routes obligingly provided by nature (those which we had been exploring in the first part of these travels). The western third of Armenia, together with the adjoining south-western districts of Georgia, was therefore singularly ill-placed to resist the pull of the greater or lesser powers established on the Anatolian plateau to the west. Armenia was a giant causeway. Her fate was to be overrun and, if there were no single preponderant power in the Near East, to be partitioned.

The outer walls of mountains, however, acted as powerful natural defences of the whole region against invasion from north or south. The Caucasus kept out the predatory nomad powers who controlled the great bay of the South Russian steppe, which runs south between the Caspian and Black

Seas, in late antiquity and the early Middle Ages. Their irruptions – whether those of the Sabir Huns in the early sixth century, the central Asian Turks in the 620s, or the Khazars in the eighth century – were occasional and did not result in permanent conquests. The Zagros and Taurus to the south proved even more effective barriers, mainly because the Fertile Crescent, arching between the mountains and the desert, held many more attractions for expansionist powers than the bleaker lands north of the mountains. With the single exception of the Arabs whose outward drive to conquest was supercharged by their commitment to *jihad* and rode over natural barriers and the normal geographical constraints on the size of states in the pre-industrial age.

But it did not take long for even the Arabs to realise that they could not storm Armenia from the south. There were too few natural breaches in its mountain rampart, which ran east and west from the virtually impassable mountains of Kurdistan. After their first attack in force (in 640), when they struck directly north across the Taurus at the administrative centre of Armenia, they preferred a circuitous route of invasion. They pushed over the passes of the Zagros, east of Kurdistan, and seized hold of Persian Azerbaijan, colonising the interlinked fertile basins around Lake Urmia and in the hill country to the south of the lower course of the Araxes. Azerbaijan had been the base from which the Persians had supported their colonial administration in the three provinces of Transcaucasia in late antiquity. Early seizure and rapid colonisation of Azerbaijan by the Arabs was both essential to secure their position in Iran itself and provided them with a platform from which to send out fast-moving reconnoitring forces over Transcaucasia. Over a century passed, a new dynasty took over the caliphate, before serious efforts were made to impose Arab authority outside Azerbaijan and the few, isolated forward military bases which they had held hitherto (Theodosiopolis was the first to be garrisoned).

Natural relief, therefore, delayed the conquest and subjection of Armenia. When it began in earnest, in the second half of the eighth century, the primary impulse came from central government under the new Abassid regime, anxious to improve its military position in Transcaucasia. For the allegiance of the peoples of Transcaucasia, which had been gained by economical displays of force, was increasingly endangered by the only two adversaries who were capable of matching all but the greatest of Arab armies in the field and whose ideological underpinning was as strong as that of the caliphate.

Of these adversaries, the Khazars were the more immediate threat and the main Arab thrust into Armenia was determined principally by the requirements of defence-in-depth against attack from across the Caucasus. The front line ran up the Kura valley from the Caspian shore to Georgia, and attracted the largest concentrations of troops and settlers. But a second, supporting line of securely held territory was established to the south. The Araxes valley up to and including the great plain immediately to the north of Mount Ararat was occupied. Dvin, the old capital of Persian Armenia (not far from Erevan), was thus brought under direct Arab rule, eventually resuming its ancient role as the military and administrative centre of Armenia. The second adversary, Byzantium, still clung to the north-western fringes of Armenia (the westernmost section of the upper Euphrates valley, up to Kemah) and had historic claims to much more territory. Irredentist ambitions were feared, and a subsidiary objective behind the occupation of the Araxes valley and the retention of a garrison at the forward base of Theodosiopolis was to deter Byzantium from pursuing them.

Further west other settlers were moving into Armenia. The caliphal authorities sponsored their migration for internal security reasons (which were also a subsidiary motive behind the occupation of the Araxes valley). The Armenian uprising of 774–5 had revealed the fragility of the Arab position in southern Transcaucasia, and, after its bloody suppression by a crack force from eastern Iran, encouragement was given to the colonisation of strategically important and accessible regions. However, the primary impulse probably came from the colonists themselves, their motives being the usual ones – the search for prestige by participation in bold ventures, hunger for land and wealth and subjects, competition between rival tribes and their leaderships.

Since they were going against the grain of the relief of the highlands and there were only three relatively safe passes crossing the Taurus, settlement proceeded slowly and ultimately only affected two widely separated areas within western Armenia. One group of colonists seeped across the most westerly of those passes, the Ergani pass, into the lower Murat Su valley, and was reinforced by spillage east across the Euphrates from the highly militarised region around the main base of operations against Byzantium, Malatya. Here Arab occupation was limited to the plains along the river valley, up to that of Arsomasata, and the western section of the open uplands to the north. The highlands further north, from the Munzur Dağ to the Bingöl Dağ, were untouched, as was the middle sector of the Murat valley, including the plains of Bingöl and Muş. The Arabs, therefore, were confined to an enclave in the open, more fertile lands of the south-west.

There was a similar seepage of adventurers and colonists over the easternmost of the Taurus passes, which leads up from the basin of the upper Tigris past Bitlis to the west end of Lake Van. Gradually Arab control expanded along the north shore of the lake and, over the shoulders of Mount Süphan, into the open plains with their rich volcanic alluvial soil where Manzikert was developed as the main administrative centre. This was a second isolated Arab enclave, which could not exercise permanent effective control over the plain of Muş, immediately to the west, let alone over the highlands of the north (the Bingöl Dağ and its eastern outliers) or the mountains of Kurdistan to the south-east.

The Arab conquest of Armenia was thus surprisingly limited in scope and caused surprisingly little disruption to the existing political and social order. The takeover of the lowlands was relatively easy and painless, whether swift as in the east or slow and gradual as in the two enclaves in the south and west. Large tracts of Armenia retained their independence. They were mainly the highland areas where serious resistance was to be expected but also

83

included a number of isolated plains (notably those of Muş, Ağrı and Kars). These areas were left untouched by Arab settlers and only felt the force of Arab military power for limited periods, when the authorities moved onto the counter-offensive after each of the three great rebellions (of 747–50, 774–5 and 850–2). The most dangerous assault came later, at the turn of the ninth and tenth centuries. It was not provoked by open Armenian opposition nor instituted by the central authorities, but was part of a bid for regional supremacy in west Iran and Transcaucasia launched by the Sajid emirs of Azerbaijan.

None of these repressive phases lasted long and they failed to break Armenian resistance in the highlands. They only caused limited and short-term damage, and the traditional patterns of pastoral life and localised lordship among the highlanders were, if anything, strengthened in the course of the guerrilla wars against the intruders. Concerted aggression on the part of the Arab authorities also had a beneficial *political* effect on the Armenians. It deepened a sense of national identity, created strong bonds between the traditionally rival gatherings of lordships within regions, and greatly enhanced the status of the grander of the noble families, whose members took a leading part in the struggles against the Arabs. The trials of Armenia, despite all the bloodshed and the temporary disruption which they brought, by compressing the leaders of resistance, their ramified kin, their retinues and their traditional local allies together in the mountain fastnesses to which they withdrew, and by offering unmatched opportunities for the amassing of the key component of power, prestige, promoted political cohesion at all levels. Political adversity thus counteracted to a remarkable extent the centrifugal forces of geography and climate (the long, harsh winters were the great corrosive agents) which broke up Armenia into a multitude of small districts and kept society seething with local feuds.

The grim years of rebellion, withdrawal and determined guerrilla warfare thus provided the springboard for the rise to regional dominance of a small number of leading noble families (foremost among them being the Artsrunis, who built the palace complex at Aghtamar, and several branches of the Bagratid family). They also, it has to be admitted, provided opportunities for them, if they chose to do so, to ride the wave of Arab repression, to act as loyal and energetic allies and clients of the Muslim oppressors, and, in the process, to extend their own spheres of influence (as happened in the case of the Bagratids of Kars in the mid-ninth century). By consolidating the authority of the premier families, they prepared the way for indigenous state-formation as soon as Arab power began to wane.

The survival of an autonomous Armenian society and culture through the centuries of Arab occupation is chiefly attributable to the geographical configuration of Armenia. The inflow of Arab colonists was limited and they made little impression on the highland regions outside their areas of settlement where resistance was much more effective. Throughout Transcaucasia they were confined to the lowlands, in particular the more readily accessible regions of strategic importance, on the natural avenues of east–west communication provided by the great rivers of Transcaucasia, the Kura, the Araxes, the upper Euphrates and the Murat.

But apart from the constraints imposed by limited human resources and relief, the Arabs in their political heyday showed little inclination to penetrate into mountain zones in any part of their empire and then to set about the laborious process of pacifying them. Roman techniques for bringing naturally refractory regions under direct control, involving a systematic programme of road- and fort-construction which was gradually pushed deeper into the mountains, were not copied by the Arabs. They were content to surround and isolate highland regions. Their policy was passive, not active or intrusive save in emergencies. They relied on the gravitational pull exerted by the pure monotheism of Islam and the lure of the flourishing, luxurious civilisation of the plains gradually to draw highlanders into the religious and political system of the caliphate. Their absorption would only be achieved over many generations, and in the meantime the authorities relied on diplomacy and techniques of client-management which other states deployed outside their frontiers, and occasional punitive military action to keep the highlands quiescent.

Armenia was one example among many of this unusually modest, realistic approach to the management of a vast empire by a widely dispersed colonial élite. But in Armenia hopes that the culture of the Arabised lowlands would encroach spontaneously on the surrounding highlands proved quite vain. For the Armenians possessed cultural defences which were no less formidable than the physical defences provided by their mountain fastnesses. As Christians, indeed as heirs of the first state to establish Christianity, they were neither overawed nor allured by Islam. Their own distinctive brand of belief, marked off from Orthodoxy by disagreement on one vital point of doctrine, underpinned their sense of national identity, and enabled them to turn to their great western Christian neighbour, Byzantium, for aid in crises without any real danger of absorption from that quarter. Their cultural resistance could not be overcome either in the short or the longer term.

The caliphate, under the Abbasid regime which took power in 750, compounded its problems by an understandable, but fatal policy decision. It disbanded the centrally funded Armenian levies which the previous Umayyad regime had deployed in Transcaucasia in operations against the Khazars. It was a natural response after the first great Armenian uprising of 747–750 which had sought to take advantage of civil war in the caliphate. But the consequences were baneful. The surplus of skilled fighting manpower generated by the highlands was penned in, unused. Armenian patriotism, instead of being weakened by long service in the forces of the caliphate, was heightened and the pressures for action against the alien occupying forces in the plains built up steadily until they reached bursting point. The two general rebellions which followed, in 774–5 and 850–2, and the repressive countermeasures of the Arab authorities sealed the division between the Christian Armenian and the Muslim Arab intruder. Further advances by the Arabs could only be achieved by brute force in spasms of violent aggression.

Of all the highland regions, termed *terres d'insolence* by a distinguished French historian, which studded the length and breadth of the caliphate outside its inner core (the desert and the fertile lands fringing it), Armenia was probably the most refractory. The caliphate was an agglomeration of lowland territories, connected by a transcontinental route network to the central lands. It was loosely constructed, nowhere more loosely than in Armenia where there were no secure routes linking together the three areas of Arab occupation.

But although the caliphate was a vastly overextended empire, there were two powerful bonds holding it together in its early medieval heyday, religion and trade. And as long as a reasonable degree of cohesion was maintained, its resources were such that its hold over highland regions, even if it was as fragile as in Armenia, could not be challenged save in the very short term. The basic unifying force was Islam, in particular the common commitment required of Moslems to its propagation by *jihad* and consolidation by *haj*, and a general readiness, which diminished only gradually, to recognise the ultimate religious and political authority of the caliph, attenuated though it might be in practice. But trade and the wealth which it generated proved invaluable auxiliaries.

Centuries of participation in long-distance trade had entrenched commercial interests in pagan Arab society and ensured a high status for the merchant-venturer. The economic opportunities offered by the empire won for Islam were not foregone. The caliphs gave their blessing to trade. Within a half century of the initial conquests, the *de facto* single market created by arms was enforced by legislation. Tariff barriers to the free movement of persons and goods were prohibited. New Arab currencies were issued for circulation throughout the caliphate, silver dirhams for the former territories of the Sassanian Empire in the east, gold dinars for the Mediterranean lands. Arabic was declared the official language. The absence of artificial, man-made impediments to trade, and the maintenance of law and order by the provincial authorities, provided favourable conditions for mercantile activity.

There followed a period of sustained economic growth throughout the caliphate, which was without precedent in its outer lands, stretching from Transcaucasia to central Asia. Several virtuous circles came into play. Increased exchange of processed natural produce and manufactured goods between regions encouraged increasing differentiation in production which in turn gave a further boost to long-distance trade. Meanwhile demand grew steadily as Arab colonists and local populations were concentrated in growing towns, as the general standard of living rose in the lowlands, and as local élites formed and developed an appetite for luxury goods. Urbanisation proceeded apace throughout the outer lands; the resulting increase in demand stimulated increased production, specialisation and exchange between cities and regions, which then prompted further urban growth.

It is impossible to say, for lack of quantified information, how long this benign interaction between demand, exchange and supply lasted. It is likely that the rate of growth was slowed by the increasing frequency of conflict within the caliphate which is discernible from the second half of the ninth century and that the vast transcontinental economy which had been developed entered a phase of stable equilibrium in the tenth century. But it still completely overshadowed the depressed Mediterranean and Continental European economies, and had created a dense network of cities which were to remain a permanent legacy of the caliphate in the outer lands.

Transcaucasia profited as much as any region in those outer lands from the general economic growth. Numerous local products were praised by the geographers who wrote for the urban merchant classes of the caliphate in the tenth century. They were exported all over the Arab world, from which other goods were imported in return. Transcaucasia was, as the geographers make plain, an integral part of the caliphate's economic system. One of them indeed considered Albania (now Soviet Azerbaijan) to be the most prosperous and attractive region of all. Cities sprang up everywhere in the lowlands, in Armenia as well as Albania. In the southern enclave, four new cities appeared on the north shore of Lake Van, while Manzikert was developed and became the capital of the emirate. Urbanisation spread out to the very edge of the zones of Arab occupation, reaching for example the uplands between the lower Murat Su and the Munzur Dağ in the western enclave, and stimulated analogous developments in the highlands beyond, along the routes leading to and from Arab territories (of which Ardanuç, in the extreme south-west of early medieval Georgia, and Havjij, somewhere near the western side of the Bingöl Dağ, are good examples).

The economic development of Armenia did not stop at the political frontiers between territories directly administered by the Arab authorities and those mainly highland areas where power continued to be exercised by a nexus of greater and lesser Armenian lordships. The market forces generated within the empire of Islam acted upon the refractory highland regions there as elsewhere. Difficult communications might diminish their effect, but the booming economies of the plains inevitably stimulated more exchange with the mountains and increased the disposable wealth of the leading highland noble families. The knock-on effect was, as is evident from the cases of Ardanuç and Havjij, greatest on the main commercial routes through the highlands as also on neighbouring lowland regions which had been left in Armenian hands.

The Arab occupation thus had a second benign influence on Armenia, besides consolidating political authority in the highlands. It magnified the wealth of the lowlands and allowed the most successful noble families in the highlands, whose power rested ultimately on the steady accumulation of prestige through achievement in war, high lineage and free-handed treatment of their followers, to amass larger treasures, hence to increase the size of their immediate retinues and the extent of their wider clientage. Once the balance of power shifted between the mainly Arab lowlands and the Armenian highlands, there began a period of dynamic expansion by the leading nobles of the latter. As Arab military power declined and they began to push out on to the plains, there was an acceleration in the rate of their accumulation of wealth which, by enabling them to increase their forces, gave added momentum to their advance over the lowlands, which further magnified their wealth.

The most successful managed to maintain their pre-eminence in a large, secure highland region on the northern or southern edge of Armenia, and to extend their authority over the fertile, urbanised lowlands of the interior. By entrenching themselves on the plains and gaining control of their resources, they were able to transform the nexus of clientages and alliances which had supported them hitherto into a durable principality with roughly defined boundaries and to acquire for themselves acknowledged princely status. The immeasurably increased wealth of which they now disposed also enabled them to patronise the arts and to develop courts with their own flourishing cultures. The most durable monuments to this cultural acme of Armenia are the magnificent churches which were built in the leading principalities, most under princely patronage, and the high-grade historical works which they commissioned.

Four powerful regional dynasties emerged between the early ninth and mid-tenth centuries. The Bagratids, who had long been recognised as one of the premier families in the Armenian nobility, established two of them. With Arab sponsorship, they expanded out of their mountain fastnesses around the lower Çoruh river in two directions, south-east over the plain of Kars and north-east over Georgia which thus came under the rule of an Armenian dynasty. Their greatest rivals were the Artsrunis, who steadily extended their authority over an arc of lowlands north of their highland refuge zone in the impenetrable mountains east and south-east of Lake Van. Finally the ramified Siounian family rose more slowly to prominence in the highlands south and east of Lake Sevan (of which Nagorno-Karabakh is part). The tangible vestiges of three of these court cultures are still to be seen in eastern Turkey (the exceptions being the churches built by the Siounians which are in Soviet Armenia and Azerbaijan). They were our main objectives, together with the landscape itself with its dramatic juxtapositioning of mountain and alluvial plain in the regions around the greatest of all the Armenian volcanoes, Ararat.

A certain melancholy, though, clings to these sites, impressive though they are. They were the products of courts which flared up as bright cultural centres for all too brief a time, in a short interlude of comparative freedom for the Armenians. The pressures from outside diminished between the mid-ninth and the mid-tenth centuries. The caliphate imploded in the 860s and 870s and never subsequently recovered its former power; the Sajid emirate of Persian Azerbaijan temporarily filled the void, made a bid for regional hegemony in Transcaucasia and western Iran, but then collapsed even more quickly than it had risen, in the 920s; and, to the north, beyond the Caucasus, the remarkably durable, polyglot empire of the Khazars fought a losing war against the Vikings for the allegiance of the Slavs of southern Russia, finally suffering a devastating loss of prestige and authority when Viking raiders sacked the capital in 965. Each of the four leading princely families of Armenia exploited the growing weakness of the local Arab emirates of the lowlands and set out on miniature campaigns of conquest and state-building of their own, as outlined above.

But there was no political vacuum in Armenia. Its great Christian neighbour, Byzantium, was itself taking full advantage of the divisions of the caliphate and the steady weakening of its central strategic forces. The military balance shifted decisively in the 860s, opening the way for a steady, step-by-step expansion of Byzantium, which was to last from the 870s until the 1040s. It was on a much grander scale than that of the individual Armenian princely dynasties. So too were the new resources which Byzantium acquired as it overran the emirates and cities of the Arab marches along the south-east side of Anatolia. Once the decision was made to alter the main direction of the offensive thrust and to concentrate it on Armenia – and the decision was inevitable at some stage because of the geopolitical position of Armenia, threatening Anatolia, as it did, along the easiest eastern approaches – and the full force of Byzantine power in all its manifestations (military, diplomatic, propaganda) was brought to bear, the princely dynasties established by Artsrunis and Bagratids in central Armenia and in southern Georgia, as well as the multitude of lesser lordships which had held their own, stood no chance of maintaining their independence in the long term.

Byzantium was a predator with growing strength and an attention to Armenia which only wavered in crises. It could and did deploy all the devices of statecraft which had been developed over centuries of continuous political existence to forward its interests in Armenia. The main weapon was warfare, of a particularly effective kind (localised guerrilla tactics directed with unremitting patience against a sequence of designated prime targets), but it was backed by subtle and flexible diplomacy. An aggressive form of client-management, used in tandem with military action, succeeded in extending and intensifying Byzantine authority over highlands as well as lowlands. Princes and lords were carefully cultivated, with offers of presents and titles and salaries and properties, were inveigled or browbeaten by propaganda into joint campaigns against the Moslem emirates first within, later outside Armenia, and were kept sweet for the moment with generous grants of territory when Arab lands were annexed. Meanwhile Byzantium was steadily and unobtrusively strengthening its own position. Whereas the Armenian princely dynasties had managed to turn service of their Arab suzerains to their own advantage, the connections now established worked to the advantage of the strong and determined outside power.

The political configuration of Armenia was changed slowly but remorselessly decade by decade, once the political initiative in the Near East passed to Byzantium and priority was given to the Armenian theatre of operations. This followed immediately on the annexation of the emirate of Malatya in 934. The lowest section of the Murat valley on the opposite side of the Euphrates was taken over at the same time since it had been a dependency of the emirate. It was amalgamated with a band of mountainous terrain stretching north on the east bank of the Euphrates and with the lowest section of the upper Euphrates valley beyond, which were already in Byzantine hands, to form a large base area, straddling the Munzur Dağ, from which to launch campaigns of conquest and pacification east over Armenia.

The first targets were the main part of the south-western Arab enclave, up to and including Arsamosata (now inundated by the waters of the Keban dam), and the Armenian highlanders of the uplands and mountains to the north. By 940, both areas had been overrun and the Byzantine forces were preparing for the next stage of the grand offensive. With their advance over the whole length of the highlands from the Munzur Dağ to the Bingöl Dağ and their seizure of the two main castles (Havjij and one in the Göynük valley, possibly on the site of Kale Köy) which guarded the route running from Theodosiopolis to the Murat valley immediately west of the Bingöl Dağ, they were in a position to pick off the outer areas of the main zone of Arab settlement in the Araxes valley and the emirate of Manzikert in the south at will. Their choice fell on the former. The new prime target was the forward base of Theodosiopolis (now Erzurum), the adjacent plain on the upper Euphrates, and the plain of Basean on the upper Araxes over the watershed. Within ten years, they were in Byzantium's possession, and, as an additional bonus, the emirate of Manzikert had been gravely weakened by Byzantium's successful efforts to stir up trouble within its ruling family.

A pause followed the capitulation of Theodosiopolis in 949 and the annexation of the adjoining plains. It was occasioned partly by the need to consolidate the gains already made and soothe the understandable anxieties of the Georgian branch of the Bagratids at the rapid advance of Byzantine power to their borders, partly by the diversion of much of the field army to south-east Anatolia to contain and counter a last flurry of Arab raiding on that sector of the frontier. The crisis there soon passed. The Hamdanid emirate of Aleppo, which had initiated the attacks, relied on the continuous accumulation of prestige from success in the *jihad* to maintain its tenuous hold over northern Syria and Cilicia. A serious defeat in 960 had catastrophic consequences and the emirate collapsed as suddenly as it had risen in the 940s. As soon as the position in the south-east had been secured by the evacuation in 965, agreed reluctantly under intense Byzantine military and diplomatic pressure, of the *jihad*–fighters from their chief base of operations, Tarsus, Byzantium was able to resume its offensive further north.

There were still distractions in the south and considerable gains of territory, including the great city of Antioch, were made there. But the main thrust was directed at areas immediately neighbouring Byzantine territory in Armenia. The immediate results were spectacular. The enfeebled principality of Taron, comprising the plain of Muş and a tranche of the Taurus to the south, was annexed by Byzantium in 966–7. Its ruling dynasty, once the senior branch of the Bagratids, had been fatally weakened by latent feuding over the previous generations. Acquisition of Taron opened the way for a successful assault on Manzikert which fell in 968–9 but was soon lost again. Crises elsewhere preoccupied Byzantium in the following decades – Viking intervention in the Balkans, two civil wars in Anatolia, and a general revolt of the Bulgars. These relieved the pressure on the premier principalities of Armenia and Georgia, indeed were used by one of the Bagratids of Georgia to demand and obtain a grant of a swathe of Byzantine territory stretching south from his own borders towards the plain of Manzikert in return for sending military aid to the beleaguered emperor. But diplomatic pressure was still applied to maintain and improve Byzantium's position in Armenia and southern Georgia, while the rising power of a certain Bad, a Kurdish leader whose ambitions spilled over the Taurus from his lands in the upper Tigris basin to embrace the whole emirate of Manzikert, kept the most successful of the Georgian Bagratids in check. When the crises had been weathered, and the Bulgar insurgents had been pushed onto the defensive in the Balkans, the advance eastwards was resumed.

Central Armenia, including the whole of the two premier principalities, was annexed bloodlessly. The lands of the powerful prince of southern Georgia (including Manzikert which had fallen to him around 993) were left in his will to the emperor, who came in 1000 to appropriate most of them and to receive the submission of neighbouring rulers (this was the occasion for his visit to Havjij). Twenty-one years later it was the turn of the Artsrunis to do a deal, under the terms of which the family ceded sovereignty over its principality in exchange for a high court rank and extensive lands in Byzantium. In 1045 the senior branch of the Armenian Bagratids, who had embellished their capital at Ani with impressive buildings, followed suit under intense Byzantine pressure and made an agreement on the same lines as their great rivals.

This was the final stage in Byzantium's slow march east. Byzantine control now extended over part of southern Georgia and the whole of central and western Armenia (the cities on the north shore of Lake Van having been netted by local military action in the 1020s and 1030s), except for a single, small, isolated client principality centred on Kars. The policy of steady, unobtrusive expansion had been pursued with exemplary consistency and patience. The successes came piecemeal but the cumulative effect was to transform the political map of the Near East, and prepare the way for a next stage in which, I suspect, the united forces of Byzantium and Christian Transcaucasia would have moved against the Muslim states of Syria and Iraq.

But then the unthinkable happened. The greater and lesser powers of Iran and its eastern dependencies were suddenly destroyed by the Turks, who brought a lethal combination of raw nomad fighting power and experienced high command to bear against them. Armenia was now threatened by the northern nomads, who had succeeded the Khazars as the dominant people in the west Eurasian steppes, *on its vulnerable eastern side*. It was quite impossible to defend. So too was the great plateau of Anatolia to the west, once the full field army of Byzantium had been caught and routed at Manzikert in 1071. In a single generation, all the gains so laboriously made by Byzantium in Armenia were swept away, and its very existence imperilled as its Anatolian heartland was overrun. For Armenians it was the end of independent political life in their homeland.

CHAPTER 5

10 September (Van)

After his normal morning round of silent, motionless combat against the anxieties which rose in the night, the *arkadaş* got up and gave tongue. Speech helped drive off the stragglers among the defeated enemy.

This was to be a lazy day. So we lingered over a breakfast of bread and honey and coffee. Nigel talked and conjured up other scenes . . .

The time is 1958, the place Baghdad. Nigel is working for Reuters and has been sent out to try to get the local correspondent out of jail. . . . He visits the prisoner once a week, taking him a stock of cigarettes. One of those old sten guns without a safety catch, which can shoot at the slightest jolt, is in his back each time he goes. He discovers later that the prisoner does not smoke. . . . The scene shifts to a hotel swimming pool. A ginger-haired man is broiling in the sun. Slowly he edges towards Nigel. Nigel tells him that he will burn. Speaking softly the ginger-haired man introduces himself as a loss adjuster. He works for an insurance company, which has received a claim from Iraq after an oil pipeline was blown up. He wants to establish whether it was the result of action by a foreign power – in which case his company will pay up – or sabotage by an internal opposition group – in which case the claim will be ruled invalid. The Reuters correspondent who has been put away was devilling for him . . . Nigel tells him to leave Iraq immediately, as he can justifiably be accused of spying, and puts him in touch with the embassy spook – easily recognised as such because he gets the airmail edition of *The Times* (unlike *bona fide* diplomats who got the regular edition in the diplomatic bag) and because he could not possibly have got into the legitimate Foreign Office as he only got a third-class degree at Oxford . . . Nigel recruits a replacement correspondent, a Pakistani, but has difficulty getting him accredited. The Iraqis insist that an Iraqi be appointed. So Nigel calls on the Head of Security who looks like Bulldog Drummond. He gives the authorisation. Later that day the Security chief is shot for plotting a coup d'état, but he was an efficient man and the decision had been acted on . . .

I shook my head. We were still in the café. It was 11.30, time to be setting off to visit Aghtamar, the palatine church which the greatest of the Artsruni Princes of Vaspurakan built on a small island off the south shore of Lake Van. I never discovered whether or not the Reuters man in Baghdad was released.

Aghtamar was far more touristic than on my previous visit six years earlier. Mercifully we arrived during a lull in the flow. Doubtless this had something to do with the fact that it was midday and sensible tourists had scuttled under cover to escape the brain-addling sun.

The Turkish flag flew beside the church. Two armed *jandarma* soldiers were moving quietly among the tourists. A large Swedish coach-party was clearing up after its lunch, barbecued in the cemetery. Some of the detritus was still balanced on top of elaborately carved medieval Armenian tombstones. The *jandarma* NCO was there, without his rifle. He grilled a bone with a few fragments of meat attached to it on the embers, then gnawed at it.

Nigel was bowled over by the church, which is amazingly well preserved thanks to its inaccessibility on an uninhabited island. I had been there before, and, I am afraid, looked at it with rather a critical eye. Still, no one can deny that it is an extraordinary monument, certainly not the Turks who now exploit it to the full as a touristic draw. A Turkish flag appears on postcards of the church, symbolising its appropriation by the Turkish state.

97

The church is the only building left standing on the island. When it was built, though, it was part of a large palace complex built by the greatest of the Artsruni Princes, Gagik II (908–936). A panegyrist, who doubtless goes too far, describes it as a city, which was carefully laid out by the prince with streets, terraced gardens, parks and residences for the different grades of courtiers as well as the palace itself. An artificial harbour was built, and the whole complex was fortified and made virtually impregnable.

The church is large by Byzantine standards, though on nothing like the scale of contemporary churches in Europe. It has rather an odd plan – a quatrefoil with its sides squeezed in – but a far odder external appearance. For all the outer surfaces have been as it were splashed with sculpted reliefs. These take the form of horizontal bands of decorative carving, medallions with human busts, isolated reliefs of figures and fantastic creatures, and frieze-like scenes. The human figure is flaunted, as if the Artsrunis were cocking a snook at their Arab neighbours, were deliberately and flagrantly violating the Moslem ban on religious images. Although antecedents can be found for several of the individual scenes, in small pieces of sculpted relief dating from the seventh century, there was no precedent for spreading the sculptural decoration over so much of the external surface (and without much regard for the architectural form of the building). Nor indeed was it imitated subsequently.

The whole ensemble is rather bizarre. Odd features in the carvings themselves suggest that the craftsmen were struggling to meet the requirements of an exacting patron who had firm ideas of what he wanted and was eager to break out of the traditional limitations of Armenian art. The reliefs stand proud of the walls, presenting a flat surface on which the sculptors got to work, creating images out of shallow incisions and deeper grooves. Figures and animals are not modelled but outlined, hence are largely confined to two dimensions. It looks as if the patron wanted solid, substantial sculptures affixed to the exterior – so he was given deep reliefs – but his artistic agents were principally concerned

98

with surface pattern, and shared a taste for abstract geometrical and vegetal carving with their Arab contemporaries – so they confined themselves to carving lines and grabbed every opportunity to spread patterns over garments, armour and fantastic creatures, as well as along the horizontal bands. Occasional awkwardnesses in the composition of scenes or the delineation of figures betray the difficulty of the task and the strain it put on the sculptors. Thus the small Eve who is tempted by the Serpent in one scene is suddenly inflated in the next scene where she persuades Adam to taste the apple. Elsewhere the Virgin and Child are flanked by two absurdly small archangels. The worst problems, though, were posed by the human body: Adam and Eve in the Garden of Eden have large, overhanging stomachs outlined with a deep incision; two of the three men in the Fiery Furnace have acquired breasts and no attempt is made to represent the furnace. In general the figures are stolid, with large eyes and severe expressions, and a limited repertoire of stiff gestures does not impart much movement to scenes of action.

The execution may be far from perfect but one is awed by the boldness of Gagik's conception and the determination which turned it into reality. The main themes are that Paradise lost at the Fall (which is illustrated in sculpture outside and in the frescoes of the dome inside), will be regained as mankind takes the new path to Salvation opened up by Christ and that throughout the intervening period between the Fall and the Last Days, both before and after the Incarnation, God has intervened regularly to ensure the survival of His loyal servants. A selection of loyal Old Testament servants are depicted outside – Jonah, David, Samson and Daniel feature prominently among them – alongside the four Evangelists, the saints who brought the Gospel to Armenia and three mounted warrior saints who aided the Armenians in dark days. Into this formidable company of biblical and Christian heroes, Gagik slipped himself presenting a model of the church to a slightly smaller figure of Christ, and two of his ancestors who were executed when they refused to abjure Christian-

99

ity in 776. He was thus introducing his family into the story of mankind's painful progress towards Salvation, just as he had his court historian write it into the history of Armenia in antiquity.

The external sculptures thus both illustrate the Armenians' awareness of their dependence on God's favour and their consequent sense of affinity with the Chosen People in the Old Testament story, and glorify the Artsruni family. The frescoes inside, which are now badly damaged and very faded, reiterate the theme of the loss of Paradise at the Fall in the dome, but then give a full version of the Gospel story in three registers on the walls. The New Testament thus pushes its way inside the Old and provides an appropriate visual setting for the conduct of the liturgy.

Back on the mainland we had a late lunch, a massive one in Nigel's case. There were soldiers all over the restaurant, a rather touristic one, guarding a dignitary who was lunching on the terrace above us before he paid a visit to Gagik's church. We returned to Van where we paid protection money for a small boy to guard the car while we climbed the citadel rock. Nigel kept well clear of its undefended inner face which drops straight down to the ruins of the old town. The sun was sinking towards the surface of the lake as we made our way back to the car, its reflection rising up from the waters like a huge egg yolk to meet it.

The *arkadaş* kept hold of his new relaxed state of mind at dinner. Conversation flowed from him – more sharply etched portraits of various friends, some inside information from the old news hound about apprehension in high places at the time of the San Carlos landings during the Falklands War, memories of the struggle he had once had to pay a call he had promised to make on Nadezhda Mandelstam in Moscow when his efforts to shake off his shadows got him utterly lost and his eventual arrival was far from inconspicuous, and a panegyric of Graham Greene whom he ranked with Conrad above all other twentieth-century English novelists. This seemed to be going rather too far. So out of contrariness I insisted that GG was merely a very high-class thriller writer, with a rather unnerving fascination for unprovoked acts of cruelty. An amicable argument ensued.

Afterwards we strolled along a back street. There was a large Bezik hall to our left. The lights were on. The tables were covered in green cloth. The Bezik sets were neatly arranged upon them. At the back the *patron* sat at a large desk, in a swivel chair. Small flags sprouted from a stand on the desk. Nearby a huge mosque was nearing completion, its minaret still encased in scaffolding. In the main street the post office was open despite the late hour. Jetons for public telephones could be bought from a shadowy figure sitting in a glass booth. Outside a platoon of telephone boxes, each discreetly illuminated, stood guard. Further along the street postcards of alluring Turkish *houris* were on sale. The salesmen in the carpet shops by the central crossroads exercised their charms on us in vain. We stocked up with bottled water for the night and returned to our room. Nigel read a page of *The Towers of Trebizond* and fell asleep.

I wrote up my notes on the balcony outside until midnight. An illuminated sign advertised in red lettering the presence of the Emniyet in an imposing building across the street. The carpet salesmen at last started shutting up shop. Below us, the cavernous boiler-room of the Beş Kardeş Oteli was silent and the water was cold.

11 September (Van–Doğubayazıt)

Nigel was still in an expansive mood when he woke up. The hour between seven and eight whisked by with more talk. He announced that he thought of dons as nuclei without the other components of atoms. Then he told the story of his father's last years. He was sectioned after setting fire to the things he most disliked in the drawing room – the telephone, the 'accidental' table and the TV remote control. He was found with blackened face poking the embers. Tapers were attached to the spines of the

101

books round the walls . . . Nigel got him out of the bin within four days and admired the Goya-like drawings he had made of several of his fellow-inmates. It was then that father told son that he had wanted to be an artist, but, as that was impossible, had gone into the army.

'That,' he said of one of the portraits, 'is Jones. A sound man but doesn't understand much.' (Jones was a psychopath, aged twenty-two.) The old brigadier had formed an escape party, with Jones as his right-hand man . . . He had not risen beyond the rank of brigadier, in spite of a brilliant early career, because he lifted the arc of fire at Dunkirk to allow the retreating garrison of Calais through, contrary to General Alexander's orders. He died aged ninety-one.

We paid our bill. The unshaven desk-clerk scarcely acknowledged our presence. We returned to the *pasta salonu* (cake saloon) where we had had breakfast the previous day. Nigel continued talking. Harold Pinter was now the subject. He had given Nigel a copy of his short play about the Kurds, *Mountain Language*. Some time later, at a party, Pinter accosted him accusingly, saying 'You didn't like it, did you?' At which Nigel had a brainwave and said it was like 'a razor slash'. Pinter relaxed and relished the phrase. As he was telling this anecdote, a Kurdish prisoner in handcuffs was taken out of a Volkswagen minibus and into the Emniyet building next door. A policeman went into the minibus, sat down in front of a table with a typewriter on it and did some desultory typing while talking to another policeman.

We set off on the day's journey rather late. On the way out of Van we encountered cyclists for the first time in eastern Turkey, passed a large graveyard of rusting trucks and buses on the outskirts, and, well outside the city, caught a distant view of a university campus under construction on a particularly bleak section of the always bleak shore of the lifeless lake. A lone skinny bird was swimming in the fishless waters. The only touch of colour to relieve the drabness of the scene was a Kurdish encampment a little further on.

We visited the melancholy site of old Erciş which was aban-

102

doned between 1838 and 1841 when the level of the lake rose. Erciş was one of four towns which grew up on the north shore during the period of Arab hegemony in Armenia. By the mid-tenth century two distinct settlements had developed, an older fortified town and a new, apparently unwalled trading centre. They continued to flourish until the late Middle Ages, through all the political vicissitudes of the region, as it passed successively under Byzantine, Turkish and Mongol rule.

A deep ford has to be negotiated on the way to the town's cemetery which occupies a low mound at its northern end. In the distance, two kilometres or so away, four chunks of massive masonry still protrude from a small island which emerges from the waters of the lake. Waterlogged meadows, feasted on by cattle and sheep, stretch away to the south-east from the cemetery mound.

We then drove back the way we had come two days earlier through Patnos, a bleak garrison town, to Tutak where the tea-house was rather emptier than it had been before. All but one of the clientèle were unshaven. Then we turned north-east, along the easy natural route leading to the plain of Ağrı, a route which follows for most of the way the Murat Su as it winds through the intervening hills. There being no standing monuments of any distinction from the Middle Ages to visit, we sped over the long undulations of the eastern half of the plain towards the still invisible mass of Ararat. Our only halt was at the village of Taşteker, which was the site of a monastery in the Middle Ages. We had been asked by a colleague of mine to look over whatever remains were left. There was a lot of activity when we arrived. For once most of a village's able-bodied men were at work, winnowing and building haystacks. A group of them guided us to the site of the monastery church. This has been completely destroyed in the search for buried gold. All that can be seen now are three fragments of foundation walls and the odd cut stone block lying in the large contiguous pits which have been dug.

We continued on our way and climbed the easy saddle which separates the Ağrı plain from three smaller, lower-level ones to the east. Ararat suddenly materialised ahead, above and to the left. The *arkadaş* swerved for fear at the sight of the monster with its two great hunched shoulders, then tried to belittle it by likening it to a gigantic boil surrounded by pustules or a vast pudding with a topping of cream. Below the saddle we entered a weird landscape of bare, sombre-coloured rock. Lava, with basalt boulders tumbling over each other, had congealed in mid-flow. Green slag-heaps disfigured the plain. Jagged, blood-red ridges and low grey cones rose out of its flat surface. Behind us the sun was setting in an orange sky.

There was room for us in the plush Isfahan Hotel and the water was hot. Outside the Turkish secular state flaunted itself near the border with Iran. Large illuminated signs advertised different brands of beer in the main street. Goods were piled up on the pavement fronting the shops, to display Turkish plenty. A beggar boy with sores on the left side of his mouth pursued us down the street. In the post office a plump, bearded Englishman mindlessly dialled again and again on a telephone which was not working but had swallowed up his money. Scavenging dogs sorted through rubbish not far from the hotel, while nearby a water-lorry leaked in several places. A shopkeeper poured a large quantity of grey seeds straight into a customer's jacket pocket. Silver paper was in vogue for window displays. Circular neon lights were in every room and burned into the eyes. Two Iranian ladies with expensive silk scarves for *yashmaks* slipped out of a shop into the dark . . .

12 September (Doğubayazıt-Kars)

The day was cloudy. Only the massive shoulders of Ararat were visible. We visited the late eighteenth-century palace of Ishak Pasha which looks out over a desolate, boulder-strewn plain. The town which once surrounded it has vanished, except for the heavily fortified citadel built against the cliff behind it. The palace seems to have doubled as a grain store, since it has seven huge rectangular subterranean silos. There are too many Italianate motifs and too much repetition in its carved decoration for my taste, with the striking exception of the entrance to the harem quarters where each gourdlike design is different. We had it to ourselves apart from a silent pair of Iranian tourists.

We then sped over the plain and climbed the saddle running west from Ararat, beyond which lies the Araxes valley. The Turkish army was in battle formation on the pass. All guns were trained on the great mountain, as if the troops were intent on attacking it with those puny weapons or thought that they could hide from it under camouflage netting.

The Araxes valley below Ararat is vast, fertile and irrigated. Armenian politics have always tended to revolve around this largest of its plains. Here stood Dvin, its administrative capital in the periods of Persian and Arab direct rule, and here stands its modern successor, Erevan. Vegetables and sunflowers are grown in large quantities as well as grain. Wherever one looks, trees, mainly poplars, bestride the landscape.

The small town of Tuzluca, medieval Kolb, commands the defile through which the road leaves the plain for the west. The citadel rock above it has been picked clean of ancient and medieval stonework. The modern town is another of those places which thrive at road junctions. It is set amid hills and mounds of bare orange rock spewed out by a volcanic vent immediately to the west. An extraordinarily well-mannered and dignified boy came up to us as we drank tea and addressed us in English. He told us that he went to the Anatolian Lycée at Erzurum, and was in the same class as the boys we had met at Bayburt and Erzurum. When Nigel said he wanted to buy a melon, he carefully chose the best from the large pile outside his father's grocery shop. The pile was growing steadily larger as melon after melon was passed along a human chain.

'You won't forget me?' he appealed as we prepared to leave and we promised to write.

Almost as soon as the frontier with the Soviet Union abandons the left bank of the Araxes and turns north, following the line of the Arpa Çay, the road to Kars follows suit. In the distance we could see the towers of the Soviet frontier guards and, once, illuminated in a patch of sunlight, a well-preserved early Armenian church right on the frontier. We were crossing a vast stony wilderness, occasionally fissured by ravines, where vain attempts have been made, by piling up the basalt stones into cairns, to clear the land for cultivation. The wilderness continues beyond the small town of Digor, though here the attempts of man to master it have been more successful and it is punctuated by larger cultivated areas. At last, we came to the easiest of passes, between two low volcanoes, and looked out over the plain of Kars which stretches west as far as the eye can see and east to the Arpa Çay and the Soviet frontier.

CHAPTER 6

The harsh, grey outline of the formidable citadel of Kars, stone walls ringing a stony hill, was in keeping with its blood-soaked history. Here in 1855 a garrison led by English officers held off a Russian siege while waiting for a Turkish relief column that never arrived. In one day's attack the Russians were beaten off, leaving 6,300 dead. It took the burial party under Doctor Humphrey Sandwith, the chief medical officer, four days to dispose of the corpses. In the course of the siege the Russians intercepted the garrison's mail, before forwarding it with apologies for the delay. After two months of starvation, cold and cholera, the garrison capitulated.

The formal surrender scene is described in Doctor Sandwith's memoirs. The Russian commander addresses his British opposite number as gentleman to gentleman: '"General Williams, you have made a name in history, and posterity will stand amazed at the endurance the courage and the discipline which this siege has called forth . . ."' The doctor goes on: 'I leave my readers to imagine anything more touching than the interview between these gallant leaders, whose eyes were suffused with tears, while their hearts were big with the sentiments of high honour and graceful benevolence.'

For his heroic stand the said General Williams was knighted, made a Freeman of the City of London and awarded a pension of £1,000 a year by a grateful nation which admired nothing so much as an honourable defeat. A similar débâcle had been celebrated a decade earlier by another physician, Doctor William Bryden, the sole survivor of a British force of 15,000 massacred by Afghans who doublecrossed them. Bryden's blood-curdling account unhesitatingly gives 'our side' the moral victory. (Echoes of the same high Victorian values lingered on into my own childhood; I could recall being mystified by accolades bestowed on the First Eleven which, despite being soundly thrashed by the local village team, was deemed to have upheld the honour of the school.)

An added reason for British enthusiasm over the siege of Kars was perhaps that the casualties were mainly Turks. (At least one was inflicted by a British officer, Major Teesdale, who cut down a Turk about to dispatch a wounded Russian officer. For this act he was publicly thanked by the Russian commander and awarded the Victoria Cross.) Not surprisingly Turks themselves took a different view of the incident. One military pasha described it as unwarrantable interference by British officers in the legitimate Turkish command over a valuable army and an important but untenable position. 'By placing the one in the other they lost them both.'

We decided to head straight for the deserted Armenian city of Ani, on the frontier inside a Turkish military zone, rather than waste time going into Kars to ask permission. The gamble almost cost a day. At the large military post near the frontier we were turned back. The glamour, though not the grimness, of Kars dimmed as we reached the ring road round the town. Grassy plain gave way to the wasteland that heralds Turkish urban development. We crossed a scummy river with grassless banks and a railway line with blackened siding before rounding a corner leading us into a grid system of steep mud streets. To either side were low featureless buildings. Rubble and waste were flung anywhere. Kars had survived, but at a price.

On the second floor of the empty concrete Tourist Office building a haughty youth told us in excellent English that he would take care of our case. While we were waiting for his colleague to sign a form to take on to the Emniyet he explained that cameras were banned at Ani, since it was a military zone. He could sell us some postcards instead.

Alternatively he could be our guide. When we declined he suggested meeting at our hotel later in the evening. Far from having authority he was probably destitute. He seemed the very embodiment of shipwrecked dignity – another relic of a patrician race.

Outside the Emniyet Ataturk stood like Kitchener in iron-grey stone, the colour of Kars, with brows furrowed, eyes piercing the veil of Turkey's future. One arm was out-stretched, inviting all good Turks to share his vision of a new Turkey. Inside sat the old, immutable Turkey, a line of peasants waiting patiently on a bench in a long corridor, the silence broken by the sound of a typewriter, slow as the ticking of a grandfather clock, as a police clerk filled up a form in triplicate. We watched the scene for a few minutes. Then I cleared my throat. The clerk looked up in aston-ishment.

The Scholar stated our business, and handed over our form. The clerk signed it without reading it and went on typing. Half an hour later we entered Ani.

My first, overwhelming and lasting impression was of a very grand melancholy. Standing in the heart of Asia, a mag-nificent ghost 1,000 years old, half a dozen ruined churches are all that remain of this capital city, once the focal point of one of the richest and most advanced civilisations the world had known. From here the Bagratid kings, who claimed descent from David, established their suzerainty over the whole of Armenia.

Ani stands on a triangular plateau a mile long by half a mile at its widest point, protected by a double wall on one wide in which is set the great Lion Entrance Gate and by deep gorges on the other two. One of the gorges forms the frontier with the Soviet Union. Through a hole in the wall of the Church of the Holy Apostles, I could see a Russian sentry staring at us through binoculars from a watchtower a few hundred yards away. Both of us stood in ancient Armenia, separated by a leap of history across the ravine. The paradox was that the clamour behind the Iron Curtain for Armenian autonomy contrasted with the silence here in the free West: the silence of the grave.

The Scholar drew my attention to the detail of Ani's architecture – the quality of the masonry, the fineness of the carving, the sophistication of design. Inside a drum-shaped shell we found the remains of a four-leafed-clover nave, with space for side chapels in the hollows thus created. We wandered till near nightfall among the elegant ruins: the cathedral, the mosque, the three churches dedicated to St Gregory the Illuminator who converted Armenia to Christianity. One of these stands dramatically on a headland looking over the Arpa Çay cascading beneath a broken bridge that once crossed to what is now Russian soil. Nothing else remains: Ani's glory lasted a century. Weakened by Byzantine intrigues, it was sacked by Seljuk Turks in 1064 – two years before William the Conqueror landed in England. After a brief revival it was shattered again in 1319, this time by the hand of God in the shape of a terrible earthquake. After that it became uninhabitable. Clearly visible to us less than twenty miles to the north was the Soviet town of Leninakan. Three months almost to the day after our visit Ani was to feel yet another earthquake that would destroy part of Soviet Armenia taking a toll in human life equivalent to the entire population of Ani at its height, and sending out shockwaves that would reverberate throughout the Soviet Empire. It is another irony of modern history that the Cold War that once seemed to threaten Ani had in fact protected it. For by being in a restricted zone on the NATO frontier it had not been accessible to Turkish villagers to pillage for their building materials. Instead it stood as it had for over 600 years, a monument to a dead empire, the grandest ruin known to me.

The only sign of local life we came across in its ghostly precincts was a young boy gathering in cows for the night. I remember him particularly because he slipped and fell heavily. He was on the point of tears when he caught sight of us and hid his face. Instinctively I put an arm round him while he recovered. A second later he was off again with a great shout. At the gates a girl of perhaps four put her hand out for a coin. I pressed one into it. She closed her fist on it, bent over to inspect her treasure, and doubling up, clutched it to herself in a silent paroxysm of glee. There were no other tourists. Ani also appears to have been the grandest ruin known to Aristakes of Lastivert, who wrote nine centuries ago, mourning its fall:

'Where are our kings? They are nowhere now. Where the legion of soldiers massing in a cloud before them, their uniforms the colour of flowers in spring? They are gone forever. Where now is our wondrous pontiff's throne? Today it is filled only with dust, its rightful occupant a prisoner in a foreign land. The priests' voices have fallen silent. The lights are dimmed, the smell of incense has gone and the altar of the Lord is covered in dust and ashes. . . . Now if all we have related has befallen us because of our wickedness, then tell heaven and all that abide in it, tell the mountains and the hills, tell the trees in the woodlands so that they too may weep over our destruction.'

Though only early September it was chilly and dark as we walked along the shattered main street of Kars in search of food. We could already imagine the ferocious bite of winter. The impression left in my mind: ill-lit waste space, rubble, drains. No flowers or gardens. Old buildings with no hope of a lick of paint. New buildings raw unfinished slabs with built-in decay; nothing designed to please the eye, even impress. Indifference of humans to their surroundings and vice versa. We peered through a window with the sign 'BILI-ARD' into a dim, neon-lit room with peeling wallpaper where men played cards. In another they sat in ranks watching television: aping Europe, but not of it.

Kars had long been a strategic prize forever fought over and changing hands – a battle-scarred, temporary home for a traditionally nomadic population. Why look for familiar Western credentials in such a place? Yet its very oddness drew us. It had a vitality of its own. Somewhere in Kars' stony heart there was warmth and life. The key to finding it was to suspend expectation.

We had settled for an unpromising, ill-lit restaurant in a building near to collapse. It had a picture of a Swiss mountain scene on one wall. (Seeing it, I recalled 'The Monarch of the Glen' at Erzurum. Another traveller, Philip Glazebrook, came across a Swiss scene in these parts, as well as 'The Hay Wain', and suggested they were symbols of Moslem paradise – the limpid stream and the heavenly cart in a lush Suffolk setting contrasting with the green slime of the local river.)

We were sitting in a draught, so I went to shut the front door, only to find there wasn't one. A few feet from the opening where it should have been two cats fought over a scrap, not identifiable, beside an open drain. Yet we dined off delicious lentil soup, *köfte* – lamb minced on the spot – and *ayran*, for the cost of the coat check in a London restaurant.

We were on the point of going to bed when the Scholar found that he needed to take on water for the night. Across the street from the hotel was a long, low concrete building where a scuffle was taking place: some police came, and a knot of young Turks dispersed. We strolled over to find ourselves in a two-storey shopping mall, with small shops, booths, television parlours and cafés, all open for business. It was nearly midnight: public apathy, private enterprise. We wandered along the concrete corridors and up the stairs, past a barber's shop, a group of tailors sewing cross-legged, until we came to a general store laid out Western style for customers to help themselves and pay at a checkout – unnecessarily, since the storekeeper's whole family together with children was at hand to serve or chat.

The Scholar picked out a pair of litre bottles of mineral water, and handed them over for payment. The storekeeper demanded the equivalent of forty pence. The Scholar was outraged: we had not paid more than thirty pence since leaving Ankara. Why should Kars charge this exorbitant price? The Scholar gave the man one of his haunted looks. But the storekeeper was adamant. By now we had the attention of his whole family who were clearly enjoying the exchange. The Scholar turned to me. I looked the other way. He tried again, but in vain. Finally he succumbed, but with the parting words, in English: 'I shall pay the price you have asked. But, – this as much to me as to the storekeeper – 'I am not pleased!' Up came the minatory figure: 'I am not pleased!'

I slept uneasily and woke several times. The first, I found the Scholar sitting in a pool of light, head stock still, eyes

112

glowing like coals. Our last exchange of the night had been about the map he had promised to make for me of the region demonstrating how natural forces had governed its history.

'A simpleton's map,' I had asked.

'Yes. It will be a very complicated task.' He had set to work at once. Paper was prepared and laid out, coloured pencils assembled. I looked to see if he was tracing. There was no movement. The eyes did not flicker. I wondered if he might be dead and if so what I would do with the body.

The second time was to the familiar crashing sound of falling water. I pictured the Arpa Çay at Ani in spate emptying into the great Araxes to the south. I opened my eyes. Once again the great gallons were flowing down the Scholar's throat. Closing them again a confused image came to a mind of three As, Arpa Çay, Araxes and Aesophagus, merging to form a single mighty flood. Work resumed at daylight. There were visits to the car for stationery and maps. I imagined Procopius and other vital elements from the source material being assembled for my benefit. My heart swelled with importance.

Finally the Scholar announced it ready.

'I found the solution to the problem of the source map. I decided to use the car atlas.'

After expectations of Procopius it was something of an anticlimax to settle for Avis. However, I was soon reconciled. The Scholar's was the first physical map I had ever been able to follow – arrows showed which way rivers flowed, green circles marked alluvial plains and the symbols for volcanoes would be eminently recognisable to a twelve year old, looking like the boils schoolboys develop at puberty.

Despite his labours the Scholar was in excellent spirits at breakfast. It was his turn to hold forth. We had no way of knowing how prophetic his words would soon seem. He spoke of the twin forces vying to determine the destiny of Armenia: man in the form of the human spirit, building; and nature in the form of earthquakes and volcanic eruptions, destroying his work. His thesis was that while nature limited the scope of man's movement, sweeping aside his plans in a trice, the constant resurgence of the human will was responsible for consolidating the power of the Armenian Bagratid dynasty, ruthlessly rebuilding their fortunes and bringing together disparate fragments of client states in the fight against invaders. It was the oratorical zenith of our trip, as much for manner as for matter. The peroration reached its climax as, despite a crust of bread and liquid honey in his hand, he nevertheless contrived to raise the familiar index finger to declare:

'Friability! Friability is the key! It was the friability of Armenia's social groups that enabled the Bagratids to emerge triumphant!'

We made one last stop in town to see an Armenian church, again fine and elegant: but after the spectacular settings of Aghtamar and Ani it seemed more sad than splendid. A coachload of tourists arrived. The Scholar recognised them as a group run by the Serenissima organisation. As he greeted their leader, a fellow academic from the British Museum, I experienced the sense of quiet superiority of the learner taking private lessons who has met up with the regular ski-school class.

Then we packed to leave. Assembling my lighter luggage more quickly than the Scholar's, I offered to assist him with his suitcase. He declined with the little cry of alarm that he gave whenever an alien hand came near the Source Material, so I waited for him beside the car. He soon emerged from the hotel carrying several bulging plastic bags and his heavy old case breaking at the seams which I knew to contain documents, scholarly pencils, walking shoes, tweed suit and tie, washing bag predating the zip fastener. He was wearing the cast-off coat of a mutual connection acquired in slimmer times and very old gym shoes. With the straw hat crammed on his head he looked just then like a cross between an overgrown schoolboy and the cook between jobs.

Perhaps it is not surprising that, as we turned to leave this violent biblical land, the hand of nature should have reached out to smite us. I was at the wheel when I became aware of a muffled groan. Beside me the Scholar lay with head back and face hidden under a clamp of tissues down which a tell-tale trickle had begun to flow. The sight of blood set off a spontaneous train of thought – I had heard no shot; a silencer perhaps? – before I recognised the symptoms.

Earthquakes and nosebleeds have much in common. Both are unheralded natural eruptions. Both transform the surrounding landscape. I stopped the car. It looked like a battlefield. From underneath the tissues there came a muffled cry, 'No! No!' I drove on. There was a long silence. We halted again at a traffic light where a policeman stood idly watching us. There were no other cars in sight. The Scholar haemorrhaged quietly beside me. The policeman stared steadily. I smiled with feigned unconcern, wishing I knew the Turkish for 'nosebleed', inventing headlines in my head ('Wounded Terrorists Seized By Vigilant Patrolman, Feuding Armenians Make Full Confession'). An eternity later the light turned green.

As suddenly as it began the nosebleed ended. It was forgotten by the time we reached Horasan to wonder at the Mongol bridge spanning the Araxes in six elegant arches, still used today by traffic. At Erzurum we turned north to complete the circle we had began at Trabzon's airport. Soon we were plunged in the mountain scenery I had loved on our outward journey. The Scholar pointed out how the local farmers put their haystacks, for warmth, on top of their houses. We lunched at a charming restaurant in Tortum, an unusually prosperous-looking town with ornate lamp-posts. It was like eating on a hot day on the French Riviera: good food served in welcome shade. One of two lone, unexplained Japanese tourists ate in silence at the next table making gestures at each mouthful as if, said the Scholar, casting a spell over his food.

At the end of lunch the waiter went out to find us coffee, but returned empty-handed with an apology. I noted down the Scholar's reply in my exercise book.

'My dear fellow, it is I who am sorry. I shouldn't have put you to all that trouble. But thank you all the same. *Teşekkür. Teşekkür.*' He was his old self again.

Tortum stands at the entrance to a long gorge that cleaves northwards ever more deeply into the mountains. At times our road, following the river on its journey to the Black Sea

115

at Batum, grew dark as the towering walls of rock closed in 1,000 feet over our heads. After an hour we turned off, and took a winding path high into the mountainside to Öşk Vank to see the shell of quite a large tenth-century Georgian church. It was a mystery even to the Scholar why those medieval Christians had chosen so inaccessible a site for such an elaborate place of worship. We paused to photograph a telegraph pole planted in the middle of the road. Smiling children offered us fruit. I felt an extraordinary sense of well-being.

An hour later we came to a sign to Işhan. The road up the mountain ran even higher and steeper than at Öşk Vank; and the church itself was even more moving, an elegant cruciform shell with a hole to the sky for an apse: another Christian ghost in a Moslem country that was not hostile but blankly uncomprehending. Turkey had simply forgotten its past.

We were caught by nightfall on the slow winding road and in the dark could not at first understand the layout of Artvin, a fortress town built on an incline so steep that we parked our car on one side of the hotel and had to take a lift for three floors down in order to reach the street on the other.

Travel writers have recorded eating badly in Turkey: or perhaps bad food is a more entertaining topic than good. Our own experience was in the main of delights. That night was only our second disappointment in ten days. Dinner began with a soup of mutton fat into which the waiter poured a jug of vinegar. For both of us eating stopped abruptly there. Breakfast of honey and fresh bread made up for what dinner lacked, but in part only, as we found ourselves sharing it with a small swarm of what looked like killer bees.

Artvin houses the military headquarters of the province bordering Russia. The main street was filled with soldiers and cars flying senior officers' pennants: also brand new banks. In a marble palace carrying an American Express sign, I presented an American Express traveller's cheque for $50. Behind his grille the counter clerk compared it with printed replicas in a book brought to him by a minion. He turned a page on which a $100 version of my cheque was displayed.

After a few moments of scrutiny he handed mine back shaking his head sternly.

Our last detour of the day was to Ardanuç, a mountain village dominated by a spectacular fortress. It was searingly hot. We stopped the car beneath the final cliff face and walked round it to the foot of the ruined keep. Near the summit a village woman was tending a lone cow placidly munching tufts of grass on the overhanging edge of a death drop. She spotted my camera and angrily waved us away. In the village the Scholar found vestiges of the original settlement. He was quickly surrounded by a group of children; a boy with shaved head appointed himself our escort. I was besieged for photographs. As we left the escort formally shook and then kissed the Scholar's hand.

The return journey to the Black Sea reminded me of going back to school. As we cut through the mountain pass at the bottom of the gorge poetry turned to prose. The booming blue of the mountain sky turned to flannel-grey cloud. The cloying atmosphere descended once more. Dry scrub gave way to claustrophobic evergreen, and the warm, damp smell of tea plants greeted our nostrils. Uniform, cheap apartment blocks of the kind I imagined on the other side of the Soviet border replaced the lively mess and squalid mysterious alleyways that we had grown used to. The only thing I liked about the Black Sea coast towns was their names. In a succession of disappointments we drove west along the scrappy coast from Hopa to Of, finding more of the same, the chief source of variety being the range of attitudes struck by Ataturk: beckoning, scowling, galvanising, mesmerising or piercing the veil of the future.

We spent our last night in Of. Our *otel* had a *lobi*, a *recepsyon*, a stained-glass window, a lavatory seat with hand-painted water lilies, and a formal dining room with more waiters than diners. Here and there in the town were a few shattered churches and ruined castle walls among the mosques, empty shells of Christianity, all that remained of the Greek merchants who had once given life to the region. It seemed deader than Armenia. There the ghosts cried out louder and haunted me still. So much did they that at Artvin

117

the day before, while talking to our hotel proprietor, who spoke good English, I decided to mention the unmentionable. After all, we were leaving the next day.

'There used to be a million Armenians in Turkey.' The proprietor nodded gravely.

'Yes. Now there are none left.'

'What happened to them?'

'They were resettled following the uprising.'

'Where were they resettled?'

'The next country. Greece.'

'Those were the Greeks. What about the Armenians?'

'Also the next countries.'

'Perhaps also the next world?' He nodded again.

'Yes. It was a savage uprising.'

The Scholar . . .

. . . and the Gypsy.

Bus station . . .

. . . hotel.

Above: On the trail of Citharizon: the Scholar questions the inhabitants of Harabe Köy.

Left: The clue: a block in a courtyard at Yeni Köy.

Below: The walls of Citharizon.

The brigand (on the morning after), Sefket Durak and our host at Yeni Köy.

Tombstone at Ercis.

Above: Ishak Pasha Saray.

Right: The mosque and minaret of Ishak Pasha.

Country near Ardanuç: dung-pats.

An old man of Of.

Rila monastery.

Street scene, with Chevrolet, at Kütahya.

The Scholar enjoys his food . . .

. . . the Gypsy takes his rest.

CHAPTER 7

My confident assertion that the formalities to get to Ani could be gone through at the military post turned out to be a fantasy. Two precious hours of daylight were lost as we retraced our steps from the military post and sped on to the tourist office in Kars. There forms were filled in, and we were kept waiting until the senior official decided to saunter out of his office, which had the regulation desk, swivel chair and flag-stand, and appended his signature. We were told to take the form to the police headquarters for their authorisation.

The police chief's limousine had levitated onto the high pavement fronting the building. Its polished bodywork gleamed. The seats were covered in a thick, black-and-white patterned pile, which matched the livery of the patrol cars. We made our way inside where we were directed upstairs and along a corridor to a cramped office. One of the three officers there got up and went as we arrived. A second put three sheets of paper, separated by carbon paper, into a typewriter, adjusted them and began typing slowly. The third studied a brochure intently. Eventually we spoke and the studious character looked up in mock surprise and stamped our forms.

The sun was sinking towards the horizon when at last we reached Ani. We had only a little over an hour there, but we had the site to ourselves, apart from a boy watching over some cattle and a sentry who suddenly materialised when we went towards the gate leading into the citadel area, which is barred to tourists. We picked our way around the ruined city of the Bagratids.

It stands at the south-east extremity of the Kars plain, on the edge of the Arpa Çay just before it enters a series of gorges on its way south. It occupies a naturally well-defended, triangular site in the angle between the Arpa Çay and a western tributary, the Alaca Çay, which meet immediately below its southern point. It lies below the general level of the adjoining plain, so that travellers are surprised and impressed when its magnificent outer fortifications suddenly come into view. Inside, the ruins, which have been saved from the attentions of predatory villagers by their position in a military zone on the frontier, stretch away to the inner line of fortifications defending the citadel. All the houses, workshops, storerooms, baths and palaces have collapsed, but a few churches still stand and leave the visitor in no doubt that he is entering the capital of *the* premier princely family of Armenia in its later tenth– and early eleventh-century heyday. The ground plans and lower elevations of other important monuments are known thanks mainly to excavations conducted by the Russians between 1892 and 1917, when they occupied the Kars region.

The city grew rapidly in the years following the Bagratids' decision in 961 to make it their capital instead of Kars. A high percentage of the wealth generated in central Armenia in the period when the economy of Transcaucasia was at its apogee was concentrated in the city. A large number of noble and merchant families naturally clustered around the Bagratid court. Their traditional rivalries, now taking the form of competitive patronage, and the determination of the princely family to demonstrate its pre-eminence by the magnificence of the buildings it commissioned, were the driving forces behind its development.

The Bagratids installed themselves in the citadel, in a substantial palace complex which included a number of grand rooms on the first floor, one of them with a fountain in the middle, as well as a chapel and a bath suite. The city which grew up outside soon overflowed its first set of walls. A much enlarged area (150 hectares) was enclosed by massive new

120

defences, built in 989, which blocked the northern approach from the plain. Housing, commercial and public buildings were probably arranged around the residences of the nobles and merchants, only one of which, at the north-west corner of the city, has been investigated. Two sets of baths have been found as well as more than twenty churches, four of which are recorded as having been endowed by individual families: a small circular church overlooking the Alaca Çay ravine, dedicated to St Gregory, was built by the Pahlavunis in the late tenth century; the same family was responsible for the slightly later church of the Holy Apostles, which has five domes (over the central crossing and four corner-chapels), and the slender polygonal church of the Redeemer, completed in 1036; much later, a rich merchant, Tigran Honents, founded a monastery on the slope down to the Arpa Çay which included an elegant church, finished in 1215.

The most impressive buildings, though, were put up by the Bagratids themselves. They constructed two large churches of very different design as part of the city's initial development. The same architect, Trdat, was responsible for both. He was the finest architect of his day in Armenia and his services were also in demand in Byzantium. He seems to have drawn inspiration from different buildings erected in the seventh century which saw the first flowering of Armenian architecture. But his designs were no slavish imitations of ancient models. They incorporated major modifications of his own.

His most important project was the cathedral, completed in 1001. It is a massive basilica, some three times larger than Aghtamar. It has survived the depredations of time remarkably well, only losing its central dome and much of the supporting drum. Trdat altered the traditional design, by increasing the width of the nave and emphasising the vertical thrust of the whole structure with pointed and stepped arches rising from tall clustered piers. The interior is far grander than one expects on first viewing the exterior. But the exterior too testifies to the architect's skill. Instead of the flamboyance of Aghtamar, there is an admirable restraint in its decoration. Blind arcades and carved bands framing or arching over the windows serve to bring out the overall articulation of the building. The carving itself is abstract, delicate and elegant, with none of the fumbling evident at Aghtamar. It also avoided giving offence to Moslem visitors.

Similar high standards of craftsmanship and sobriety in decoration can be seen in the other church known to have been built by Trdat. This was a huge rotunda, 32.65 metres in diameter, dedicated to St Gregory, which he built for Gagik I between 1001 and 1013. The Russian excavators uncovered the bottom three metres or so of the structure, thus gaining a good idea of its design. It was modelled, with variations, on the most famous of the churches built in the mid-seventh century, that dedicated to the angels of heaven at Zvartnots. In both a circular ambulatory surrounded a two-storey central space of quatrefoil plan, which was surmounted by a dome, rising to a height of forty-eight metres. A larger-than-life-sized statue of Gagik was found inside, tempting the Russian archeologists to suppose that it was designed as his mausoleum.

The construction and embellishment of Ani marked the re-emergence of the Bagratids as the leading princely dynasty in Armenia after a period of temporary political eclipse in the first half of the tenth century. Traditionally they were the most circumspect of the Armenians in their dealings with foreign powers. Deference and loyal service had kept them at the very apex of Armenian society during the period of Persian direct rule over central and eastern Armenia in the fifth and sixth centuries, and through the more turbulent centuries which followed. The invaluable aid which they gave the Arab authorities in the crack-down following the third great uprising of 850–2 brought them rewards, in the shape of land and political authority, which they used to gain hegemony over the whole of Armenia as well as Georgia (ruled by another branch of the family since the early ninth century). Their position was almost impregnable, resting as it did on a lineage which no other family could match, the favour of the preponderant foreign power, and the possession of a secure redoubt in the formidable mountains on either side of the lower course of the Çoruh river, where they could weather political storms. Artsruni claims to descent from Senacherib were easily trumped by a genealogy which presented King David as their ancestor.

Night had fallen and it was bitterly cold when we got back to Kars. The streets were ill lit. There seemed to be no shops open. The Hotel Yılmaz, the best in the city, faced a large concrete building with a few neon-lit windows. The street in between looked like a back street. We hurried into the first *lokanta* we found, a few blocks away. The cold air rushed in through the doorway which had no door. They closed at eight when we left.

Where was the city centre? we wondered, as we retraced our steps through the dark streets to the hotel. . . . Then we realised that it was crammed into the Soviet-style concrete building with neon-lit plate-glass windows facing the hotel. One of them gave on to a café where all the faces were staring out – at the television just above the window. Two policemen went in. We followed. It was the Kars shopping mall. Water had spilled from the gents on the ground and first floors, and was spreading along the walkways. A group of running youths kept appearing and disappearing up or down the stairways. Each shop unit was filled with bluish light. Tailors and cobblers were still at work. A barber's shop was open. So too was one selling electrical goods and two grocers. It was a hellish place, as heartwarming as an underground car-park, suffused with eerie light, echoing with the sound of running feet.

Before dawn I was woken by the *muezzin* of Kars. Their discordant calls sounded like the drunken singing of rowdy youths echoing among concrete buildings.

13 September (Kars–Artvin)

Once again our plans for an early start were thwarted. But this time the talk was pouring out of me. Ani must have inspired it, for it was about the volcanic 'shakings' which reminded Armenians that they were but puny playthings of

123

God and about the long, bitter winters which broke down their society into small feuding groups . . .

We were looking up at the citadel of Kars when a flabby, pale-skinned, reddish-haired man came walking by. Where, we asked him, was the church of the Holy Apostles? A stream of instructions, quite impossible to follow, came in reply. It was evident that he was directing us to the far side of the city. As he talked, we became aware of a conical roof, the tip of an Armenian dome, half-hidden behind some trees nearby. So we thanked him warmly for his help. He had the carefree look of a man on a long holiday. He was a management consultant, he told us and asked us what we did. When the *arkadaş* said he was a writer, his eyes widened and he gazed at him with awe, hesitantly admitting that he too wrote poetry. Just then a supercharged bus drew up and discharged a Serenissima tour party dead on schedule. My friend, the tour leader, made some introductions, then gave a highly professional short lecture on the architectural features of the church. A girl engaged the *arkadaş* in conversation about a dinner party they had both been to in London. Then they were off on the way to Ani. We waved at their bus and re-entered Turkey.

A long journey lay ahead. So Nigel drove at a fair lick with masterly skill. The large villages of the plain of Kars flicked by. In one of them large piles of bricks which had been left to bake in the sun were being uncovered. Another was suffering from a plague of crows. The crows had come when poplars were introduced, the tour guide had told us. Soon, the plain behind us, we were speeding through the belt of hills which shields it from the main east–west route along the Araxes. As we neared the river, the hills were increasingly denuded of their pines, covered instead with glistening black stones. Then they opened out into the plain of Horasan, remarkable for an elegant and well-preserved Mongol bridge over the Araxes and a petrol station which was adorned with flowers (a rare sight, for virtually no one bothers about the external appearance of buildings in the east). Next came the larger plain of Pasinler, medieval Basean, then the yet larger one of Erzurum over the watershed. Beyond to the north, lay the bare and rugged mountains of south-west Georgia (medieval Tao).

The day was still young when we entered the narrow valley of the Tortum river. After a few kilometres, we reached the town of Tortum, a charming place set amid cliffs, and halted for lunch. So too did a bus, which discharged its passengers into our *lokanta*. There were two Japanese among them, one of them so tanned that he almost faded into the darkness at the back of the *lokanta*. Only his arms and hands were visible. They moved back and forth over the table and the food on it, as if he were casting spells or warding off evil spirits. The *arkadaş* remarked that he had had many such strange habits when he was young. One was 'looking at everything with his nose.' This means he had to sweep his nose across every object he wanted his eyes to take in. Outside, Tortum was drowsy in the heat of the day. Neat too, with rather chi-chi municipal lamps.

Our direction, east-north-east, was now determined by the grain of the landscape. The mountains, stripped of vegetation, are packed tightly together. They have jostled and shoved into each other, so much so that in places the rock strata rise and fall almost vertically. Small rivers have had to cut deep trenches to make their way, generally east but with occasional thrusts north, to the Çoruh which then flows into the Black Sea on the Turkish-Soviet frontier. Their valleys, each a series of interlinked gorges, provide the only practicable routes for travellers. It is forbidding country. How anyone apart from shepherds can scrape a living from it beggars the imagination. But they do, and occasional oases, cramped into a narrow strip on the shaded side of an open tributary valley, or perched on a well-watered ledge high above a canyon, support flourishing villages.

We visited two such oases in search of medieval Georgian churches. The village of Öşk Vank lies at the head of its long side valley. As we drove towards it, fruit-pickers, mainly girls and women, came out of the orchards which stretch along the sheltered south side of the valley and welcomed the strangers with captivating smiles, begging us to eat of their fruit. The village spreads out around its great domed church. Immediately behind it some elderly wooden houses cling to a steep slope above a small stream. İşhan, our next stop, was more remarkable still. It is reached by a vertiginous track, just wide enough to take a car, which climbs up a bare mountainside with hairpin bends for seven kilometres. At the top, one suddenly enters another world. There are trees everywhere. So much greenery that one scarcely notices the houses. Only the large episcopal church forces itself on the attention.

The church at Öşk Vank was built between 963 and 973 by the leading prince of southern Georgia, the Magister David, in his own name and that of his brother Bagrat, who died in 966. It was part of a monastic complex which included an academy, a library and a scriptorium. It is a gigantic building, almost fifty metres long. Its plan is that of a cross, with the west arm elongated to accentuate the east–west axis of the building. The central crossing is surmounted by a dome which rests on four free-standing piers. The sanctuary and transepts end in clusters of three apses. It was well-engineered and has survived relatively unscathed by time. Though rather gaunter than the (later) cathedral at Ani, with deep niches gouged out of its façades and soaring pipelike blind arcades affixed to its exterior, it is a most imposing structure and set a standard for church-building which rival princes in northern Georgia strove to emulate. It was decorated inside principally with frescoes, which were illuminated by a larger than usual number of windows, and outside by stone-carving, which, as in earlier Georgian churches, included reliefs of the donors. These are placed in a prominent position on the south side of the sanctuary where the sun picks out their ceremonial presentation of the church to Christ, who is flanked by the Virgin (now dislodged) and John the Baptist. An elaborately carved octagonal column, in an open gallery on the south side of the nave, glorifies the Bagratid family, illustrating their descent from David and the favour shown to them by the hierarchy of heaven.

The cathedral at Işhan was completed in its present form in 1032. It is not quite as large as Öşk Vank (over thirty-five metres long) and has a simpler version of the cruciform plan, with a single large apse at the east end. But the beholder is awestruck at the scale of it, at the symmetry of its exterior detailing, and at the quality of the stone-carving, more ornate than at Öşk Vank (and Ani) but still subordinated to the architecture. The presence of the church, high above river valleys gouged through the scrunched up landscape of Tao, seems little short of a miracle: which in a way it was. For it was built by the two premier princes of Georgia acting together in a rare phase of harmony, as well as the local bishop.

Both churches are rightly recognised as masterpieces of medieval Georgian architecture. They were the last of the great monuments put up in the early medieval heyday of Armenia and Georgia which we visited. All that remained to do was to complete our circuit of north-east Turkey, with a detour to Ardanuç, the medieval capital of the district of Klardjeti. We hastened on our way to Artvin, capital of the modern province.

Night fell as we followed the Çoruh through its canyons. Then, Artvin suddenly appeared, a constellation of lights hanging above us in the darkness. It took some time to ascend that far. Most of the hillside below seemed to be occupied by military base, but eventually we arrived in the centre and installed ourselves in the smartest hotel. It pulled rank with an extraordinary display of fitments. The loo cover in our room was adorned with a picture of several sparrows sitting on a spreading branch, decorated lavatory seats clearly being a feature of this area. A bulbous yellow light hung from a small ship's wheel in the centre of the ceiling. Purple flowers festooned the shower curtain.

Disoriented, we went out to the nearest restaurant, where much heavy drinking was going on. For once no one was attending to the ever-riveting spectacle presented by the television news. All eyes were on glasses of beer and *raki*. Nigel gazed with fascination at one man who was particularly far gone. His eyes fixed themselves on a friend who joined him, then he rose slowly and walked with measured, unsteady steps across the room, a short, stocky, unshaven figure, with great bags of debauchery under his eyes. Meanwhile a large cast of juniors were watching their boss lounging in an armchair as he gave an interview for the benefit of the nation, but not for our companions. Then came long extracts from a speech by the Prime Minister, which was filmed by a single unwavering camera to his right. Some soup was brought, swimming in fat. Nigel's appetite died at the sight of it, not to be revived when the *patron* poured in a large quantity of vinegar. Now at last the news turned to foreign affairs, with an item about the Lebanon, which was read out without any footage of film. Nigel took refuge in drink, half a litre of beer chased by a large slug of *raki* . . .

When we emerged, lights were flashing around a yellow inflated Bambi in the window of a shop selling sneakers. The Security Police were playing cards in their building. A plainclothes officer, disguised with a lot of stubble on his chin, came up to us as we watched and asked us where we were staying. We had forgotten the name of the hotel. He smiled and disappeared. Still we knew how to find it. Back in the room, Nigel caught sight of his slightly enlarged body in the mirror and cried out, 'Jahosophat, great rolls of fat'.

14 September (Artvin–Of)

We breakfasted on bread, butter and honey as usual. This morning we were outside, on the veranda of the hotel, looking out over the Çoruh valley far below. The *arkadaş'* hair, freshly washed, had sprung up in uncontrolled fashion. Soon, attracted by the smell of honey on this warm morning, bees began to circle round the bouffant head and sip at the honey on our plates. A decoy plate, put on a neighbouring table, where the sun would heat it up, failed to lure them all away.

There was less conversation than usual. Nigel recalled an English woman of seventy whom he had seen on a steamer in the Aegean. She was looking frantically for her lover. She had been doing so for twenty years, searching every ship for him. She was allowed to travel free throughout the Dodecanese.

We made a short detour up the valley of an eastern tribu-tary of the Çoruh, to visit Ardanuç, the last site of particular interest to me on our itinerary. It is a place of some historical importance, though without monuments to compare with those we had seen at Aghtamar, Ani, Kars and in the high-lands of Tao south of Artvin. It commands the most difficult section of the direct route connecting the Black Sea coast, at Batum, with the upper valley of the Kura river (around Ardahan) and the plain of Kars. The Georgians had wrested it from Armenian control in late antiquity, and by the ninth century it lay well inside their territory which had expanded as far as the Çoruh valley in the south-west.

Ardanuç and the route which it controlled were by then very valuable possessions. For the growth of the transconti-nental market created by Islam had stimulated trade with the surrounding world. The flow of goods along the roads lead-ing to and from the caliphate had in its turn promoted urban life at key points on these routes. Aradnuç, which was one such key point on a major thoroughfare, profited immeasur-ably from its position. By the beginning of the tenth century, a substantial town had grown up below the powerful castle which had occupied since time immemorial a flat-topped rock overlooking the entry into the narrow, winding gorge leading west to Artvin and the sea. A source of unimpeachable auth-ority reports that an enormous customs' revenue was gener-ated by the passing traffic which came from Trebizond, Georgia, Abasgia (the increasingly powerful northern neigh-bour of Georgia at this time), Armenia and the central lands of the caliphate. Whoever controlled Ardanuç was therefore in the enviable position of being able to extract a massive revenue for himself, by virtue of its position just outside the frontiers of the Moslem free-trade area. It was a prize, though, which would have to be defended against predatory neighbours of all sorts.

Life was indeed far from uneventful in medieval Georgia. Before a short, successful phase in the second half of the tenth century, when the Georgians turned their old alliance with Byzantium to their advantage and expanded south, past the Bingöl Dağ, towards Lake Van, members of the various

129

local branches of the ruling Bagratid family were engaged in a ferocious competition for position and prestige, which could erupt into open feuding between them. Two such rivalries, one of which was an open feud, were going on simultaneously in the general area of Ardanuç in 923. They provided Byzantium, the most powerful predator within striking distance of Ardanuç, with an opportunity to intervene and establish a presence in the area which was far too tempting to ignore.

Two deaths, that of the head of the northern branch of the Georgian Bagratids, Adarnase II, who had received the title of curopalate or premier prince of Georgia from Byzantium, and that of Gourgen, head of the southern branch of the family, who held Ardanuç, heightened the tensions which already existed. When a Byzantine mission arrived, headed by a senior official (who later became the top-ranking admiral in the Byzantine navy) and escorted by 300 troops, suspicions flared in the northern branch of the family. They feared that the title of curopalate was going to be reallocated to another Gourgen, who was emerging as the most powerful prince in southern Georgia. The second of the four sons of the late curopalate intercepted the mission, demanded to know what it was up to, and was only mollified when he was told, truthfully, of its overt purpose, which was to present Gourgen with the inferior title of magister. However, it also had secret instructions from the emperor to take up the offer made by a certain Ashot Kiskasis to hand over Ardanuç which he had just inherited from his brother, the Gourgen who had died. His main motive seems to have been to spite his son-in-law, Gourgen the honorand, with whom he was at feud.

The Byzantine mission and its large escort were allowed to continue on their way and duly invested Gourgen with his title. Then it was time to act on the secret instructions. The mission and its escorting force turned north, ostensibly to pay a courtesy call on another local ruler whose lands marched with those of Byzantium, but then occupied Ardanuç, and advertised the fact by raising a Byzantine flag on the walls. It was an extraordinary coup, which bloodlessly brought Byzantium the most important fortified place on the main route leading east from its possessions on the west bank of the lower Çoruh and a large source of additional revenue. The strength of Ardanuç and especially of its citadel, the old castle, was such that there was little danger of it falling to a counterattack, and it was close enough to Byzantine territory to be resupplied and reinforced without too much difficulty. Its acquisition was calculated to weaken, perhaps fatally, the rising power of the southern Georgian princes, at a time when the Abasgians were already pressing back their cousins in the north.

But the Byzantines had not bargained on the sense of common danger which now swept over the fractious princes of Georgia and led them to bury their differences temporarily. Hopes that the holder of the lands between Ardanuç and the Byzantine frontier on the lower Çoruh might follow Ashot Kiskasis' example and submit were soon dashed. Worse was to follow. For the senior princes of both the northern and southern branches of the family sent a joint letter to the emperor, warning him that they would go over en bloc to the Arabs and launch a joint attack on Byzantium, unless Ardanuç was forthwith evacuated. The emperor had no choice but to back down and took the obvious course of disowning those who had acted on his instructions, and ordering them to restore Ardanuç to Ashot Kiskasis. This was duly done. The mission continued on its homeward journey. And an important lesson was learnt by Byzantine policy-planners. Henceforth they pursued more cautious expansion throughout the east, preferring to offer generous concessions in the short term so as to win or retain goodwill for the future rather than extract immediately every ounce of advantage from favourable circumstances.

Ashot Kiskasis' position was far from comfortable after the departure of the Byzantine mission. He had imperilled the security of all the Georgian principalities, already under threat in the north from the advancing power of the Abasgians. What made things undoubtedly worse was the fact that he was the brother-in-law of George, ruler of Abasgia. The suspicion must have arisen that an ulterior motive of his action might have been to further Abasgian expansion by weakening Georgia. At any rate, despite the strength of Ardanuç's defences, he was forced before long to abandon it, first for territory adjoining that of his Byzantine friends, then for a more secure refuge in Abasgia. Freed of this threat, the Georgians were to have a very different future. Instead of struggling to maintain an increasingly precarious independence, they were able to exploit the growing weakness of the Arab emirates of Armenia and the new, softer-handed policy of Byzantium to extend their territory far to the south and mark the medieval apogee of their power by grandiose church-building in their heartlands.

The Ashot Kiskasis episode, a rare case in which the Byzantine documentary record allows us to penetrate into the tangled family history of Georgia, had long assured Ardanuç a special place in the affections of historians of tenth-century Transcaucasia. So I had to see it, even if a visit told me nothing new.

The sun was blazing down when we emerged from the tight winding gorge which runs directly below the north face of the citadel rock. Ahead the valley opens out and offers agricultural possibilities which doubtlessly encouraged a modest growth of population at Ardanuç long before the boom times brought by trade with the Arab world. The castle rock, which became the citadel of the early medieval town, is an extraordinary piece of natural military handiwork, flat-topped, oval-shaped, sloping gently from south to north, surrounded by sheer or almost sheer cliffs on all sides. There are very few points, where the height of the cliffs diminishes or vertiginous paths provide hazardous access, which required strengthening by man-made fortifications. These included caves converted into fighting platforms with parapets, in the north-west face of the cliff, which are connected by a series of tunnels to the summit, and a massive perimeter wall on the south-west side which reproduces every curvature of the rock platform beneath.

We made no attempt to inspect the defences at close quarters, preferring to stroll below and contemplate the citadel from a distance. There was, in any case, no need to struggle

132

up, since an American scholar had already carried out a meticulous survey of the citadel with funds supplied by Armenian foundations in the United States. The straw hats were needed as we viewed it first from the modern town which has migrated south-east to the far bank of the river, then from a saddle to the west. We were more interested in the village which huddles inside the remnants of the medieval town walls. A few sections of the walls are still visible, from which it is plain that the original circuit enclosed a large area of sloping land beneath the southern half of the east side of the citadel rock.

A small boy appeared and offered to guide us. He was much smaller than my seven-year-old daughter. So I was astounded when I saw that he could write well, equally so when he told me that he was ten. When we went into the village, he did his best to protect us from the children and women who crowded round, begging us to photograph them again and again. The importuning redoubled when we were seen to be taking far more interest in the remains of an old *hamam* than in the inhabitants. However, that seemed to be the only visible memorial of the village's past urban life. So we took our leave with a flurry of photography. Just before we got into the car, our small guide kissed my hand and touched it with his forehead.

We set off back towards Artvin, observing the base of a massive pier lying in the wide bed of the river just before it enters the gorge. It must have belonged to a bridge which allowed traffic using a route along the easier right bank of the river through the gorge to reach the old town of Ardanuç beneath the citadel-rock on the left bank. That bridge or a predecessor was once used by early medieval merchants of many nationalities as they made their way to and fro between the Black Sea coast and the rich, open lands of Moslem Transcaucasia east of the mountains.

Below Artvin the modern road follows the narrow valley of the Çoruh as far as Borçka (where Ataturk gazed pensively out of a poster at the plastic bags filled with bread which dominated every table of our *lokanta*). North of Borçka the road veers west, away from the river and the nearby Soviet frontier, crosses a pass 1,000 metres high and descends towards the Black Sea. Clouds hovered over the pass but beyond the sun was shining on what French sailors used to call *le pissoir de la Mer Noire*. Low hedges of tea ran in neat ranks along every hillside. Nigel fell asleep, unaware that I was going into historical shock.

Years before, in 1965, I had struggled along the Black Sea coast from Samsun to Trebizond. The car was underpowered and all the heavy traffic between Turkey and Iran was crowded onto the coastal road. It was quite impossible to overtake anything as the road wound its way in and out of the folds in the sides of the mountains as they fell steeply into the sea – a miserable day which taught me that no military force of any size would ever choose to advance along the Black Sea coast if its commander was in his right mind.

But here, not far from the mouth of the Çoruh, there was no corniche road. The mountains sloped gently and evenly to the sea. The road stretched away to the west, inviting the motorist to speed and offering the easiest of routes to roving armies. *So there was another natural invasion route running east–west, in the far north.* All my interpretations of the strategic manoeuvres of the great powers in late antiquity would need to be reviewed with this new truth borne in mind. My heart sank, as I steered along the gleaming road, and each long shallow concavity in the coast turned out to be as easy to traverse as the one before . . .

But then I began to cheer up. Roman offensives directed against what is now western Georgia at last made military sense. The young Emperor Justinian was not suffering from absurd overconfidence when he sent his armies this way in 528, and his distant successor Heraclius was not taking a desperate gamble when, in 627, he instructed the last fighting force available to the Roman Empire to march east from Trebizond in the hope of linking up with the forces of his great Turkish ally in eastern Georgia.

The *arkadaş* slept on as we sped west. The Black Sea slapped against low rocks, interspersed with thin beaches. It seemed to be as dead as Lake Van. Almost all the fishing boats were hauled up on dry land. The only vessel visible at

134

sea was a dredger. No one sunbathed. A small group of boys were standing on one low rock. Otherwise nothing. Inland, black smoke belched out of the chimneys of the tea factories on the outskirts of each small town, and blocks of flats lined the dual carriageways by which they were all approached. The central crossroads were all dignified with traffic lights, the essential mark of urban status in this region.

The sun was sinking towards the horizon as we neared Rize, the first large town we came to on the coast. It introduces itself with a dualled bypass alongside which runs its approach road. A giant bronze Ataturk holds up a torch in the main square. A barber whom we asked for directions to the citadel invited us into his shop for tea. . . . A customer came in, a tall, substantial figure with curly hair. Our host set about pomading it. An intense desire came over me – to sit in another of the chairs and to have the sensuous pleasure of an ordinary haircut magnified by this prolonged working in of unguents. But loyalty to a man's only hairdresser (his wife) forbade it and temptation was just resisted.

When we reached the citadel, we found a handful of people looking out at the sombre sea and a horizontal pall of black smoke spreading out over it beyond the town. We joined in and looked out too. The heavily restored town walls running down from the citadel presented little of interest. Then we were off to the town of Of.

Of seemed pretty dead at night. So we dined in a white, bemirrored room in our hotel. The tables, all but two unoccupied, were arranged around the instruments and electronic equipment of an absent band. Three chefs, a head waiter and a manager looked after us. Afterwards the *arkadaş* finally got down to writing postcards. He started one to new friends of his – 'You can't possibly imagine the glories of Eastern Turkey' – and stopped, because, of course, they could. So he returned to his copy of *The Towers of Trebizond*. He had reached page fifty. Rose Macaulay and her friends were approaching Trebizond (as indeed we were, for the second time). Soon he fell asleep and I scribbled my postcards.

Our travels were almost over. There was nothing much to see between Of and Trebizond airport. So our start was hyper-leisurely. As the time of our flight drew near, the *ark-adaş* drew out the leisure and went off on a long search for a colour film, so as to photograph the water lilies decorating the hotel lavatory seats. Of was now crowded. Everywhere women were to be seen wearing identical shawls with jagged red and white stripes. At last Nigel reappeared and made several studies of the water lilies. We had to drive at high speed to catch our plane.

Below us, once we had crossed the coastal mountains, the harvested hills of Anatolia stretched away in all directions, pock-marked with threshing-floors. Beside us an old man was reading a garishly coloured tabloid – the first newspaper we had seen since we had left Trebizond for the east. At Ankara, a few hasty words and the *arkadaş* was off on the first leg of a complicated journey to a slothful existence on an Aegean island. *Arkadassiz*, without my *arkadaş*, I tried to while away the time until my flight the following morning.

Then an Israeli scholar materialised whom I recognised from the colloquium. He had slipped away a day early from the study-tour party, which all this time had been penned together in three midi-buses, struggling over bad roads between the scanty vestiges of the first Roman frontier along the Euphrates. A big man with tousled black hair on a balding head, he was on his way to Omaha, Nebraska. Talk, not as variegated or amusing as that of the *arkadaş*, helped us through time. We met again in the evening and fed on Iskender kebabs in a fast-food restaurant.

'Better than anything served up in the hotels visited by the study tour,' muttered my new companion. Then we made our way uphill through dense smog to the new Kocatepe mosque, past a shop the proprietor of which had devised a novel way of enticing customers in – he had placed a snarling, stuffed wolf in the window where it bestrode bags of flour and cans of olive oil.

The mosque is a gigantic traffic island, swathed in noise

and fumes. The plinth upon which it stands is an under-ground car-park. It is revetted in grey marble inside and out. Marble has only been skimped on the paving of the platform outside the mosque enclosure. There the concrete is merely framed and criss-crossed with marble strips. Some work remained to be done in the courtyard inside the enclosure. A great fountain was not yet working. Patches of marble paving were still to be laid. A lone telephone box, its yellow clashing with the grey of the marble, still awaited a tele-phone. Silence reigned when we went into the mosque. Its interior was a void which sucked all sound and pollution out of the air. A single figure moved noiselessly from gallery to gallery. Thick pile carpets deadened our footsteps. Low lights spread a glow behind the stone fretwork masking off the galleries and the stained glass in the upper windows. Over-head there hung an enormous ball faceted with mirrors, with four smaller ones in attendance, like those which shiver and scatter coloured light over nightclubs . . .

We slipped out silently into the enveloping smog and made for the hotel. My new companion was so anxious to get out of Turkey that he decided to come out to the airport with me at an early hour, although this would entail a long wait for him. The airport was only half-Turkish, he said. I downed large slugs of whisky and ruminated about Turkey.

The single most impressive achievement of the Turkish state since my last visit in 1982 has been the development of a telephone network which embraces the whole country. The yellow telephone box is ubiquitous. It is the first sight which greets the traveller at the entrance to Sumela. In towns, small and large, they stand on sentry duty outside the post offices which stay open into the small hours to sell jetons. And the telephones work and provide instant access to international lines. Yet this is the country where post offices have not conceived of the letterbox, where one of the two main post offices in Ankara is staffed by only four clerks at midday and they go into shock if a customer asks for more than two or three stamps, and count them out two by two.

The hierarchy of power in provincial towns is displayed in their buildings. The most imposing are the Security Police headquarters. Next come local authority offices and, in the back of beyond, government blocks of flats built to a standard design, painted cream with a broad vertical brown stripe on each face. Banks come next, vying with each other to impress their customers. But the mullahs are counterattacking. Mosques are either under construction or have recently been completed almost everywhere. Even in Karayazi, the most run-down small town we passed, there was a smart new one. Doğubayazıt is one of the rare exceptions, with no sign of a new mosque, but then it seems to have set itself up as a defiantly secular town, cocking a snook at Iran across the nearby border and holding out against the rising tide of Islam inside Turkey against which the naval traveller had railed for denuding more and more of his favourite restaurants of drink.

Every town strives to pull rank by the grandeur of its approach roads, dualled if at all possible, and sweeping up to roundabouts or traffic lights. Otherwise little thought is given to appearances. Houses are not painted or white-washed. Almost no one grows flowers for pleasure. At the night the feeble neon strip light fills the inhabited spaces of restaurants, cafés, shops and workshops with an eerie light. Yet appearances can be all-important and great care taken over them. Buses wear smart livery to tout for custom. Inhabitants of the remotest villages wear impractical leather slip-on shoes; and brightly-coloured dresses and *chadors* enliven the populated landscapes of the high pastures.

The changes since my first visit in 1965 are enormous. The ox-drawn cart, its wooden axles screaming, is a rarity even in the Kurdish east. The television has killed the cinema stone dead in provincial towns. No longer does one go to sleep with the sound-track of the movie being shown in a nearby open-air cinema drumming in one's ears. Instead one wakes up to the sound of more or less melodious *muezzin* summoning the faithful to prayer at dawn. And there is bottled water for sale everywhere.

But some things remain the same. Small boys still scurry in and out of shops, carrying trays of tea. Shepherds still guard their flocks, motionless in their thick, broad-

shouldered capes. And there has been little stylistic development in the postcards of alluring girls – they are just much
harder to find.

Not much of western Turkey could be seen in the early
morning as the plane flew to Istanbul – only the huge lump
of Mount Olympus, the premier holy mountain of Byzantium
before the rise of Athos in the tenth century, which pushed
up above the mist, and the shadows of the Princes Islands on
the shimmering waters of the Sea of Marmara. Aged aircraft
belonging to small independent airlines were dotted around
Istanbul airport, reminding travellers that Turkey is a country
where the market reigns supreme. My last sight was of three
wolflike dogs scavenging on the edge of a runway.

My neighbour was a Moslem Canadian, who had been
drilling in vain for oil in the mountains south of Lake Van.
His team was guarded by upwards of a hundred troops, who
shot Kurdish 'terrorists' every now and again to maintain
their authority in the area. At night the perimeter of the camp
was illuminated by arc lights. If oil were found, the well
would triple Turkey's production, but the company was losing patience and exploration would have to halt by mid-
November when winter set in.

Behind us, in the smoking section, sat the Turkish team of
weightlifters and wrestlers on their way to the Olympic
Games in Seoul. Their massive frames were relaxed. They
chatted amiably. The centre of attention was a small man, a
Bulgarian Turk who had been reportedly bought from Zhivkov for an enormous sum. He could generate more power
per pound of weight than any other man in human history.
My neighbour began talking to an American lady about his
Malaysian wife and I dozed off . . .

139

PART 2

TURKEY 1989

CHAPTER 1

The young man in the open-necked shirt with the collar tucked outside his jacket introduced himself as the acting British Consul. He had been invited to the party in honour of the Scholar by virtue of renting a flat belonging to our hostess. He came from Woking. I asked him the name of Britain's Ambassador and he said he hadn't a clue. He was on assignment from the Home Office and he concentrated on the job in hand, which was curbing illegal immigration. He said there were 5,000 'illegals' from Turkey a month, and if the Turks didn't put a stop to it the British would have to. I asked how.

'For a start we're introducing visas with an application fee of £20 – non-returnable. That should make the undesirables think twice. You get these Anatolian peasants saving just enough for the air fare, then coming in and saying they're political refugees. Next thing you know they are living on the taxpayer.'

I said I did not envy him having to turn back hopeful young men who had been given all the money their families could raise for a better life.

'The humiliation, too, trailing back home.'

'I'm not bothered,' he said. 'That's their problem. Chancers, that's what they are . . .'

'What about the genuine political refugees – Kurds and the like?'

'They have to prove their status.'

'Doesn't do much for Anglo-Turkish relations to put them

in jail when they land at Heathrow while you make up your mind.'

'There's the accommodation problem.' I wondered aloud how British tourists would feel about waiting in Turkish jails while the authorities checked their papers. 'That's what I'm here for. I interview them before they leave – that is, the ones that apply through the proper channels.'

'You must speak pretty good Turkish.'

'Not a word. That's Lina's department.' He indicated the pretty, dark-eyed girl next to him. 'But when you've been in the game for a bit you learn to smell out a fake from a genuine political. Besides, it's up to them to convince me.' He paused, squaring his shoulders. I wondered if he did that when he was interviewing suspects. Evidently wanting to change the direction of the conversation he went on: 'I used to speak some German once. I think I might go over and pick it up again in the holidays.'

And after that, no doubt, on to the next job in hand. I wondered what: who better equipped to handle repatriation of Hong Kong boat people? Was this was the authentic face of the Home Office?

Lina had already explained that she was Italian by birth, Yugoslav by passport and resident in Turkey. She spoke six languages and had taken the job of interpreter at the Embassy in the hope of getting British nationality. I said she had a pretty good contact, indicating her neighbour. She shrugged politely and made a wry face.

I asked the man from Woking how he liked Istanbul.

'I'm not bothered, really. We can pretty well shut it out in the compound, especially at the weekends. There's tennis courts and facilities. You can't hear a sound. You wouldn't know you were abroad.'

Something stirred in my memory. It had to do with a standard British Rail notice, 'DO NOT FLUSH TOILET WHILE TRAIN IS STANDING IN A STATION', across which someone had scribbled the words: 'EXCEPT WOKING'. Silently I raised my glass to the unknown graffiti artist.

From the balcony, where the party had overflowed, there floated a sound like heroic verse. The bold declamatory style, the grand statement leading into the labyrinth of qualifying clauses, the sweep of the subject matter, the occasional ringing laugh at once established the Scholar's unmistakable hallmark: levity of manner, gravity of matter. It was, as always, an impressive performance, but with a dimension new to me: the language he had chosen to address his audience in was French, which he spoke fluently, in a high, metallic voice and English public-school accent. The flow, borne on the summer night air to the sofa where I sat, seemed never to dry up. It was as if a mighty wind had stirred the Marmara sending its rollers crashing against the balcony of the little flat. The Scholar's subject, appropriately, was Byzantium, and his listeners, who included a textile manufacturer with patient blue eyes and a Dunhill pipe, and a blonde lingerie tycoon married to the son of the hanged Prime Minister, Adnan Menderes, sat round him in awed silence. Nobody could say the evening's guest of honour had failed to rise to the occasion.

At last there was a pause for breath. Turning to my neighbour, a Turkish banker called Kemal Ozkent, I observed, hoping to amuse:

'The words of Racine, the accent of Winston Churchill . . .'

The banker turned and said without smiling:

'Oh no, I think he's very interesting.'

The reason for the pause emerged later. It was not that the Scholar had run out of information, but that the textile manufacturer had been stung in the leg by a bee that had got inside his trousers. Such were his fortitude and good manners that no one had noticed until he whispered something into his wife's ear and tiptoed off. The Scholar never quite got back into his stride after the bee incident, when the textile manufacturer's place was taken by a former ambassadress, part-Dutch, part-Mexican, who arrived fighting drunk. Now reduced to near-speechlessness, she punctuated the scholarly flow with expletives directed at present-day Turkey.

The party, to mark the Scholar's return to the scene of his

triumphs of the year before, was being given by an aunt of my friend Eleni in her flat in a once leafy fishing village on the Marmara long since swallowed up in the exploding sprawl of Istanbul.

The evening began badly for my new acquaintance, Kemal. He sat for supper at a little table that included Eleni and myself. The son of the founder of a leading Turkish bank, Kemal was a man apparently in need of constant reassurance. When those around him failed he supplied it himself. He began by explaining solemnly that although his wife was a good sailor he was himself a master professional yachtsman; he added that he was also a champion skibob rider and close friend of the late Lord Brabazon of Tara; and he openly rejoiced in his good fortune at being able to get on with everyone he met.

'Take Greeks,' he said. 'We are all Europeans, I always say, so what the difference? If I went to, say, Milan and introduced myself as a Turk, people would greet me just as they do here. So why not in Athens?'

But Eleni was not Greek for nothing. As he spoke her eyes grew larger and darker. When he finished silence fell. She took a deep breath.

'Well,' she said, 'I used to live in Milan and we had an Italian maid from the mountains. When there was a thunderstorm she would run into the house with wild eyes, screaming: "Help! The Tur-rks are coming! The Tur-rks are coming! We shall all be mur-rder-red!"'

Momentarily deflated, Kemal redeemed himself with a joke. To deflect attention from his discomfiture I drew another distinction, between northern and southern Europeans, and told a story to illustrate my idea of a warm Mediterranean welcome. At Athens airport that summer I had been greeted by my friend Eleni holding a pole with a blown-up photograph of myself taken on holiday, in dark glasses and straw hat, at the arrival point where drivers wait with signs bearing their passengers' names. During the wait a taxidriver had inquired who the celebrity was and she said it was a writer. The whole incident greatly perplexed Kemal

146

and he had fallen silent. But after a few moments he turned to Eleni and said:

'You know, I have been thinking what the taxidrivers were saying to one another when you told them it was a writer. They were saying. "He is a writer, but he cannot read!"' At which everyone laughed. And for the rest of the evening each time he caught my eye he would point to me, doubling up with laughter: 'There is the writer who cannot read!'

At a nearby table I spotted another new acquaintance. This was the doctor, a benign and portly figure whom I had been sent to consult professionally about an onset of dizzy spells and round whom a plot had since been hatched.

The doctor wore a hearing aid and spoke careful, emphatic French, quite loud, as some deaf people do. He had made light of my complaint, waving aside my theory of a brain tumour.

'It is all quite simple. It is a question of construction. The cause is your shape. Since you are long and thin, it takes time for the blood to reach your head when you rise to your feet. In my own case,' – he added, glancing wistfully downwards – 'the body being approximately spherical, the problem does not arise. And now, since this is not a terminal illness, I shall cure it immediately.' He handed me three small pills with the air of a conjuror. 'Take these, and ascend or descend, as the case may be, more gradually. The phenomenon should then disappear. That is all. And if it does not,' he went on carefully, 'then nature will effect the cure instead. You should always begin with the understanding that, like patients, doctors know almost nothing. Take the inner ear, said to control the balance . . .' But we never did take the inner ear, because at that moment his eye was caught by my copy of Flaubert's *Egyptian Journal*. 'Do you like Flaubert?' The face turned purple, and seemed about to explode. 'Horrible egotist bourgeois monster! I do not love Gustave Flaubert!'

'You do not think he is a genius?'

'Yes, yes, genius!' he said testily. 'I talk of the man, not his work. I hate him. *C'EST UN AFFREUX MONSTRE EGOISTE BOURGEOIS.*' The outburst made me forget my dizzy spells and concentrate on the doctor. He told me that he spent hours at a stretch reading, and became so personally and passionately involved in the process that he formed an inextricable relationship with each author in turn. He spoke of reading as others speak of travel. Every book was an expedition in the company of the author. He eagerly looked forward to the winter for which he appeared to have booked himself on the journey of a lifetime. He was about to embark on the complete works of Proust. 'Flaubert is a cruise,' he said, 'but Proust is a round-the-world voyage.'

So taken were we by the doctor that we invited him to the party to meet the Scholar. Eleni had something else in mind as well. He was a recent widower and Aunt Celeste, a smart widow in her eighties, openly declared herself not at all averse to another liaison. A Greek of Maltese descent, she had already had five husbands – though admitting only to three, the other two being Turks. The elegant, silver-framed photographs in her bedroom showed her as a young woman of a startling beauty. She still had sparkling good looks, with long nose and lively, interested eyes set close together like a bird's, and a carefully orchestrated thatch of nearly credible fading gold hair. Small, chic, feminine, she had an abundance of worldly charm; but above all, punishing energy.

Aunt Celeste's day did not begin early, but it began with vigour, after a morning spent in bed surrounded by her photographs. First came gym. After half an hour of exercises, she lunched at home unless she had an invitation, and then her chauffeur arrived. Mehmet was a slight, unobtrusive man in his middle-fifties with built-up heels and impeccable manners. He had his own stately rhythm. After showing Aunt Celeste into the back of the car he would settle himself in the driver's seat, pushed as far back as it would go so that he could clasp the wheel with arms straight. He set off slowly and with great deliberation for the crown of the road, and once there yielded to no man.

On the first of several hair-raising journeys into town with Aunt Celeste she invited me to agree that he was an expert driver. She had the habit of pausing during a sentence that began in French and lapsed, according to whim, into Turkish

148

or Greek, to berate him for losing the way, which it seemed he regularly did. To me she confided that although *'il manque le sens du nord'* he had soon found his way round her neighbourhood, where he had cut a swathe through the womenfolk. Throughout all this the improbable Romeo's face remained benignly impassive as he carved his way through the Istanbul traffic, sending pedestrians diving for their lives. They made a formidable pair.

Aunt Celeste was renowned for her business sense. The first stop in town was Celestia – her not quite eponymous boutique where she sold baby clothes. From there she would go to her Istanbul *pied à terre* from where she arranged wedding parties and social functions. I gathered that both enterprises were a great success. I never visited them; for a while I enjoyed the fantasy that they were a front for a string of high-class bordellos.

Late in the evening she would return home to change and social life would begin. She immensely enjoyed eating and had a sweet tooth. After the succession of traditional exotic Turkish dishes, guzzled with little cries of delight, she would settle into what she liked best of all: a box of After Eight chocolates. The picture of her animated face under the tidy bird's nest of hair, eyes twinkling with pleasure, remains fastened in my mind. When it was suggested it was time to go home she would pout.

Aunt Celeste's chief regret was that she spoke almost no English. Had she done so I suspect she would have gone to live in New York where, she told Eleni, the two of them could have started up a clothes-making business. Instead she settled for visits. When the Scholar and I last saw her she was about to leave on a trip to Disneyland (her eyes lit with excitement at the prospect), New York, Barbados and Marrakesh – and from there to Patmos, provided Eleni had enlarged and modernised her kitchen in time for her visit so that she could spread herself to make Turkish dishes.

Aunt Celeste loved jewellery. Her fortune was invested – and her person encrusted – in it. Precious stones flashed on her fingers as she ate her After Eights. She educated her nieces to believe that it was the hallmark of femininity to be able to spot real stones from fake at twenty paces across a drawing room. Distrusting banks, she carried her hoard in a carpet bag when she went about in strange cities. Warned of muggers in New York she was outraged.

'They wouldn't dare!' she said. Once when leaving home in Athens she set the bag down outside the house while she locked the door and did not remember it until she was on the way to the airport. Eleni told of the terrible silence in the back of the family car as the uninsured aunt, together with her white-faced heirs, raced home to discover the family treasure sitting in the flowerpot where she had deposited it.

Aunt Celeste's house mirrored her personality. The sitting room was a riot of elegant clutter. Cheap and priceless carpets overlapped one another on the floor; bibelots, from Fabergé to Marks and Spencer's, were scattered on tables. For the party the transparent plastic covers had been removed from the Victorian silver teapots and bowls. An ostrich egg, said to dispel spiders, hung from an arch. Cabinets crammed with Chinese and Turkish porcelain lined the walls. Generous bunches of fresh flowers stood beside Aunt Celeste's favourites, nylon gladioli carried by hand from New York. The house looked lived in, for so it was, by someone who understood both Levantine show and *les petits soins* of daily life.

The buffet consisted of a succession of small dishes, mostly unknown to me. At a certain moment I observed Aunt Celeste placing a bowl of crystallised fruits in front of the doctor, and watched eagerly for developments. But before she had time to engage him in conversation the ex-ambassadress had lurched into view and slumped into the empty chair beside him. I sought out Eleni to report the setback. When I looked again the ambassadress, in full flow now, sat facing the doctor who, to my surprise, was smiling with every sign of contentment. Then I noticed that he had removed his hearing aid and almost eaten his way through the crystallised fruits.

We never heard the outcome of the matchmaking. But as we were leaving the good doctor told Aunt Celeste:

'My mission is to prolong life, yours to enrich it.' She looked delighted. It seemed a good enough start.

CHAPTER 2

Our second journey was much more frivolous than our first. We had to resume the interrupted search for the late Roman fortress of Artaleson and the early medieval town of Havjij which we had failed to find in 1988. We had to make up for our faint-heartedness at Çukuryayla and return to follow the obscure leads we had been given. But otherwise the plan was to steep ourselves in varied experiences. We would spend a few idle days in Istanbul, which I last visited properly in 1965, then, after returning from the east, we would motor along the western edge of the central plateau of Anatolia like old-style tourists, seeking out whatever sites of interest there were from prehistoric to modern times. A short visit to Bulgaria would round the trip off. I was eager to take up the offer of a distinguished archeologist to show us round an important early medieval town which she had excavated, as well as to see the archeological museum in Sofia which had been closed when I was there before. The *arkadaş* was happy to add Bulgaria to the East European countries which he intended to visit on the way out to Istanbul.

The most interesting part of the journey for me was going to be our motoring tour of western Turkey. I had never seen the swathe of open plains and hills separating Ankara and the central plateau from the mountains which back onto the Aegean and Marmara coastlands. And I should have. For the fate of this area in the early Middle Ages determined that of Byzantium, the Roman successor state in the east, and I purported to know something about that.

The western edge of the plateau contained the main assembly points for the fast-moving cavalry armies which conducted guerrilla operations against Arab invasion forces from the mid-seventh to the mid-tenth centuries. It also formed the inner line of defence, guarding the approaches to the rich coastal provinces of the Aegean and Marmara from attack by land. Such cities as survived the catastrophes of the seventh century, when the Arabs dismembered the eastern Roman Empire, leaving only an impoverished rump centred on Anatolia as the heartland of Byzantium, were transformed into heavily fortified military bases. Their garrisons and the troops guarding the villagers who were evacuated together with their livestock at times of danger to the nearest defensible highland massif played a vital part in the defensive struggle.

I was eager to look at the remains of the fortified towns and to see what information could be gleaned from their material remains about urban life in Byzantium outside its two great cities, Constantinople and Thessalonica. No less important, I wanted to gain a better understanding of their strategic functions by examining their sites, the relative strength of their defences, and the extent of the territory which they commanded. Finally the best way to grasp the military articulation of the landscape was to travel over it and to see for myself where the relief of the western mountain zone provided natural defences for the coastlands beyond and where, by contrast, breaches in it opened up thoroughfares for advance westwards and north-westwards towards the sea.

5 September (Oxford–Istanbul)

The *arkadaş* met me at Istanbul airport and whisked me past apartment blocks surmounted by satellite dishes and a derelict factory built onto the Theodosian wall to a plush pension behind St Sophia. Half an hour later I joined him and his first travelling companion, Eleni, in the garden of the Yeşil Ev, a

152

pastiche Ottoman *konak* (mansion). Beer did nothing to dispel the disorientation brought about by the flight. Dazed and befuddled I wandered off on my own.

It was early evening. The Topkapı palace was closing. So I made my way into the park below. It was unbeatable as a re-introduction to Turkey. The flowerbeds were small and filled with garishly coloured plants (mainly crimson and orange). It was a flashier version of the English municipal. Several families were packing up picnics which they had had on the tables and benches provided by the city authorities. They all seemed to have brought one or more large, thin-skinned, shiny metal containers. The families were poor and had a slightly hunched look. Further on there was a long, low stage-set among the trees, facing a level amphitheatre of short concrete benches arranged in concentric rows. A largish audience was gazing at the set, which consisted of a row of pastel-coloured clapboard houses. A formidable array of black loudspeakers stood on each flank. The rapt audience listened as the sound system was tested.

I walked on round the base of the high wall enclosing the ancient acropolis which is now occupied by Topkapı. The park was in shadow and cooled by its many trees. Stalls were being dismantled either side of the main path. Halfway up the slope a man was trying to extract red iron posts from their concrete foundations, hammering steadily but futilely at the underneath of their flat tops. Ahead sentries guarded a gate in the Topkapı wall at the Seraglio point. Nearby the Gothic column reared up from the middle of a gloomy café in the trees. This had its own, rather inferior stage-set with smaller loudspeakers. Rubbish spilled from waste bins and stank. 'VICTOR DEVICTOS GOTHOS' declared the column base to the empty café chairs.

Boats large and small busied themselves at the mouth of the Bosphorus. A large statue of Ataturk stood in the sunlight on the edge of a small waterside park. Ataturk's pose is one of assumed nonchalance, one hand on a hip, the other clenched at his side. He wears a bow tie and what look like spats. Two or three boys were swimming in the Bosphorus: an act of folly. Istanbul, with a population now approaching eight million, discharges almost all its sewage untreated into the sea.

A large ferry was loading up by the entrance to the Golden Horn. Some passengers hurried across the quay. Others were taking a short cut, climbing around a spiked fence courtesy of an old man who had laid a plank across a void at the right angle where the quay changed direction and gave them passage in return for a fee.

I walked back through the thoroughfares of the inner park. Most of the stalls were gone. The main path had been washed clean. There was a funfair off to the right. It ran to dodgems, which were crammed into too small an arena, and a great swing in the form of a galleon, the motions of which, by some miracle, did not make its passengers sick. But the centrepiece was a roundabout, from which rose a gigantic, bright-eyed, busty girl with short black hair and a swirling black skirt (the roundabout itself) – like an enlarged version of a ship's figurehead, updated (to the 1960s) and deprived of most of her torso. Nearby were some fenced enclosures with a few mangy creatures – geese, stork, listless Kangal dogs, and two camels at which some boys were throwing pebbles and dust. Beyond this degenerate, diminished zoo, in the centre of a small formal garden, stood a naked female statue, crudely but sensuously carved, with slightly sagging breasts and a fig leaf over her parts.

That evening the three of us went to Galata for a drink in the Pera Palas Hotel, built in the 1880s, and revetted in rich brown and purple marble. Nigel shied away at his first attempt to ride the lift up through the marble ceiling. He did so later, fortified by a drink. A violent wind rose just before we left. We climbed hastily into a taxi, telling the driver to take us to the smart new hotel in the old city, the Ramada. He took us to the right area but had no idea where the hotel was. We went round in circles searching for it, repeatedly passing a hamburger bar. Our driver clearly put his faith in Allah, expecting the hotel suddenly to materialise. He asked passers-by how to get there but the instructions were complicated and failed to deliver us there. He never asked for the *address* – either he had not conceived of the notion of places having addresses as well as positions, or he didn't know the street names, or he couldn't read them. Eventually the Ramada did materialise and we entered an unreal world of transparent lifts gliding silently on pistons, of bright lights, of an artificial stream lit from within, and rich tourists. After a long wait, we ate shish kebabs.

6 September

Nigel spent the morning at work on his processor. I went to the Archeological Museum. A shoeshiner offered to polish my gym shoes. Two men led two panting moth-eaten bears slowly down the cobbled street behind St Sophia. Most of the museum was closed off when I arrived. At twelve, the barriers were removed from the entrance to the classical galleries, but the late Roman and Byzantine rooms upstairs remained sealed off.

The museum houses what is basically an Ottoman collection. It dates in the main from the late-nineteenth century. It includes the whole of the nondescript narrow frieze of fighting men from the temple of Artemis at Magnesia-on-the-Maeander, which was excavated in the 1890s. The most impressive exhibits were assembled from the outer reaches of the Ottoman Empire – for example several magnificent Hellenistic sarcophagi from Sidon which have multiple layers of action crammed into their bas reliefs. The most imposing object of all is a gigantic sarcophagus from Iconium, dating from the third century AD. It must be fifteen foot or so high. Husband and wife (or what remains of them) relax on top, attended by four plump *putti*; reliefs of family devotions and hunting scenes fill the panels on the sides, framed above and below by narrow friezes of figures wrestling, racing chariots and doing more hunting.

I joined Nigel and Eleni for a drink and sandwich at the Yeşil Ev. Its shamness could not be disguised. Reproduction olive-green upholstered chairs in the lobby looked pretentious and out of place. The bannisters on the stairs were flimsy. A powerful smell of heating oil seeped out from the basement. The walled garden at the back, shaded by trees, seemed more attractive, but canned Mozart emanated from every side and figs were ripening in the trees overhead, ready to open and allow their viscous, pink juices to fall, drop by drop, on the human beings eating and drinking below.

Afterwards, we went on a touristic foray to the quarter of Blachernae, where we saw the Kariye Camii (the early twelfth-century domed nave, reminiscent of late antique buildings with its marble paving and marble panelled walls, holds the eye longer than the mosaics crammed into narthex and exo-narthex or even the famous Palaeologan frescoes in the mortuary side chapel), and two of the great Ottoman architect Sinan's finest mosques, the Mihrimah Camii, visible from afar behind the highest section of the land walls, and the stupendous Süleymaniye Camii. Two Heath-Robinson lighting contraptions spoil the interior of the Mihrimah Camii – a grimy chandelier of upturned glass cups each with a small light bulb, and a large iron circle, festooned with more bare bulbs, two storm lanterns and two loudspeakers. Both are suspended from the dome and hang just above one's head, thus forcing themselves on the attention in place of the soaring arches, the *minbar*, the *mihrab* and, high above them, the stone fretwork fronting the stained-glass windows.

7 September

I got into St Sophia the morning after the party before the worst of the tourist rush. I had resolved not to make the mistakes of my first visit twenty years ago: not to make anachronistic comparisons with the mosques built by Sinan in the sixteenth century, which defy gravity effortlessly; not to seek out the odd patches of Byzantine figural mosaic which are quite out of place (and utterly out of scale) in this huge building. The immediate overwhelming impression is indeed of the scale of the building and of its Roman-ness. The barrel-vaulted exo-narthex and narthex are magnificent Roman structures in their own right. Their subordinate function as mere antechambers is only betrayed by the great doorways, each surmounted by a massive, bulging lintel, which lead into the nave. It is above all the *mass*, the *weight* of the main structural elements of the building which mark it out as a Roman work of unmatched grandeur, in spite of being rushed up at jerry-building speed (immediately after the bloody climax of the Nika riots in January 532 when the Emperor Justinian lured the rioting crowds into the Hippodrome, set loose his troops upon them and turned the great arena into an almost hermetically sealed killing ground where some 35,000 died). There is no attempt to hide the engineering achievement of enclosing so vast a space. Indeed, the only appropriate way to decorate it is to encase walls and pillars and arches and vaults in simply patterned or patternless gleaming materials, thus both glossing and displaying the forms beneath. Such appears to have been its original adornment. It consisted of silver revetment, marble panelling, and fields of patterned mosaics, with crosses scattered on gold space or small bright-coloured polygons and stars spangling a dark blue background. Such figures as there are (dating from later periods), even the Mother of God in the apse, seem small, puny creatures, pinned like intruder moths to the great sweeps of stone. Paradoxically the six gigantic Ottoman medallions with Koranic quotations placed high up above the nave are much more in keeping with the building than all the Byzantine mosaic patches on the walls.

We lunched in a bustling *köfte* restaurant recommended by Kemal, though how he knew of it beat me, since the clientèle were far from rich. Nigel had spent another creative morning on the processor. It was now time for a second touristic foray, this time to visit Byzantine monuments of the tenth to the twelfth centuries. Our taxidriver seemed not particularly knowledgeable about the old city, and became confused when I showed him my map which dated from 1960. We never found the Myrelaion church which the Emperor Romanos Lekapenos built around 920 for a nunnery, which he established in the house where he had lived before his successful putsch. All we saw were different kinds of shops

157

and a loo packed into a massive structure honeycombed with brick-vaulted chambers; massive stone eaves protruded from the sides, and a circle of well-cut Roman blocks of stone emerged from a patch of grass next door.

We went on to the next objective, the Fenari Isa Camii, which consists of two churches conjoined. The northern one was built in 907 by a certain Constantine Lips, a great figure at the court of Leo VI, for a monastic foundation of his. The southern one was added towards the end of the thirteenth century by the wife of Michael VIII, the first Palaeologan Emperor, and was probably intended to be the new dynasty's funerary church. The interior of the original, northern church used to gleam with glazed, multi-coloured tiles, inlaid marble and mosaics. All that now remains *in situ* is some of the original marble carving which picked out the main interior features of the building. It seems that the crosses in the narrow marble strip running around the cornices of both churches have not been noticed and are going to coexist with the Moslem fittings which two *haji* workmen were installing in the southern church. These gleamed as brightly as the Byzantine decoration had once done in the northern church, so brightly indeed that the marble of which they were made acquired the sheen of plastic. There was a large, deathly white *mihrab*, flanked on either side by two immense deathly white candles which stood on bronze bases and bore aloft two neon-lit circles. The axis of the building was disregarded. Both the *mihrab* and a bright green, striped carpet were set at an angle and aligned on Mecca (too small an angle though, so that they seemed to me to be likely to miss the target).

Finally, there was Zeyrek Kilise Camii, a triple church built between 1118 and 1136 by the Emperor John II Komnenos and his wife Eirene, at the centre of a monastic complex dedicated to Christ Pantokrator. Besides the church and the residential quarters of the monks, there were a number of charitable establishments – a fifty-bed hospital, a home for twenty-four elderly men, a hospice, a bath-house and a home for lepers. The whole complex was placed in a conspicuous position on what is now called Fatih hill, overlooking the monumental centre of the city. There the generosity of the ruling dynasty would be very visible. From there John Komnenos and his successor Manuel would preside over the city in death as in life, from their tombs in the chapel which linked the two main naves together. The northern, to which women were admitted, was somewhat smaller than the southern and has lost almost all its original decoration. The southern was built on a grand scale and sumptuously adorned inside. It seems to have had stained-glass windows, marble revetment all round the nave, and a magnificent *opus sectile* pavement of interlace design which is well preserved. Some of the finer elements of its marble fittings have been incorporated in the *minbar*.

The surrounding quarter is now a poor one: narrow lanes snake between tenement blocks; ragged children play in the streets; no sound of traffic penetrates from the bloated city below which is strangling itself with congestion and exhaust fumes.

We hurried back to the Yeşil Ev to receive Celeste and her nephew, Bora for tea. She was a study in pink and cream with touches of glitter: pink woollen dress, pink frames to spectacles, cream silk jacket spangled with white and coloured beads, necklace of ivory cylinders, and fair amount of gold round neck and wrist. The bright green eyeshadow over the twinkling eyes was the only discordant element. She had been at work in her antique shop and arrived in her chauffeur-driven car. The chauffeur drove with arrogance at a stately pace, with his arms out straight and his seat laid back. He was known as Napoleon.

Bora arrived separately. He is an ex-*Gastarbeiter*, of a grand sort. He spent forty years as a chemical engineer in St Louis. He now lives off his *kaynak* (spring) which is on the European side of the Bosphorus; he gets a good rent from the lessees, narcotics *mafiosi* who use the water-business as a front and are 'not particularly interested' (as he puts it) 'in maximising their profits'. Like other former *Gästarbeiter*, he has plans to invest in a hotel – though, in his case, it will be created by converting the family's derelict forty-bedroom house on the Bosphorus into a palatial establishment, and will need to be backed by vast sums from other investors. Unlike most rich metropolitan Turks such as Kemal and the textile manufacturer, he has no fear of the countryside – the years abroad have both disengaged him from the narrow world of urbanised, bourgeois Turkey and made him more curious and more affectionate towards the peasantry. He likes talking about politics and local affairs to villagers while his son climbs up to visit ancient monuments.

Nigel and Eleni talked with Celeste, while I listened to Bora. Periodically pink blotches besmirched my white trousers. A sign of good luck, said Bora, if they come from birds. Finally I worked out the source overhead – irregular discharges from the burst underside of a ripened fig. Bora reflected on the good and bad in Turkey. He admired the Cappadocian peasants who always voted for the loser in elections, to ensure that there are checks on the government. He liked competition, even conflict, between state institutions – that between the PTT and the two TV channels (for once, acting in concert) over use of satellite transmissions for cable distribution was then erupting in a bitter lawsuit. Above all, he praised the Bosphorus mayor who was confronting the establishment and demanding that one-million-pound villas built in his district for Ozal and other great men be altered within thirty days to conform to planning regulations. He had already got a court order and demolished four, to prove that he was in earnest. On the other hand, the chemical engineer regarded the level of air and sea pollution around Istanbul with appalled amusement, and presented Turkey as surrounded by enemies – he ticked off the neighbours one by one, giving reasons, historical or current, for their animosity.

Bora and Celeste went their separate ways at six o'clock, he on foot with a slightly waddling gait, she sitting behind the impassive Napoleon in her Peugeot. I went on a hurried tour of the Hippodrome area as dusk fell. We then had dinner in a restaurant outside the sea wall. Eleni reminisced about a Sudanese cook who had given her a bag made out of a whole baby crocodile – leaving it on the table showing the belly and flattened legs.

160

CHAPTER 3

Istanbul's daily awakening has been likened to a beggar stirring in the gutter, then staggering to his feet to reveal his dazzling raiment. But at the Yeşil Ev Hotel, a Ministry of Tourism re-evocation of Ottoman ascendancy, the rubble and the beggars, touts, men selling postcards, boys selling fresh bread were sadly hidden from our view. Here, in the old quarter near Topkapı where the Scholar and I were lodged the first sounds of the day came from the *muezzin* loudspeaker on top of the Sultan Ahmed mosque, which was visible from my window. Advertised as a renovated pasha's residence, Yeşil Ev was in fact merely a good counterfeit. Five years before there had been nothing there.

This in no way lessened our comfort; it was an elegant enough counterfeit with a handsome green and white wooden façade. My room, reached by a generous winding staircase, was almost filled by a brass-railed double bed. It had six sash windows that fell like guillotines, heavy slatted shutters and a jungle of brass and cut-glass lamps – I counted fifteen light bulbs. Marble table-tops, two sets of curtains, heavy brown velvet and plastic lace (in the home of the genuine article), added an erotically louche touch. Room service was assiduous, even pressing. One morning a waiter burst in with a tray of beer for six. Though I was clearly alone it was all I could do to persuade him that I had not ordered it; it quickly became a matter of honour, and had it not been for his burden I might have had reason to fear violence.

For the ears it was Scylla and Charybdis – when the piped

Vivaldi stopped a bald, black-bearded pianist with a truckdriver's touch struck up with classical medleys. At nightfall there was a Son et Lumière half-hour in the open air café beneath my window presenting the story of Sultan Ahmed mosque in a whispered boom with trumpets – English on Monday, German on Tuesday, Turkish on Wednesday, double bill at the weekend.

We usually ate in the garden where well-to-do townsfolk came. Inside the guests were mostly foreigners. Breakfast was a choice between plastic airline containers in the bedroom and delicious fresh preserves served downstairs. I shared breakfast in the dining room on the first day with an American couple who turned out to be not man and wife, but fellow Evangelists. When I complained of the pianist the man said he preferred to regard it as the will of God. I learned that after a week in Istanbul they would be stopping off in Bulgaria on the way home.

'Business or pleasure?'

'Our business is a pleasure,' he replied. The pair smiled serenely. Next day I ate breakfast in the garden.

The Scholar was lodged nearby, in an even newer establishment just outside the walls of the Topkapı Palace, also with piped music, but more Peter Jones than fake bordello. However, no one could have complained of the location: we were a minute's walk from the great museum, the Blue Mosque, Sultan Ahmed, the ancient walls of Constantinople and the extraordinary underground Roman reservoir with a Medusa head laid sideways forming the base of one of its pillars, the effect marred by theme music.

However, I had not allowed in my calculations for the disciplines of the Scholar's calling. Byzantium was his subject, and to Byzantium he kept. Eyes averted as he passed the great palatial entrance, he resisted the temptations of Topkapı, the Sultan Ahmed and all that had passed after the fall of Constantinople. Instead he devoted his full attentions to the ruins of the Roman Hippodrome. The Blue Mosque, which he had seen before, was too crowded. There was no time for the reservoir. Instead he took us on a tour of little known Christian churches in the interstices of the capital,

162

some being converted into mosques. In one the work was complete: it had been realigned to face Mecca, so that the new green nylon carpet ran at an angle to the old nave, while neon strip lighting was trained on to the medieval stones as if to flush out infidel ghosts lurking in the shadows.

Aunt Celeste was waiting to have tea with us under a fig-tree in the garden of Yeşil Ev. With her was a man with a mournful face and the hips of a Keystone Cop, who spoke English with a Brooklyn accent and turned out to be a mine of information on Istanbul. Aunt Celeste introduced him as Bora, her nephew. While she was warning me of the dangers of travel in Eastern Turkey – the fact that I had already been there and she had not made no difference – Bora gave the Scholar a historical account of the capital's plumbing and irrigation. He had found a series of horizontal tunnels on his own property which had probably been used to bring clean water to the old Constantinople from the north. Today it was safer to drink bottled water; and the city which had grown from two to eight million inhabitants in twenty years, had the same sewage disposal arrangements as in Roman days: namely the Bosphorus and the Marmara. So absorbed was the Scholar that he failed to notice the series of tiny explosions overhead as the fig-tree released the zest from its fruit, allowing it to fall in indelible drops on to the crotch of his white trousers.

It was at Yeşil Ev that I came across the English language newspaper, the *Turkish Daily News*. What first caught my eye was the headline 'TORTURE' spread across two columns. The left-hand one, subheaded 'The Theory', stated that Turkey was a signatory to the international agreement that torture should be banned whatever the circumstances, and to a convention that all prisoners should be brought before a judge within forty-eight hours of arrest. With some scepticism I turned to the right-hand column, subheaded 'The Practice'. I was in for a surprise. Its opening words stated baldly that of sixty prisoners consulted in a *Daily News* survey forty-five said they had been tortured, and all claimed they had no access to a judge or a lawyer within the stated time. Some claimed they had been held incommunicado for weeks.

163

Amazed at such frankness in a state that, since *perestroika*, had overtaken the Soviet Union in the league table of Human Rights offenders, I was even more astonished to find the next day that the newspaper's proprietor, Mr İşhan Çesik, had been awarded an Outstanding Service plaque by the Turkish Foreign Ministry 'for his valuable service in promoting Turkey and the views of the Foreign Ministry to the outside world during more than twenty-nine years of publication'. Was some Byzantine Foreign Ministry plot afoot?

Not long afterwards the Scholar pounced on an item on sewage supporting Bora's testimony. Ninety per cent of Istanbul's sewage system was in urgent need of reconstruction (in one paragraph an apparent Freudian misprint omitted the first syllable to read 'construction'). There was a note of pride in the announcement that in the six south-eastern provinces where enteritis had broken out a sewage system would be completed by 1990 to 1993. The enteritis 'apparently resulted from leakage of sewage into the drinking-water system'. However, no bid had yet been received for the sewage work out to tender in the Antalya area since 1973; while in the Bingöl area (to which we were heading) it had yet to be planned.

Another article we came across in this delightfully anarchic publication reported with no trace of irony that Turkish Airline authorities had been 'upset' to learn that all old DC–9 airliners had been grounded in the United States 'for structural repairs to ensure their safety'. However, there was no suggestion of Turkish Airlines, which used the same machines, following suit.

Inability to speak the language prevented me from judging the rest of the Turkish press. A few newspapers looked as respectable as the *Financial Times*, while across the front pages of the populars there cascaded each day a technicolour avalanche of breasts and buttocks. I never ceased being taken aback by the double standards operating under the rival influences of Moslem piety and market forces.

I raised the issue of human rights at Kemal's house during a conversation with an adviser to the Prime Minister, suggesting that either way, true or false, public allegations of torture were likely to damage Turkey's bid to join the Common Market. The adviser nodded solemnly and said doubtless the allegations were in part true, and the torture was probably the work of ignorant young jailers who believed Kurds were responsible for murdering their families.

The explanation seemed likely enough, but I had the feeling that no one thought the matter was of much importance. It was not so much the behaviour as the acceptance of it that struck me as profoundly un-European. (The contrast between sensibility and cruelty in the Turkish make-up had been brought home to me by the story of a Turkish art dealer whom I had met recently at a party. He was a rather squat man with soft hands and smouldering eyes. I was told he had an extraordinary eye for porcelain. He was polite, but unsmiling. I assumed he was homosexual. I left him talking to our hostess. Afterwards she told me that far from homosexual, he had a legion of women whom he drew with his hypnotic gaze. One of these was a French model whom he had invited to his house; when she refused to share his bed he had broken her nose. He had made a proposition to our hostess at the party. Rejected, he had glowered and said: 'I shall find a way to hurt you.' 'What, will you break my nose as well?' There was a long pause. 'I think I shall bite you.')

All of which brought home that, despite Kemal's words, Turkey is every bit as much Asian as European. A great blurring of continents had taken place since my first visit to Istanbul thirty years before. Two soaring bridges crossing the Bosphorus had turned the capital into a great lung that inhaled daily commuters from Asia. The old European inhabitants felt threatened by the in-rush which had swollen the population to ten times its size. Sitting in an immense traffic jam on one of the bridges, sampling the especially vile exhaust of ill-refined fuel, I could no longer distinguish the pretty villages that once led the eye up the Bosphorus towards the entrance to the Black Sea, in the endless new suburbs now covering either shore.

On the Asian side we stopped for tea at a showpiece, a grand early twentieth-century hotel, memorable for a lamp of the date that outshone even the ones on my own hotel room, consisting of a cluster of brass stems rising in a bunch from the centre of a round marble table and culminating in a dozen flower-shaped crystal shades. We ate small sweet cakes served with tea on a dusty terrace overlooking the Bosphorus before crossing back into Europe by the second bridge. We admired the city's incomparable skyline in the evening light, passed an elaborate gateway that so pleased the Sultan who commissioned it that he is said to have ordered its builder's hands to be cut off to prevent duplication. After that we followed the European coastline towards the Black Sea, past the British and Soviet Embassies, both splendid enough, and the heavily guarded official presidential residence. On our way we paused at the local equivalent of a wishing well. Aunt Celeste explained that young girls would come here to pray for a husband, bearing a gift, and would take away with them a small piece of gold thread. While we were there two young couples arrived by car in their best clothes, perhaps to say their thanks, perhaps to ask for a child.

It had been winter for my first visit thirty years before. Now it was late summer. Mud had given way to dust, and unguessable smells filled the air. I liked the city for its mystery as well as its monsters. Each day it yielded a little more of its secret self. I especially liked the little island of old Istanbul behind our hotel where the railway following the shoreline disappeared into a hole in the old Byzantine walls. On our last night we walked down through its crooked streets in search of a fish restaurant on the sea, passing the True Blue Pension where the guests sat like boat people in tiers on bunks watching television in their underclothes. The six high minarets of Sultan Ahmed (to build which he had to have special permission from Mecca) stood against the skyline like a giant upturned crab. Here the air smelled of salt and fish. The streets hummed with social life; outside one house, scarcely more than a cave in the old wall, a group of women tried to restrain a youth who had apparently got the worst of a fight. A line of tiny girls squatted on the windowsill of a magnificent old schoolhouse in the space between the glass pane and the iron grille to watch a game of football between some slightly older boys and two men, apparently passing pedestrians co-opted on their way from the office, one carrying his briefcase, the other with his jacket held in one hand. A train lumbered by on the double-tracked line with carriages marked 'Belgrade': another using the same line stopped at the local station to drop off some commuters from the end of the line five minutes away, the last station in Europe, where on his stone pedestal Ataturk stood in spats glowering into the future. As deep night fell I watched the pigeons settling in on the roof of St Sophia.

CHAPTER 4

8–9 September (Istanbul–Erzurum)

We set off at 8.15, halting for a minute or two while Nigel made a frantic search for his address book, which he found. Eleni dropped us at the airport before going on to her aunt's. Nigel and I flew to Ankara. The flight on to Erzurum was first delayed, then cancelled because of storms. We hurried to the bus station. Nigel cased the joint and chose the Eş Adas company. We were told later, at Erzurum, that it had the best reputation. The gleaming, ultra-modern, turbo-charged bus drew in to load up, a quarter of an hour before its scheduled departure at 4.30. The passengers gradually moved to their seats: a middle-class husband and wife sat with teenage and ten-year-old daughters immediately in front of us; two men of position, both quite craggy and weather-beaten, struck up an animated conversation behind us; a beer-bellied man, wearing low-slung jeans, shepherded in his wife and daughter – he looked like an irascible retired British army officer, with a balding head of light brown hair; there was a *haji* several rows ahead of us, who never took his woollen hat off and spent a great deal of the journey with his head bent and propped against the seat in front; right at the back, a child with a broken leg was laid across three seats. Only two seats were empty as we pulled out on to the main road at 4.30. The great engine murmured. The driver – a tall man who was bottom-heavy like Bora – drove at a steady pace. He had a quiet authority about him. He cracked and ate nuts as he drove, throwing the shells out of the window.

The seats were well designed to support the back, and reclined. I let mine back a bit, relaxed and relished the sensation of effortless, comfortable travel on the long road to Erzurum. I looked forward to a night of deep sleep, the mind evacuated of thought and suffused with trust of the two drivers (for there was a second, relief driver on board who doubtless had almost as much skill and pride in safe driving as this one).

The last seats were filled as we picked up the missing passengers on the way out of Ankara. There was an amenity stop some time before dark. Nigel looked out and observed that the driver was having a long pee; however, as he then picked up his prayer mat he had evidently been ruminating silently, face towards Mecca, at the end of his formal prayer. We drove on. Darkness fell as we passed Yozgat. Soon there was a second halt, at a mosque for prayers. A large number of men filed out but many just stood about outside while the pious prayed. We stopped for supper at 9.45 at a large roadside cafeteria in Akdağmaden. Dark wood panelling and a chandelier of neon circles gave it a gloomy appearance. We bought lukewarm stuffed peppers and yoghourts, and carried them to a table on a large metal tray. The *haji* spent a long time pulling his beard after he had finished eating. A short, rather rotund man, with a small Hitler moustache, wearing a shirt with broad brown stripes, came up to us afterwards outside. He spoke good English. He told us he was an agricultural engineer who worked as a consultant in Erzurum *vilayet* and ran the university farm. I tried to pump him for information about conditions around the Bingöl Dağ. His silence about trouble there was reassuring, though I got the impression that he had never ventured as far afield as Çukuryayla. He was, he told us, one of only two graduates with English degrees living in Erzurum. His was from Aberystwyth. He then lost interest and only spoke to us briefly once thereafter. We each paid a short visit to the ill-lit, stinking loo.

We set off again. The engine growled with a resonant bass. Our driver was still at the wheel. The conductor came round with a bottle of eau de cologne, pouring it into our cupped hands. Mine sprang a leak, and splashes of the stuff fell on the white trousers. Large pale orange stains appeared among the pink from the Yeşil Ev fig. The central lights were switched off. Small red lights glowed on the underside of the luggage rack above our heads. I pushed my seat back further, took some swigs of whisky, ran through my exiguous Armenian in my head, thought of my wife and daughter, took some more swigs, tried various positions, envied Nigel who was fast asleep leaning against the window, took several more large swigs and shut my eyes. . . . Sleep would not come. The half hours passed. It was now midnight. I doused the mind with more whisky. The same driver was still at the wheel. He would be changing soon. I tautened my will, drove off thought and tried again to sleep . . .

The clock above the driver glowed 12.30: still the same figure at the wheel. We seemed to be going slower than before. I looked ahead. The great bus was moving in a sinuous way through the night. I became more alert. We were going down the middle of the road, occasionally veering slowly to the left before being jerked back to the right and slowly slipping towards the middle again.

All traces of sleepiness vanished. I watched dispassionately, as if a disembodied presence, as our massive vehicle literally meandered along – now only pulling back to the right side when headlights approached. The sleeping humanity, tight packed behind the driver, was drawing him too towards sleep – just as a naturally active and combative catfish will become torpid if it joins a huddle of other relaxed catfish. Ten, twenty minutes passed. While I took in the evidence of the eyes, I could not give full assent to it. Then apprehension started to grow but had little effect – I continued to sit motionless and to watch enthralled. Finally, I made my way forward and knelt close to the driver – within reach of the steering wheel. A soft *'effendi'* came from my mouth . . . and something about *durmak* (stopping). I had forgotten the Turkish for tired (*yorgun*).

A passenger sitting in a front seat spoke quietly in English, a pint-sized professor of political economy from Erzurum with mongoloid features and receding black hair. He too was

170

awake but relaxed and fatalistic. Yes, he said, the driver was falling asleep. Yes, he too had noticed the erratic course of the bus. He then gently asked the driver to hand over to his relief. Slurred, almost unintelligible words came in reply. The driver was saying he would continue but would change over soon.

The professor did not press him, but told me about his recent visit to England, his first. He had spent £50 going by rail to Cologne and back in order to get a cheap £60 flight back to Turkey. Otherwise he was in the British Library reading the works of Robert Owen, his chief research interest for many years. I mentioned my interest in the Bingöl Dağ and got no hint of trouble in reply. Where was the relief driver? I asked him after a while, infected increasingly as I was by his fatalism. Behind somewhere, he said and pointed vaguely. . . . We talked a little more, I still ready to spring to the wheel. He thought a large man two seats behind was the spare driver, leant out and touched him. No, he was not, he said, but got up immediately, went forward, sat on a stool and talked to the driver. He was a former *Gastarbeiter* and spoke German.

More passengers woke. One of them was a young doctor from Erzurum, a neck-specialist. We were beginning to climb – which slowed us up. The former *Gastarbeiter* asked me something. I referred to the soporific condition of the driver, who was staying put. My German gave out. A few disjointed phrases emerged in a mangled mixture of German and Turkish – with heavy sarcasm I said, 'We go left, we in England' – Turkish – 'this is very dangerous . . . I have driven for many years. He drives most dangerously' – German. The ex-*Gastarbeiter* got angry. We raised our voices. More passengers woke up, including Nigel who heard a confused altercation going on ahead. The wakefulness of massed passengers now began to have an effect on the driver who was pulled back towards alertness. But still he couldn't keep us confined to the right half of the road . . .

A lady sitting behind him asked him to hand over the wheel. Still he refused.

The handover finally took place around two a.m. The new

171

driver seemed to have trouble changing gear. There was a welcome crispness in the motion of the bus and I fell asleep. I woke at dawn, when the bus stopped for more prayers. Again a lot of passengers disembarked, some to stretch their legs, most to pray. I counted nine heads bobbing up and down, but there were more. I dozed for the last hour. We arrived at 6.30. The prayer carried on the back of all buses – *Allah Korusum*, may Allah help us – had been answered.

A bearded young man, with sallow cheeks and hollow eyes, was at the desk of the Büyük Erzurum Oteli. He recommended the Büyük Erzurum *hamam* to us. Off we went, down an empty grand avenue. The chief masseur fussed around us, showed us to a cubicle and then waited to work upon us. Nigel claimed to be an old hand at Turkish baths and said that in his youth he had often spent the night in one in St James, after dances . . .

Did we want a massage? we were asked. Yes, was our immediate reply. We went into the hot room, a large domed square chamber, entirely revetted in grey-veined marble. Cold water dribbled from brass taps placed at intervals around the walls. In the centre was a low, circular platform, burning hot. The steamy atmosphere took our breath away. The sweat poured down. Gradually we extended more of ourselves on the burning platform. There were not many clients about. Everyone was decorously clad, with a thin, striped towel wrapped round his middle. The masseur got to work on Nigel. Built like a wrestler and used to 'handling truckdrivers' (as Nigel put it), he scraped off sweat, dirt and skin, compressed every ounce of exiguous muscle of the *arkadaş'* frame, doused him with bucketfuls of cold water, cricked his neck, and bent legs and ankles to the limit. I looked on and apprehensively awaited my turn. I survived, cerebellum shaken up inside cranium but all limbs intact. Back in the cubicle, wrapped in innumerable towels from head to toe, laid out on benches, we relished our escape and remained inert, vaguely looking out at the brown and ochre-coloured octagonal outer chamber and the surrounding cubicles, at the gallery above with more cubicles, and at such figures as moved about calmly in the cold air . . .

172

Back at the hotel we had breakfast, fended off the desk clerk who tried to persuade us to rent a car privately from a friend of his and took a room. We idled the day away, renting a car from Avis, lunching at the restaurant where Nigel had discovered food a year earlier and walking through the bazaar.

The up-market streets are adorned with clusters of lamps on short columns. There are over sixty goldsmiths in one street, their wares packed together, brightly lit but unpriced in the windows. A few other prestigious traders have a toe-hold in that street – the makers of wedding dresses (three of them), gunsmiths (two of them) and some retailers of expensive electronic goods. The bookshop section of the bazaar is on Republic Street near the hotel – not quite as impressive as the goldsmiths'; there are half a dozen booksellers, cheek by jowl with sweetmeat sellers, the windows of the latter displaying enormous parades of aged, unappetising chocolates and boiled sweets. The bookshops seem to envisage only one category of reader – the school pupil; their stock consisted largely of exercise books and textbooks, with a scattering of translated foreign fiction in paperback, this ranging from the *Odyssey* and Dostoevsky through Camus and Mauriac to a lone representative of Britain, J. T. Edson, the Melton Mowbray author of Westerns; this relatively highbrow stock was camouflaged with pastel-coloured covers, so that it merged in with the mass of exercise books on display.

We had dinner in the grandest restaurant, the Güzelyurt. The windows looking into the street were curtained off. A large illuminated fish tank offered trout to the diners. A long gallery upstairs provided a secluded space for parties with women. The waiters were middle-aged and sinister; they were both attentive and brusque; they looked like stocky prize-fighters; their muscular frames strained against the dinner jackets which contained them; small eyes looked suspiciously out of close-cropped heads. The English version of the menu included 'lamp' and 'Turkey'.

No *muezzin* greeted the dawn. The only sound was the crowing of cocks. But perhaps I was dreaming and in my dream erased the ubiquitous human chorus which woke me in the early hours every day a year ago. I woke properly to a stormy morning: high winds, steel-grey clouds, driving rain. The sky cleared at 7.30. The peaks of the mountains surrounding the plain of Erzurum glinted with their first covering of snow.

We set off along the broad avenues which encircle old Erzurum and separate it from the new housing estates sprawling out on all sides. Erzurum has gone one up on other cities of the east, by installing traffic lights at the roundabouts on the ring-road to regulate the far from voluminous vehicular flow. Two wedding parties were belting along, horns blaring, taking little notice of the lights. The second, smaller convoy included a man playing a skirling pipe.

The *müze* (museum) is not overstocked. Nigel was ravished by a brown Ottoman dress. The only relic of the Armenian past is a single inscribed tombstone. Outside amid Roman tombstones from Satala stands a small black statue of a sheep with a scalloped body – a small head protrudes from the front as if it were suspended inside. Nearby stands a lion, which is all head, grinning from ear to ear. Nigel thought of Eleni's smile.

We drove south to Çatak in the valley of the upper Peri Su and stopped at the teahouse to ask for directions to Viranşehir, one of the three remaining possible sites for Artaleson, the more northerly of the two Roman fortresses built in the early sixth century to stop up the gaping hole in Roman frontier defences between Theodosiopolis (modern Erzurum) and the Taurus. An important-looking figure, wearing a brown suit with well-creased trousers, engaged us briefly in conversation (he spoke German); he did not know of any castles in the area, he said, but remembered that the old caravan route had crossed the Peri Su downstream at Çinik; then he rose and left us.

A man with fair hair and bright blue eyes then talked to us.

He too spoke German. He had spent fifteen years working as a building labourer in Germany – part of a 300-strong peripatetic workforce employed by a good German boss. He had once visited England for three weeks, he said with a smile, carrying a consignment of hashish. He came from a village near Karakoçan some 200 kilometres away, which he described as rich and capitalistic. His wife's family lived in Çatak and he had come to work with his tractor for two months. It was the only one in the four villages of the area. He was dressed in black trousers bespattered with small coloured tufts, a worn thick shirt and a filthy yellow cord jacket. There was a good growth of fawn stubble on his face. He offered to guide us to Viranşehir.

He led the way on his tractor, stopping when he met his father-in-law's brother. He was the local specialist treasure-hunter. He climbed into the car with alacrity, along with a tall, thin, very dark-skinned man clad in jeans and a dark green jacket. We drove through Viranşehir to the village's old site on the hillside above. There was no trace of any ancient settlement there and the site was indefensible. After walking over it and seeing nothing but thick-scattered red field-stones, we drove back to the modern village.

The tall, dark man asked us into his house. His most precious possessions were on display in the reception room: a red telephone; three cassettes; turquoise-coloured china in a cabinet; a sofa; an armchair; and a bed with a large cushion. Soon lunch appeared on a huge round silver tray which our host balanced precariously on an upturned wooden box. We drank tea and tucked into hard-boiled eggs, which Blue Eyes' piratical-looking uncle-in-law peeled for us, bread, butter and cheese. The women of the household peeped round the corner at us. The uncle talked expansively in a loud, grating voice. A shapeless nose protruded between dark glasses and pockmarked cheeks. He wore jeans, a jersey and a kerchief on his head concealing his receding hair. He could not remember from one minute to the next what he was told.

'Where do they come from? Holanda? Fransa? Almanya?' The answer would be given, promptly forgotten, and he would ask again. Finally the information lodged in his head and he claimed once to have had two beautiful English girls to stay for two nights. Our host spoke little. In answer to a question he told me he had six children and wanted to have at least ten altogether. The uncle boasted that he had dug three holes at the site of old Viranşehir up on the hillside and had found a bracelet.

In the course of lunch the uncle and Blue Eyes told us that there were vestiges of churches on the mountain above the village. We'd like to visit them, we said, and our silent host felt obliged to offer to guide us there. The uncle found he had something else to do. Blue Eyes remembered that he had an appointment in the afternoon. With our host, we drove a kilometre or so from the village, parked the car and started walking under the baking sun up a stream towards a bare mountainside. Our host moved at a worryingly slow pace, as if a long journey lay ahead. How far was it? I asked. An indistinct answer. The rules of hospitality forbade our host to deter us by saying three hours, let alone abandon us. He was saved, though, by Blue Eyes who drove along the track past our parked car, waved, stopped and made his way after us. Our host moved with loping strides to meet him, then returned and Blue Eyes explained how long it would take. The expedition was abandoned, and after warm thank-yous from us, Blue Eyes and our host drove off on the tractor.

There was a police road-block outside Karlıova. In the town the main street bustled with life, as it had done on our previous visit. Two wastebins by the school playground were on fire. A learner driver came round the corner in a JCB. An armed policeman in jeans guarded the police station.

The town has four hotels, at least six restaurants, three offices plastered with advertisements for rival political parties, a shop selling Tüborg beer, another full of sewing machines and flimsy furniture. At dusk, cows walked slowly along the freshly surfaced roads, crows wheeled in the sky and geese waddled below the balcony of our room. One *muezzin* called the faithful but his voice was faint and seemed to come from outside the town. We stayed in the Hotel Atlı, the smartest hotel and the one closest to the police station.

The other patrons were policemen – I saw one bring his submachine gun with him into a bedroom across the passage – and tall, dignified, silent figures wearing white headdresses – Arab sheep-dealers who had arrived to supervise the shipment of sheep to the cities of northern Syria. Through the night, three-decker lorries crammed with flocks from the western flanks of the Bingöl Dağ ground through the town on their way south. We had seen several loading up between Çat and Karlıova.

11 September (Karlıova–Varto)

I dreamed we arrived in the well-appointed lobby of a hotel. It was full of people drinking tea and coffee, and talking animatedly: a cheerful place. Then I noticed streaks of blood on the shoulder of one jacket, bruises on faces and blood oozing from cuts . . . I went across to ask if the police had done it, at which point several officers came in and I froze in a bent position, hoping not to be seen. Nigel also had a police dream; in his they were Chinese and they arrested a pretty girl; Nigel intervened; the outcome was not known.

We had breakfast in a restaurant which flaunted empty whisky bottles – three Black and White, one Whyte & Mackay, one Johnny Walker. Ahead lay a second day of fruitless searching for Artaleson – not that our researches could be described as methodical or meticulous. First we drove across the stream which drains the upper, eastern Karlıova plain, then skirted the southern edge of the plain, scanning the hillsides for traces of a castle. The eye lit on nothing. We retraced our steps when the road gave out. Now came stage two. We raked the mountains behind and west of Karlıova which rose ahead of us, but only saw bleak, unbroken ranges, without any visible sites suitable for a great fortress (no well-watered green platforms on the hillside, no long promontories running out towards the plan, no isolated crags on which a castle could perch).

Kale Köy, which we revisited the previous evening, still

had vestiges of a castle early this century, but can be ruled out as a candidate for Artaleson since there are no tell-tale blocks of carefully cut stone to be seen in any house walls in the village. The castle there was probably medieval, i.e. Armenian, and, if forced to suggest an identification, I'd plump for Oulnoutin – a stronghold which the Byzantines were eager to take over early in 938 as they slowly closed in on Arab-held Erzurum. Their next step was to advance and seize in 939 Havjij, the nearest important stronghold, to the north-east, before tightening the noose and blockading Erzurum for seven months in 940. Havjij was built by the Arabs and commanded the route, presumably the old caravan-route, running from the Göynük valley to Erzurum. A wild surmise – that its Arab name Havjij may be preserved, deformed but recognisable, in the Turkish placename Haciyusuf – could not be checked out as Haciyusuf is deserted (so our Viranşehir informants told us) and is far from the nearest decent track.

Stage three was to drive east to Varto, over a pass which would not have posed serious problems to an army advancing in good order in either direction. The climb from the Çaylar plain is long but easy. The valley is well-watered and attractive. Villages occupy sheltered sites on the hillsides or platforms cut out by the stream. They may be poor and denuded of much of their population now, but in an age of subsistence farming and perennial disorder they would have had considerable attractions. The upper reaches of the valley may well have contained the large settlement of Artaleson, abounding in water, which the Roman military engineers decided to transform into a military redoubt. Certainly they would have acted quite out of character if they had not sought to establish a base in a position to command this east–west route, especially as it is one of only two relatively easy routes connecting the open country of the upper Murat Su in the east to the valley of the Göynük Çay in the west, thus one of only two militarily useful routes between the Taurus and the Bingöl Dağ. The other is followed by the main road from Muş via Solhan to the Bingöl plain. It was the route which Citharizon was built to guard.

178

We drove down from the pass. A stream has cut a deep winding valley to the right. Ahead there is a good view down the valley. Beyond, isolated rounded peaks can be seen. Soon we came to a large village, built on a flat, green site. A channel carried fast-flowing water around its northern edge. The houses looked modern, too uniform in design to be anything but the product of a relocation and reconstruction programme after an earthquake. The walls looked solid enough. . . . Embedded here and there were rectangular, well-cut blocks of stone . . .

We halted and asked the way to the teahouse. A large number of able-bodied men were playing card games at small tables. Twenty-five, according to Nigel's count. The maths teachers at the village school spoke good English. We talked about this and that. The village was called Onpınar (Ten Springs), he told us. His tour of duty there was to last five years. His previous posting had been to Samsun. The school covered several villages in the valley; it had 100 pupils and four teachers. He had just returned for the start of term. The French teacher was introduced to us. We shifted rapidly out of French, when a blank look greeted an opening remark – and pretended that we had never left off speaking English. I asked vaguely about castles. Was there one at Onpınar? The maths teacher thought not, but asked those at the next table who had the air of being village bosses. There was nothing at Onpınar, came the reply, but a few kilometres down the valley, at Dağcılar, there was an ancient castle. . . . My heart beat faster. That would explain why there were only a few ashlar blocks to be seen at Onpınar. As we got closer to Artaleson, there would be more of them bespattering house walls. We said our goodbyes and hurried off.

It was puzzling to see no more ashlar blocks in a village we passed. Still, the engine was only firing on three cylinders and we concentrated on reaching our destination. It was a struggle to get up to Dağcılar which stands some distance above the main road. Irrigation channels crossing the road and steep inclines were surmountable obstacles, and added to the thrill of anticipation. We parked the car and walked across a green sloping field towards the village. No ashlar blocks there either, we noticed. The *muhtar*, an oldish man with a much-creased face, came to meet us and led us to his house . . .

Soon his nephew came in and sat down, a quiet, well-spoken man who was back on holiday from Hamburg and was looking after his two-year-old son. One child was quite enough, he thought – in stark contrast to our host of yesterday, or the citizen of Muş, who was reported, in the previous Friday's *Turkish Daily News*, to be having second thoughts only after having fathered forty-four children by the age of forty. The *muhtar* offered us meat. We asked for cheese and bread instead. It appeared along with tea on a bent circular silver tray. ... Eventually I asked vaguely about castles. The *muhtar* had shown no surprise about the visit by foreigners and had refrained hitherto from asking questions, as had his nephew, as if it were the most natural thing in the world for Englishmen to drop in on Dağcılar. Was there a castle at Dağcılar, I asked? No, was their answer, there was no *kale* in the village, though there was one at Köprücük a little further up the valley, on the opposite side, on the way back to Onpınar. . . . Hope was not extinguished. We thanked the *muhtar*, shook hands on the edge of the sloping water-meadow, and set off for Köprücük. But why on earth had the bosses of Onpınar misdirected us to Dağcılar? Were they deliberately tricking us, or were they anxious to conceal something at Onpınar? Fears were kindled that travelling strangers might fall foul of local powers of which they knew nothing.

The welcome we got at Köprücük from two oldish men allayed them. They pressed a second lunch upon us. Soon two silver trays appeared, one battered, one in pristine condition, loaded with plates of bread, butter, cheese, honey, tomato and onion salad, yoghourt, as well as a teapot and glasses. We tucked in with gusto. The wife of one of our hosts came into the reception room and watched over us as we ate. One gained the impression that she was the dominant character in the household as she stood there, thick-lensed spectacles glinting, smiling and making her own interventions in the conversation. A young man was also there.

He offered to guide us to the *kale* above the village. Nigel took a group photograph.

We thanked our hosts and started off climbing the hillside above the village, skirting a plantation of young fir trees. The *kale* turned out to be a few prehistoric burials on the edge of a small artificial lake. They had been explored long ago by the locals and were now only marked by heaps of rough stones. We tried not to look disappointed. In my halting Turkish I asked whether there were other *kales*, whether any had walls or well-cut stones still standing. The young man led us back to the top of the ridge, then along a track which he said was prehistoric and which ran in the general direction of Onpınar. There was a *kale* of some sort buried under a ploughed field in the valley, a little upstream from Onpınar, he told us, and it was there he was taking us. He pointed out another, which he said was larger, on a low, flat circular hill on the opposite bank. And, yes, he said, there was a *kale* above Dağcılar, as well as another two hours' climb up the Bingöl Dağ. We walked on for a while. I stared at what I took to be the ploughed field with a *kale* concealed beneath it and could see nothing of interest. The other *kale* seemed to have had two roughly circular circuits of field stones, traces of which could be picked out from our vantage point high up on the far side of the valley. None of these sites seemed promising. It was now late afternoon. We decided to return to the village and try to get to Varto before dark. The young man guided us down and refused all payment.

Night had fallen when we reached Varto. It has doubled in size since 1982 when I spent a night there. It now boasts the regulation block of Emniyet flats, three hotels, six restaurants, three banks, a shop selling cassettes for tape recorders, a billiard-saloon, a high school and the only mosque in the area. But TV has not reached it. We ate *shish kebab* as soon as we arrived. There were a surprisingly large number of moustacheless faces to be seen. Then we wandered around, looking the hotels over. Men were still at work in the dimly lit workshops of the carpenters' street. Running off it was the alley of fruit-sellers, whose stocks were piled up and lit by gaslamps. In the main square, where the restaurants competed for custom by grilling their *shish* outside, the solitary figure of a doctor sat at a desk in a tall, bare, glass-fronted shop unit – motionlessly advertising his craft in front of a curtain. Patients were not queuing up outside. A huge exhaust pipe protruded from the basement of the building with the billiard saloon. Bouncers ejected a drunk, who expostulated and attacked them. A young *Gastarbeiter* showed off to his friends by making a long and repetitive telephone call. The friends were clean-shaven. One was barely capable of standing, wore a slight, sinister smile on his thin face, and leaned up against the door of the telephone box. They piled into the *Gastarbeiter*'s Audi and sped away. Only one of the telephones worked. The post office had no large jetons – so I made a hasty call to my wife, to the background noise of jetons dropping down every ten seconds.

12 September (Varto–Erzurum)

I woke before dawn to the sound of a virtuoso *muezzin*. The hotel director's dog joined in from the other side of the garden at the back. Each new *coloratura* from the *muezzin* was answered by a long-drawn-out yowling. We were up and off as soon as it got light.

We stopped for breakfast at Hınıs; with a population of 18,000 it is considerably larger than Varto and was bustling with life. A butcher's shop window presented decapitated sheep's heads with their severed necks forward. A statue of Ataturk, the first we'd seen since leaving Erzurum, was this town's claim to modernity. Appropriately there were many cloth caps in evidence.

Soon we were off again, speeding over the watershed to the Araxes valley, then west past rich water meadows and over bare hills to Gökoğlan. There we stopped to ask about castles in general and to get directions to Hamzalar, a village near the headwaters of the Araxes, from which a track leads west to the valley of the upper Peri Su. There was a faint possibility that an alluring *harabe*, marked roughly half way

182

between Hamzalar and Çatak on pre-First World War German army maps, might be the site of Roman Artaleson or Arab Havjij. So it was worth finding out if a car could negotiate the track. Apart from that, I had heard from a colleague of a sighting of a castle high up on the north flank of the Bingöl Dağ; if it existed, it should be within reach of Hamzalar.

We parked near a broken-down post office. Modernity has not touched Gökoğlan save for two bleak, peeling blocks on the edge of the town – one belonging to the *jandarma*, the other to the medical service. The caretaker of the medical building took charge of us, leading us through empty corridors to the doctor's office. He was sitting at a desk, contemplating a table of statistics which he had evidently just compiled. He was attended by a respectful, besuited and clean-shaven assistant. The doctor spoke rapidly and precisely in Turkish. He knew a fair amount of English. He ordered some tea for us, which the caretaker went off to make. We explained our interest in castles. He turned to his assistant who said that there was a *kale* near Hamzalar, but knew of none other. We asked the doctor about his life at Gökoğlan. He was not overburdened with work, he said, although he had to cover twenty-two villages. The villagers did not come to him and he couldn't visit them since he was not allocated a car, unlike his colleague at Tekman. He came from Istanbul, and seemed remarkably cheerful for a man confined to the back-of-beyond with little to occupy his mind.

There followed a day much like the previous one, though this time the castle-hunt was conducted largely from the seats of the car and the reception was not as warm (no-one offered us anything to eat or drink). We visited three villages in the course of the day. Three men greeted us at Hamzalar, told us it was quite impossible to get to the Peri Su valley by car, and offered to show us the *kale*. They jumped in and took us up on to the open uplands which run south towards the Bingöl Dağ and which are drained by the streams feeding the Araxes. The car rode easily over the extraordinarily smooth ground, until we were within easy walking distance of the *kale*. It turned out to be a small Urartian castle, on a long, narrow, flat-topped rock between two streams.

As we returned to the car, we came across representatives of the Turkish underclass: first a tall figure at whose approach our guides told us to hide our cameras; then a group of three trout-ticklers – a *castrato*, an old man with an astonishingly pink face and a boy – who between them had managed to catch no more than half a dozen, none of them more than four inches long.

Next stop was Çukuryayla, a village at which we had been lavishly entertained a year earlier. No adult appeared, just ten– to twelve-year-old boys with sores on their faces and running noses who crowded round the car. We had forgotten the first name of our host of a year before – his second name being less easily forgotten since it was Bingöl. Nigel got out his portable processor and looked up the relevant entry in his 1988 diary and found the name – Mevlut – while I walked off a little to distract attention. Where was Mevlut Bingöl? we asked. Working on a building site in Istanbul was the answer. Still no adult appeared. Did poverty overcome curiosity and keep them indoors, and leave us without hosts and protectors? Whatever the reason, we got into the car and drove off.

The final stop was at Harabehallo, now given a new Turkish name, Erence, three kilometres or so from Tekman. A middle-aged villager, with very long teeth, met us and led us up to the top of a conical hill which commands the Araxes valley: no trace of any fortifications, though. They had all been scooped up by the provincial highway department, he told us, and had been used in the foundations of the new road below. The only traces of military occupation dated from the First World War: there were hollows in the ground where Russian soldiers had dug trenches; our guide's father had seen them firing from the top.

We took the direct mountain route from Tekman to Erzurum. Near the top of the pass over the Palandöken range we were flagged down by a taxidriver. He asked us for petrol and dismantled his engine looking for a length of piping which would reach into both cars' tanks. He swilled large quantities of petrol in increasingly desperate attempts to siphon some into his car. Nigel repositioned the piping and a litre or so made its way from tank to tank. The taxi-passenger showed considerable equanimity through it all, stranded as he was in a remote range of mountains. They have the rounded curves and grass cover of hills but rise at a vertiginous angle to an immense height; a scattering of yurts seeks such shelter as can be found in the hollows of their bleak and windswept slopes. The taxidriver offered to pay us from a bundle of notes. We refused to accept anything and drove on.

The taxidriver rapidly reconstructed his engine, turned round and overtook us before we reached the outskirts of Erzurum. In the Grand Erzurum Hotel, the familiar desk-clerk smiled and fell into conversation with us. He was an archeologist, doing graduate work at Erzurum University on Urartu. We exchanged names and addresses. Across the road from the hotel we noticed one of Erzurum's wonders – a plush butcher's shop. Seven whole sheep carcasses were displayed in two brightly lit windows. Inside the shop brass downlighters hung low over the counter before which stood pots of tall roses. The proprietor's imposing desk with small flagstand imparted a rather official air to the place. Neon light from a profusion of bulbs flooded the interior.

13 September (Erzurum–Polatlı)

The *muezzin* of Erzurum sang this morning – at first, soft, soporific voices from a distance; then one near at hand disturbed some birds which made brief responses; soon it became a cacophonous chorus, above which there rose a distinctly *soprano* voice; a good half hour passed before silence returned.

A mullah, in full rig – an elegant cream outfit with a turban – was standing on his minaret as we came out of the hotel after a long breakfast. An Avis official took us to the airport – a journey which involved driving some distance the wrong way down a dual carriageway and an excursion to see a girl in

the city. Emotional farewells were taking place at the airport –
yashmak could not conceal the distress of children and
grown-ups at the thought of the perilous journey ahead for
one oldish lady. A general with his son awaited the flight
with the rest of the passengers, his beflagged car parked
outside until he left.

CHAPTER 5

The Scholar's lips moved as in prayer as Anatolia slid by below us. He sat with eyes half closed, a priest reciting his office. After a while he saw me staring.

'Vowel harmony,' he said, holding up the book in his hands. It was *Teach Yourself Turkish*. 'I was testing myself. The best way to learn.' The day before he had mastered the possessive pronoun; tomorrow he would grapple with the subjunctive. As we came in to land at Ankara he explained that vowel harmony, whereby a vowel was altered to match the others in a sentence, was a matter of the greatest importance to the literate Turkish ear. I thought of the doctor and his love of words. However, the Scholar added sadly, the rule did not apply to foreign words that have invaded the language, nor to the new technical generation that used them.

We were on the first leg of our journey to Erzurum, in Eastern Turkey, another hour away by air, to resume our search for the second of Anastasiu's great sixth-century forts. The year before we had found Citharizon, the southernmost, near a Kurdish village outside the sewer-free town of Bingöl. Now we were looking for Artaleson, which the Scholar had tentatively placed in the mountain range closer to a road running south from Erzurum.

At Ankara we were abruptly told our onward flight was cancelled owing to a dust storm (or perhaps Turkish Airlines were grounding their DC-9's after all?). We decided to defy Aunt Celeste and take the overnight bus. Sadly the Superman Turbo coaches that had caught my fancy the year before were being phased out. Instead I secured two seats in a giant new Mercedes for the 500–mile journey from a young man in exchange for the equivalent of £7 and my advice on how to emigrate to Australia.

As we set off the assistant driver came round and sprayed eau de cologne on our hands. Night fell after two hours as we began the bleak journey eastward along Turkey's long undernourished spine. In a few minutes I was asleep.

My next memory is of the Scholar's voice delivering a lecture in German, loud and cheerful. I thought first, why German? Then, that there was no particular explanation, as is often the way with dreams – just another language to add to the Scholar's armoury of French, Armenian, Russian, Bulgarian, Greek, Latin and budding Turkish.

Then I realised I was not asleep. The Scholar really was talking, and very loud. And in German. I opened my eyes and saw that he was standing in the front of the bus like a tour guide addressing the passengers. I closed them again. The decibels rose. I woke fully with a start and went forward. The Scholar explained to me that he had been about to sleep when he became aware that the driver was in no condition to drive. The bus was weaving across the road; the man was clearly drunk or in need of sleep. That had been an hour ago, since when, to alert the passengers to the danger, the Scholar had been talking to them. He had managed to secure the attention of a professor from Erzurum who had recently completed an academic visit to the United Kingdom.

He eyed me accusingly.

'Under these circumstances I consider it an act of sheer folly for any of us to remain asleep.'

All this took place at the top of his voice. I looked at the driver, a large man, who was indeed yawning cavernously, though whether from boredom or fatigue I could not tell.

'He doesn't look drunk.'

'I caught him veering all over the road. Had I not been here we might have plunged long ago over a precipice to our certain death.'

188

'What are you planning to do about it?' I wondered if he had in mind to take the wheel himself.

'I am trying to persuade the passengers to demand that the auxiliary driver takes over. So far I have enlisted the support of the professor. He is going to assist me.'

But the professor, who was extremely small, did not look a likely persuader. The Scholar appeared excited, but in excellent spirits. Perhaps it was heredity. His father had been an escort commander in the Battle of the Atlantic. Now, fulfilling some psychic need to emulate him, he was standing by to take over on the bridge. I noted that he had emptied a quart-sized bottle of water purchased for the journey, a familiar prelude to intense activity.

Standing in the dark the Scholar took the little professor aside and asked him to impress on me the seriousness of our plight. The professor, who seemed to be more intimidated by the Scholar than the driver, blinked for a moment in silence before making a pronouncement:

'In other countries you die by accident. In Turkey we stay alive by accident.' I thought it a very good joke for the time of night.

Light rain began falling. The Scholar remained at his post, poised to seize the wheel, supervising the operation of the big windscreen wiper. All the while he continued speaking in a loud clear voice. After a moment of guilt, I fell once more into a profound slumber. Somewhere 150 miles or so short of Erzurum the first driver handed over to his relief driver and, apparently oblivious to the drama he had caused, fell asleep at once in a spare seat. The Scholar now felt free to doze a little, his mission completed. The next time I awoke it was to the strangest possible sight. Dawn was breaking, and by its streaking light I could see a dozen male sterns in a neighbouring field, as the passengers bowed towards Mecca. Leading them in prayer was the driver.

At Erzurum we checked in at the Büyük Erzurum Hotel and asked for a bath, only to discover that our rooms were not ready. The receptionist, an archeological student at the university, directed us to the local *hamam*, much favoured by long-distance truckdrivers coming in from Europe. It was nice to be back in the old Roman capital, and we walked with light hearts to our next adventure, the Scholar's first Turkish bath, my first in Turkey. The building was like a converted church, tiled, complete with apses, an altar-like central marble slab on which steaming bodies lay largely covered up in towels, side chapels where men washed discreetly in rooms of different temperatures. I was struck by the towelled Moslem prudery of the Turks, a contrast with the steaming naked flanks I had become accustomed to in Turkish baths elsewhere. Uncertain where to begin we had settled for the all-inclusive service and waited apprehensively on the hot central marble slab for the beckoning finger of the attendant, a hirsute figure built like a prize-fighter. I went first. After a sluicing that made me feel like a long-distance lorry he began to administer a massage of such vigour, moving my reluctant limbs into positions unknown to nature, that I heard myself crying out. My honour was partly salvaged when I heard the Scholar in turn protesting, though with more reason: he had a damaged leg from a skiing accident.

We emerged surprised to feel so well, glad to be still alive, and staggering slightly returned to the Büyük Erzurum Hotel in time for breakfast in the top-floor restaurant. We sat by a window from which we could see down into the local prison yard which backed on to the butcher's shop opposite the hotel entrance. It was a dilapidated parody of an old-fashioned jail complete with watchtower and armed guard, but no sign of prisoners. Also visible and filling the horizon to the south was the formidable range of mountains to which we were heading in our quest for Artaleson. As we looked out over our Nescafés the sky above us turned to slate and it began to rain.

Our plan was to retrace our steps of the year before, travelling in a clockwise circle first to Tekman, on the eastern slopes of the mountain range, working our way round to Çat on the west side, where the Scholar had lost his map. New evidence had now persuaded him that somewhere in the unmarked mountainside between the two the missing fort might have been built: equally we might discover the site where the emperor Basil II had stopped on a journey east 500 years later.

Leaving Erzurum was easier said than done. The delay of the flight meant that our Avis hired car had been given to someone else. The hotel's rival car, at one-third the price, was uninsurable and ruled out by the Scholar who pictured waiting in a prison cell after an accident for travellers' cheques to arrive by post. By mid-morning Avis had relented but the weather had descended. We decided to stay the night. We had lunch in the excellent restaurant remembered from the year before, where the frosted glass door at the back still said 'LAVOBA'. We shared a table with a young national serviceman who ate his food like a hungry bloodhound.

Next morning we tried again. Our first stop in the Avis car was the local museum. It did not detain us long. Two millennia of history were represented by a few dozen nondescript statues and a collection of peasant clothes modelled on blue-eyed tailors' dummies evidently imported from Europe. A weighing machine, for the use of visitors (for a small fee), stood beside the dusty booth where an attendant sold entrance tickets. Having sold off the exhibits, the curator presumably had to find new ways to augment his salary.

After the museum we turned south. But the handover between town and country in Turkey is seldom smooth. While rural highways are good and authorities are clearly well funded, their remit stops at the edge of towns. Here funds seem to run out, roads die and signposting takes on a dreamlike quality, beckoning the motorist like a sleepwalker through strange streetscapes that seem somehow increasingly familiar, until he realises he has been travelling in circles. Soon we were lost in Erzurum's unloved outskirts. The map did little to help, apparently reflecting intention rather than reality. Confidently indicated destinations lured us to hydra-headed junctions where they were abruptly forgotten, along roads that expired in mudded streams or concrete walls.

Finally at a garage we were told that our road south had been closed by a snowfall in the night, so we amended our plan so as to make our three-day tour in a reverse direction, travelling anti-clockwise. Finally breaking out of the labyrinth we were soon bowling along the road to Çat where we had begun our search the year before.

We felt like old hands as we drove past the spot where we had first turned uncertainly off the main road to look for a fort. Now, under the Scholar's tuition, I even knew what to look for: terrain commanding a view, perhaps a hill, suitable for defence, then masonry. But telling the works of God from the works of man was another matter. Time and again the early promise of Byzantium faded on inspection into another tedious outcrop of dead rock. The Scholar had also taught me to look for tell-tale signs of oblong stone being used in a village wall or as a coping stone for a house after being plundered from a Roman ruin. He had explained that Romans built for show, so each stone was perfectly cut. The later Byzantines, more decadent and more materialistic, settled for more makeshift fortifications. Theirs was a 1,000-year retreat, an exercise in containment and management of a dwindling resource: they made do. I was gradually learning the rudiments of ruin spotting – the least I could do. Besides it made the trip more fun.

We were now in the area where the Scholar wanted to have a second look. At Çatak we stopped to talk to a knot of men having tea at the roadside. A year ago I would have shrunk from trying to persuade a group of strangers whose language we scarcely spoke to talk to us about local ruins. Now I knew better. They greeted us enthusiastically, responding warmly to the Scholar's questions. In the group was a blond-haired man who spoke German, learned as a migrant worker. I wondered if he had been sired by a visiting German soldier – you couldn't very well ask – or was part of Alexander the Great's legacy. I sat stupidly, barely able to follow the drift of pidgin Turkish helped out with gestures and, this year, the Scholar's suddenly burgeoning German, grabbing at meanings where I could. I understood that the blond German speaker had been to England, but only once, to smuggle in drugs. He offered to take us to the nearby village of Viran-şehir, which the Scholar wanted to inspect. He went off to

192

fetch his tractor. We then set off, car following tractor, and soon arrived at Viranşehir.

We were welcomed into a house at once for lunch. It was a familiar Kurdish invitation – a brightly carpeted room and a cartwheel-sized tray of yoghourt, bread, honey, butter, cheese, a stool for tea, another for the dregs, a glass cabinet for the family treasures – lurid plates, a broken clock – a picture of Mecca, another of Ataturk looking like Batman, framed photographs of relations and a soccer team; cabaret from the baby brought in by a shy mother on the insistence of a proud father, indulged for a few moments then abruptly banished. I cursed my lack of Turkish and was reduced to pulling faces to make the baby laugh. After lunch the men belched. I persuaded the Scholar that he must follow suit out of good manners.

There followed intense discussion about *harabes* – ruins – then nods, signs, 'ah's' of feigned comprehension. Our host led us off up the long hot hill they had been pointing at over lunch. Then the German speaker vanished. We plodded on with our host. After a while his footsteps slowed, then stopped altogether. He had seen the German speaker waving in the distance from his tractor. He turned back to meet him. Good manners had obliged him to accompany us, heat to turn back. We took photographs, exchanged addresses, drove off, somehow satisfied, unsure why. All in the day's work, par for the course.

Both of us had liked Karlıova, the bustling little town that was the hub of local life. The road south from Erzurum brought overloaded lorries hooting and lurching through its noisy centre day and night. The main street was lined with two-storey houses and shops, including two restaurants with deliciously cooked chicken. I found the little store where I had bought a sharp knife the year before. Curiously Karlıova had no mosque, and one shop advertising (though not sell-ing) beer – two strikes for the cap and against the fez. We settled for a hotel room away from the centre, a truly filthy place with a balcony looking on to the town: and more inter-estingly on to the headquarters of the local Security Police. I thought of the stories of torture in the *Turkish Daily News*, but the only sound to reach our ears from inside the ugly concrete barrack was distorted music from a transistor radio turned up too loud. In the street between us a sentry in civilian clothes armed with a submachine gun paced importantly to and fro, shooing away inquisitive children, chickens and citizens out for their evening stroll. His beat ended exactly below our balcony. Watching as he turned, my eye was caught by a new-looking wire leading to a bundle wrapped in brown paper and propped against the base of a lamp post a few yards away. By my calculation, if it was a bomb it would kill all three of us but leave the Emniyet unscathed. In the morning it had disappeared, unexplained. So had the armed layman. In his place a man in uniform was putting a barrier across the street, also for no apparent reason.

We needed to explore next the terrain to the east of Karlıova, so we turned off the north–south road along a minor road following the circumference of a circle on our map, and bounced along its unmade surface at five miles an hour. At a new but already derelict looking village called Onpınar my eye picked out a large well-cut stone in the containing wall that might have been Roman. We went into the village hall where twenty-five men of working age sat at tables playing a complicated card game involving chequers. It was mid-morning. We ordered tea. A good-looking man with fine hands, better dressed than the others, came over and introduced himself as the village schoolmaster. He came from Ankara and was here on assignment. He spoke halting English, and said he taught history and French, but addressed in French he looked blank. He also had arrived too recently to be of much use for the Scholar's purposes; but indicated another village where there was a castle ruin. He led us politely to our car, oblivious to the stream coursing ankle-deep through the village square.

For the rest of the day we lurched and lunged along dirt roads from village to village, in pursuit of exactly what I was increasingly unsure. At Dağcılar we were seized upon and pressed to eat lunch, at Köprücük a second lunch (unthinkable to refuse). Afterwards we headed up a near-vertical hill

194

to a castle with a moat where our host had found some arrow-heads. The castle turned out to be the rocky surround of a natural lake created by rain trapped in a ridge.

With double-lunched euphoria we walked to another com-manding site, a hill in the long valley where there might have been a fort. Perhaps there was. But the geese we were chasing were becoming ever wilder. We took stock, turned back, rewarded our hosts the only way we could, with more photographs, exchanged addresses, reversed the car on the steep incline of the village centre and headed for the town of Varto where we spent the night. We had driven twelve hours to cover thirty miles as the crow flies.

We were woken at dawn, not by cock-crow but by a dog howling at the electronic *muezzin* made further sleep imposs-ible. From Varto the road that circled the mountain range below Erzurum took us north once more towards the town of Tekman, which we were anxious to avoid owing to mem-ories of the year before of hostile vigilantes bursting into our room in the night.

We breakfasted on the way on bread and lentil soup at Hınıs, memorable for the waiter who on inquiring our busi-ness offered to accompany us. We sped past Tekman and halted at Gökoğlan. As we got out of the car, we were at once caught up in a familiar conflict between good manners and self-interest. A boy of about eleven invited us to have tea with his uncle. Another younger boy was with him. A moment later, pushing the boys aside, an older man invited us to talk to the village doctor, more likely to have the infor-mation we sought. The Scholar chose the doctor. The boys followed us at a distance to the village's only concrete house, which managed to look more downtrodden than the older ones round it built in traditional stone. The doctor was a thin young man, energetic, intelligent, serving his apprenticeship as a state servant, part of the system like the schoolmaster at Onpınar based on centralised planning rather than regional initiative. He talked at a great pace so that I could not follow: it seemed that he had almost no medicine, no drugs to speak of, and no means of transport to get around the twenty-five villages in his practice. It must have been a devastatingly

195

lonely life, but he appeared busy and dedicated to his task. While the Scholar was speaking I washed my hands at a basin in his bare surgery under the single faucet of cold water – there was no provision for hot: if these were the fruits of central planning its victory appeared somewhat Pyrrhic. As I looked round trying to imagine how a doctor could function with so little there was a tap on the window pane. It was the two boys. I waved. They seemed quite pleased. As we left the older of the two was waiting to open the car door for me: at a loss, I made an elaborate show of shaking hands with him. He grinned from ear to ear, honour apparently saved.

We were moving off the marked area of the map into virgin mountain land. The muddy track along the river bank had expired at Hamzalar, the last named village. There the cartographer's dotted line – signifying 'natural surface' – gave out, and together with a carload of cheerful villagers we swung on to the lip of a huge upturned saucer of prairie land and began threading our way between ever more strangely shaped rocks into the uninhabited regions of the Bingöl Dağ.

At the highest point a cliff came into view on the horizon. We saw water running along its foot: a headwater of the Araxes on its way to the Caspian. We stopped and got out. As we approached the line of the cliff on foot, a path cut into its face appeared below where a ruin was beginning to take shape against the skyline.

A quarter of an hour later we were standing in the plundered ruins of a prehistoric fort build of uncut stones, crude work compared with the manicured blocks of the Roman Empire designed to last for all time. Nearby, there was a Christian tombstone carved with a cross. At the foot of one vestigial structure was a series of what looked like large foxholes. The men in our party grinned and gestured. The gold diggers had not been idle.

It was hereabouts that in the eleventh century Basil the Bulgar Slayer had come to accept the submission of his local tributaries. His was not just an empty nickname. He had earned it during a ruthless war in which he had ordered that all but one of every 1,000 Bulgar prisoners should have both their eyes put out, the remainder being left one good eye with which to guide the others home. The Scholar had surmised that Basil's stopping place might well be here in the Bingöl Dağ mountains, but now was clearly losing confidence in his theory.

As I pondered the cheerful grave-robbing ethics of the gold diggers there came a distant cry. Looking in the direction of the river, we could see a boy waving to us excitedly. We climbed down the cliff face to find that an animated group of fishermen had appeared from nowhere. The boy, grinning, wanted to show off his catch to us. With him were two men, one apparently his father. The other plied us with English questions in high falsetto: Welcome, is Turkey beautiful? Where are you from? (This several times.) What is your telephone number? How do you like your meat cooked? How much is your car rental? How old are you? Since he did not understand the answers conversation was limited to a repetition of the questions.

It was our last day in the east. We stopped the car to watch the light on the Bingöl Dağ range, then turned away conscious that we might never see again its treasure house of water, light and surprises. We had not found what we had come for in these parts; but we had found other things instead. Most of the places we had visited were too uncomfortable for guidebooks to mention: yet where else would the passing traveller find the psychological comfort to match natural Kurdish hospitality? Let Eastern Turkey's hotels remain humble hovels! Long may its fearsome plumbing fend off the pollution of tourism!

We turned north through Tekman and headed over the high mountain road, now reopened, into Erzurum. A last glimpse of eccentricity on the way: nearing the summit of one of the more dramatic passes we came across a taxi that had run out of petrol. The driver flagged us down, and using his mouth and a length of pipe siphoned a tumbler full from our tank. All the while his passenger, a stout, middle-aged man, sat in the back looking straight ahead of him. As we rounded the final bend into town the taxi overtook us, hooting, its wheels screeching, both occupants waving.

We arrived at the Büyük Erzurum Hotel as light was fading. Opposite the main entrance the butcher's shop was lit to make the neatly hung carcasses look like mannequins in a Bond Street showroom.

A DC–9 (the model the *Turkish Daily News* said had been grounded for 'modifications' in the United States) took us back to Ankara. At any rate the crew would not be distracted by hunger: they had eaten our lunch. After taking our order for the meat course the waiter at the airport restaurant came back to inform us that there was none left, then served two mountainous dishes of it to the uniformed couple who arrived after us at the next table. They turned out to be our pilot and an air hostess.

Somewhere in the sky over Anatolia a squeak developed. The Scholar and I exchanged glances. After a few minutes we located the sound: there was a cat travelling two rows behind us.

Like a lock gate, Ankara's modern airport was our re-entry point to another world on another level, labelled 'TURKEY, WEST' on my map. As we picked up our newer, cleaner Avis we underwent the change from travellers to tourists. The immediate human contact we had come to depend on was a step removed. We were once more in the hands of local bureaucracy, and our guidebook.

Neither emerged well from the first test. We had picked Polatlı to the west of Ankara on the main railway to Istanbul, as our first stopping place to visit the nearby site of Gordium, where legend places the tomb of King Midas. My guidebook by Dana Facaros, usually reliable as well as lively, described it as a village. Polatlı turned out to be a town with 53,000 inhabitants, half-finished high-rise flats and a modern bypass. Trees lining the streets improved matters as we penetrated into the older part, lending it the air of a leafy French provincial town. Men with submachine guns guarding a military band playing beneath an equestrian statue of Ataturk indicated that we had reached the main square. We were given rooms high up in a hotel overlooking it, but when we got there the band had dispersed.

Nearby we could see the railway station. My spirits rose as we set out to explore it. Here was an authentic relic of the old school: grandiose booking hall (shut), waiting room and *Bufe* (marked 'OPEN 24 HOURS', also shut), generous platforms with shrubs and people sitting on benches, motionless; a line of dead carriages in a siding, a panting steam engine, also motionless, waiting to shunt some trucks. It was the quintessence of suspended animation. A big notice in English and Turkish headed 'INDIAN RAILWAY CONSTRUCTION COMPANY' announced an electrification project, for the time being at the conceptual stage.

A dismal search for food put paid to my impression of leafy France. We found a street of pastry shops, most closed for the day, but no restaurant. The whole town seemed to be watching a soccer match we could see on television screens flickering in the failing light behind closed shop fronts. Hope revived when a tailor working late assigned his assistant, a boy of ten, to take us to an open restaurant. Fortunately the match had ended, which meant service was resumed, the waiters now returning to the normal Turkish viewing habit of stopping to look at the screen only during commercials.

We were served what by our eastern standards were half portions at double prices, and wilting salad; there were no *ayran* and no smiles. As we ate I hankered for a Kurdish village with children running out to greet the car, impulsive, generous people glad to be alive, eager to meet a stranger, ready to go off with you to dig for gold, rob a grave. Exploring is better done outward bound, away from home, not towards it. By travelling west, we were heading towards familiarity instead of away from it. Even so, how could we protest when double price meant £2 instead of £1 for two dinners? But we did. We resorted to the only weapon left to tourists for avenging themselves on people whose way of life their own has robbed of joy. We didn't leave a tip.

My *Cadogan Guide* to Turkey described Gordium as a site only archeologists could love. But the Scholar and I were

199

fascinated by the rolling open countryside dotted with strange mounds of different shapes and sizes that mushroomed in ever increasing numbers up on either side of the road. The biggest was the Great Tumulus, 160 feet high, though it is reckoned to have lost about 100 feet over the 2,600 years since it was built.

At one edge of the excavations is a spectacle not just for archeologists; Cecil B. de Mille would have liked it, too. It is associated with the legend of King Midas. In the diggings, slowly being cleared of the silt from centuries of flooding from the Sakarya river, the Monumental Gateway is now clearly discernible, with behind it a row of palace buildings of the Phrygian kings, whose pastoral subjects diverted themselves with music and orgiastic cults in honour of Cybele. They claimed to have invented panpipes; one legend has it that Midas acquired his ass's ears by foolishly voting for a fellow Phrygian against Apollo when judging a musical contest. In these heroic surroundings Charlton Heston could be expected to appear at any moment as King Midas complete with ass's ears, Gordian knot and golden touch. The truth is almost certainly less spectacular: the burial site of Midas is nineteenth-century guesswork. In any case all Phrygian kings were named Gordius or Midas; the rest is speculation or myth.

On the way back from Gordium we came across evidence of the Turkish penchant for myths: as we approached Polatlı we noticed a line of uniquely strange concrete columns marching in columns of increasing height up either side of a hill. The gracefully curved silhouette, said to be a re-evocation of the monumental sculpture of ancient Anatolia, turned out to be part of a memorial to Kemal Ataturk. The concrete extravaganza had disquieting overtones to my eye of Franco's Spanish Civil War monument, the Valley of the Fallen. There was an ingredient here, more zany than menacing, that to me seemed better kept at arm's length. At its summit, several hundred feet above the town, we came to a perimeter wire where we were turned back by an armed sentry.

On the way down we took a wrong turning and found

ourselves in a well-kept military cemetery with flags flying, the dead arranged in military files in 1,000 black marble tombs. An English-language leaflet announced that it was dedicated to the glorious Turkish martyrs who had repelled the Greek aggressors in 1921, restoring peace and harmony to the fatherland. There was no mention of the 200,000 civilians out of a total Greek population of two and a half million who died in the ensuing massacre. Would Europe demand an admission about this episode, as well as the Armenian massacre, as a price for accepting Turkey into the European Community? Would this imperial nation submit to the indignity? Or would it don its fez once more and turn back to Mecca? I realised on reflection that I had missed the point. Turkey would do neither of these things. Turkey would continue on its Turkish way, muddling through into the next century with all the money for development it could lay its hands on, just like anybody else.

Gordium was the Phrygian capital and Pessinus, an hour's drive away, its religious centre. Here my guidebook's precept applied: there really was very little for the lay eye. After taking us round the sun-baked ruin, the guide showed us the model of a much later Roman temple built on the Phrygian ruin. I do not think Pessinus can have had more than a trickle of tourists; despite this – or because of it? – the guide firmly refused all payment.

Almost by chance we came on Sivrihisar. Looking for somewhere to have lunch we asked a boy who had begged a lift for a nearby restaurant. He took us to the little town's main square, a near-derelict assembly of buildings leaning against one another for support. The Scholar had been tipped off to look out for the Seljuk mosque. We spotted it by looking up to see an elegant blue and green tiled minaret built in brick poking out from a cluster of small shops that clung like barnacles to the rest of the building, entirely hiding it from view. The entrance was by a narrow passageway we eventually found between two shops. Going in, we beheld a miracle.

Seljuk architecture, more delicate than Ottoman, is relatively rare outside the region of Konya, from where the

Seljuks ruled for a mere two centuries. The mosque at Sivrihisar was a golden find, because unspoilt. As our eyes grew accustomed to the dark we counted fifty-five columns of Lebanese cedar holding up its not quite symmetrical interior, each side bordered by two storeys of wooden arcades. The stone floor was covered in fine Kilim carpets, all unprotected. The hanging oil lamps were of crystal. There was no plastic or neon to offend the eye. A knot of children sat in a corner gabbling a text from the Koran. Everything felt alive, exactly as it might have been 800 years before when it was built.

Our next stop was social, an academic visit for tea. The site was Amorium, once a military town of 30,000 inhabitants, a Byzantine Aldershot, now rubble. The director of excavations was the Scholar's colleague at Oxford, a Professor Martin Harrison, but he was away. Instead we were most formally received for tea in a delightful farm building by respectful underlings who explained that the Professor was on a visit to 'Export' University. We wandered round the acres of ruined masonry, the line of a defence wall here, a remnant of buttress there, the Scholar increasingly excited, I willing but uncomprehending, a dog in an art gallery. As we were driving away the Scholar asked me to turn and take him to the top of a hill to photograph the site, to his eye the microcosm of Byzantine civilisation, to mine dried mud.

We slept at Afyon. The town announced itself Turkish fashion with broad roads suddenly transformed into rubbish tips. We took a room, as always with balcony, looking up to the local fortress (probably Hittite in origin) perched on a rock 750 feet high. The electricity did not work. We moved, ashamed of minding, to another without a balcony. The electricity worked but the bulbs did not. I purloined some from the corridor. The plumbing sounded like a fogbound liner. We found a restaurant with an enormous mirror in a once-gilded frame and sat next to a fat American family determined to think everything wonderful, including their overweight child, a boy of unguessable age who introduced a note of

202

dissent by complaining about the food, the town and Turkey in general.

After dinner we went for a walk along Afyon's scruffy, beat-up main street, stopping at a building site where a crowd watched a young Turk manipulating an earthmoving machine with the aplomb of an Italian showing off his Ferrari. With a roar of gears the monster leapt forward, its headlight beams like feelers in the darkness, stopping on the very brink of a precipice of mud. A brontosaurus limb swung out to take an enormous scoop of earth. The gears crashed again as the earthmover backed like a ballet dancer down the narrow ramp it had made for itself to dump its load on to the back of a waiting truck. In minutes the truck was full. It drove off at high speed into the traffic. Another immediately took its place and the cycle was repeated, all at breakneck pace. After a while the star of the show appeared to have had enough. Leaping down from his cabin he lit a cigarette, straightened his cap and strode off into the night. Gawping its admiration the crowd parted to let him past.

By day Afyon revealed a labyrinth of cobbled back streets, authentic Ottoman wooden houses with overhanging upper storeys, a Seljuk mosque, later than Sivrihisar's, with wooden columns and stalactite carved capitals but without the unspoilt charm of Sivrihisar's carpets; and a memorable Ataturk depicted as a naked wrestler apparently about to eat his defeated (Greek) foe, who stood menacingly over us as we sat in a municipal tea garden. While the Scholar took a stroll I was distracted from writing my diary by the surreal conversation of an elderly English couple at the next table, apparently about the husband's holiday reading. I recorded the following exchange:

'Do you like the book?'

'Well, sex comes into everything. Take the whelks.'

'How does whelks come in?'

'Bob buys whelks, see?'

'Then what happened?'

'E ate all the whelks.' There was a pause.

'What's that got to do with sex?'

'Dunno.'

'But you said sex comes into it.'

'Yes.'

'Why whelks?'

'I couldn't say why. But 'e ate 'em.'

At this point my attention was diverted again, by an open truck passing by in the traffic with a boy on the back, his arm round a baby brother who was stuffing his face from a bag of dates, farming folk visiting the big city. From the street a much bigger boy stretched out an arm and seized the bag; whereupon the baby grabbed his hair with both hands and hollered with the full force of his lungs. At the same moment the truck moved on, and the would-be thief was dragged along beside it, part-Absalom, part-Isadora Duncan. But I never saw who got the dates, as a passing lorry blocked my view; and by now I had completely lost track of the whelks.

From Afyon we returned to Phrygia. At Ayazını and Arslantaş, a few kilometres north of Afyon, we found echoes of Cappadocia in troglodyte caves, carved with strange angular carvings typical of Phrygian art. At Midas City thin legend yields to pure mystery. Even the name is invented. Captain Leake, a nineteenth-century British traveller, thought he discerned the letters 'MIDAI' on a façade and announced to the world with Victorian self-assurance that he had found Midas' tomb. In fact nobody has satisfactorily deciphered Phrygian lettering; there is no positive evidence of tombs at Midas City, and Phrygian culture remains for the most part an enigma. Instead there are extraordinary objects resembling outsize stage props carved in rock, façades with nothing behind them including a memorably colossal slab like a seventy-foot front door with an elaborate symmetrical pattern resembling a maze carved on one side. On the other is rough rock. Nobody appeared to know what it was for, or even if the work was finished.

Seyitgazi could legitimately be described as an assembly of architectural spare parts from the Ottoman, Seljuk and Byzantine eras. That would be to miss its charm. It is a complex of buildings lovingly restored, standing on a hill beside the little town and a place of pilgrimage where locals bring their picnics. The central feature is the grand chamber with the tombs of the eighth-century warrior Seyit and his wife Eleanor, a Greek lady. Hers is a modest affair of conventional proportions. Though no wider nor noticeably higher, his measures twenty-two feet in length, presumably in recognition of his military prowess. The tomb was built in the twelfth century by the mother of a Seljuk sultan, and the surrounding buildings added by an Ottoman successor. We watched the sun go down over Seyitgazi sitting in the stone stables with a local family who insisted we share their *kebab*, while with immense ceremony the caretaker lowered the Turkish flag fluttering over its fortified walls.

There is an approved official joke about the provincial capital, Eskişehir (meaning 'old town') and a later companion site to the northwest, Yenişehir ('new town'). The Turkish government has devoted considerable effort to developing Eskişehir with the result that it has become one of Turkey's largest towns, whilst Yenişehir remains a crumbling village. My guidebook stated that Eskişehir had become so wealthy from the manufacture of locomotives and Meerschaum pipes that it can afford to water its streets twice a day to keep the dust down. As we bounced through the craters to the hotel area I could not help wondering what Yenişehir must be like.

We spent a dismaying evening exploring potholes and piles of decayed rubbish in our search for a place to eat, settling finally for a cupboard-sized restaurant run by an enterprising young Kurd with bounding energy, which made us feel nostalgic. But every dog has his day. Eskişehir's moment came for me in the bath: the hotel provided floating soap and bathplug, so that if you lost the one in the search for the other both would reappear on the surface of the water. The plug was a cunningly constructed ball of rubber held in place by suction. If accidentally dislodged the air in its hollow centre would cause it to become buoyant and rise to the surface. There seemed scope here for an enterprise to rival the steam locomotive and the Meerschaum pipe. It might even fund an extra shift of street cleaners.

The purpose of our visit to Eskişehir was for the Scholar to see the Archeological Museum, said to contain Phrygian relics. He seemed disappointed by it, but I had the benefit of a dissertation on Roman, Byzantine and Arab coins which the Scholar taught me to regard as clues in a historical treasure hunt. Style, shape and content of precious metal told much about the culture from which they came. Inside Turkey itself collections like the one in Eskişehir were rare: most were sold off before reaching a museum.

Before leaving I paid a ritual visit to the bus station. The best cameo was of a trio of old men, all white-bearded, two of them apparently brothers, helping a third who might have been their father up the steps leading into the crowded building where, as always, all Turkey appeared to be on the move. The oldest of the three, a doubled-up bundle of old clothes dragging a cardboard box tied with string, made up in length of beard what he lacked in stature. This Dickensian trio reached the rows of packed benches where a young man in air force corporal's uniform offered him his seat. The old man took it, and watched by the other two, opened and unwrapped his parcel and brought out half a dozen objects that at first looked like candles, but which were apparently homemade cigars. He offered them to each of his neighbours, including the corporal's female friend, who shrank uncomfortably into her smart outfit. It was the first time I had witnessed a Turkish crowd registering bourgeois embarrassment. Presumably Ataturk would have called it a sign of progress.

On the wall of a restaurant on the Greek island of Patmos there hangs – as far as I know there still does – a picture entitled 'The Man from Kutali'. To judge by the story of it told by Mr Vagelis, the restaurateur, it can only refer to Kütahya, the name being jumbled during the change of the Turkish alphabet followed by the translation, since it occurs in a town in Asia Minor, and only Kütahya to which we were now heading fits the description.

The picture shows a man wearing only a pair of smart blue satin striped shorts, wrestling with an animal that might be a tiger, imagined by an artist who had never seen one. The tiger's head is so twisted round that it looks as if it is about to come off. But the most arresting feature is the wrestler's careful pose, with freshly set waves and parted hair, combed moustaches and the avuncular expression of a political candidate out to dispel malicious rumours that he is a man of violence, seen glancing up from a typical day's work. The setting is a classical forum, Graeco-Roman style.

According to Mr Vagelis' account, a brother and sister were born to a Greek farming family in Kutali, or Kütahya. At first nobody realised that both had extraordinary physical strength. Then one day the father sent the boy to look after his herd of goats. It came on to rain, so the youth herded the goats into a cave and rolled a great stone across its entrance. Next day when villagers came to the cave they could not believe their eyes: what manner of man could have moved such a great weight?

The girl, too, proved prodigiously powerful. So, reckoning to turn the phenomenon to their advantage the villagers went to the church and prayed for a dispensation to allow the pair to marry, so as to breed a new strain that would ensure the future prosperity of the community.

However, the pair were not interested in the proposal; the youth ran away and became a wrestler. Thanks to his strength he became famous and went to London. There he won all his fights, putting the other wrestlers out of work. This so incensed them that they loosed a London Zoo tiger into the ring to kill him while he was wrestling. But to the astonishment of the onlookers, he strangled the tiger.

Still intent on his destruction his rivals arranged to put him in the ring with a succession of wrestlers, and when he was weakened by fighting they sent in a bull to kill him. But a Jewish woman in the crowd took pity on him and, opening her purse, threw him a knife that she apparently kept for such occasions. Gratefully he took the knife and killed the bull.

At this point in his account Mr Vagelis paused to attend to a customer's bill; and when he sat down again seemed to have lost interest in his subject. No, he did not know what happened next, whether he married the girl, nor why she

207

should be Jewish, nor indeed what eventually became of the wrestler. He only knew that this was the true story of the man from Kutali.

Kütahya turned out to be a delight. We followed the signs to a little group of old buildings forming its historical centre and were charmed by the Ottoman mosque – though nothing in my eyes could outcharm Sivrihisar – which was decorated in local tiles, renowned to this day as Turkey's finest. We lunched opposite the elegant little *medrese* turned museum looking at a fountain which was a focal point for gossip and washing clothes. Our menu was yoghourt, tsatsiki, aubergines, beans, lamb stew, baklava, coffee, accompanied by a mountain of bread. The bill: £2.80.

After lunch we strolled in search of magnificent decay. We did not have far to look. I photographed a doorway fit for a sultan leading to debris; a shattered fifties Buick abandoned outside a line of unspoilt Ottoman houses; best of all, a cinema which looked as if it had received a direct hit advertising a film entitled *Ya Ya Ya Sa Sa Sa*. To my chagrin and shame we overlooked what my guidebook described as the best bus station in Turkey with pillars tiled from floor to ceiling. But we visited the colossal Byzantine castle towering over the town, fifty-five reinforced towers (once over eighty) linked by a fortified wall. The Scholar showed me how later Christians had build a carapace of rubble and stone around the work of the castle's original builders. The notice at the castle entrance proclaimed its dates as eighth and twelfth centuries; the Scholar deemed them seventh and ninth centuries, to fit in with periods of known Arab offensives.

With the Scholar driving we turned south from Kütahya, skirted the Murat Dağ mountain barrier, paused to admire the operatic Ataturk at Dumlupınar and joined the busy east–west highway from Ankara to Izmir. Wedged between two slow-moving lorries we pulled out to overtake. Another overtaking car sped past us, so narrowly missing ours that we felt ourselves sway in the slipstream. The episode left the Scholar more shaken than I was, perhaps chiefly from annoyance that it reduced his authority to criticise my poor driving.

The fast road took us to Uşak ahead of time and we had

enough light left to visit Ulubey nearby in search of another castle; but instead of man's work found only God's in the shape of a magnificent canyon across which, with half-closed eyes, one could pretend that an outcrop of rock was the remains of a moated fort. I do not think either of us believed it was.

Uşak remains unique to me for one curiosity. We dined in a restaurant on the first floor of a conventional city block. As we left to go home I noticed, set among the tables, a double bed made up with sheets and ready to be slept in. Almost as strange was that the Scholar had spotted it on the way in but had not thought it worthy of comment.

It was my idea to go to Aphrodisias. The Scholar had only paid a fleeting visit many years before to the huge Graeco-Roman city discovered in 1961 and dedicated to the Goddess of Love, and I remembered it as an unspoilt wonder too far inland for package tourism. Our road there took us out of town by the river Menderes where it makes its leisurely way down the great Anatolian slopes towards the sea. We paused on the way to pick up petrol. (Not far away twin prefabricated breeze-block mosques were under construction; it was not apparent why – Uşak had plenty – perhaps a private endowment?) The petrol attendant had his battery of phrasebook questions ready.

'Do you love Turkey?'
'Yes.'
'Vous parlez français?'
'Oui. Et vous?' Silence.
'What is your name?'
'James.'
'How old are you, James?' And finally, 'You pay, James.'
As the pump gauge was broken we paid what he asked. His guess was as good as ours.

Tourism had made impressive gains since my last visit to Aphrodisias. Then the carpark attendant charged me the equivalent of two pennies, the man selling entrance tickets was killing a snake, and I had the site almost to myself. This time we parked in a sea of coaches and waited our turn behind tourists in fezes listening to the history of Aphro-

209

dite's Temple in Italian and Japanese. The Bishops' residence – added in the fifth century – looked like Milan
airport on a bank holiday, the incomparable Odeon Tokyo
in the rush hour. At the present rate of growth the daily
influx might soon fill the 30,000 seats of the world's biggest
and best preserved ancient stadium. The other visitors had
as much right to be there as we had; we resented them
no less for that. It seemed a comedown for the city that
had moved the Emperor Augustus to choose it as his own
from among all the cities in Asia. I fear the Scholar did
not much enjoy his visit.

I decided he would not much enjoy the neighbouring
attraction of Pamukkale either, a freak of nature in dazzling
white limestone rising in a 400-foot-high curtain of stalag-
mites and shallow pools. A frolic in its waters was proposed
by my guidebook as a highlight for holidaying children. We
steered clear, and drove on to spend the night at the town
of Nazilli, which offered a double-banked guarantee of being
tourist-repellent: it had been recently rebuilt following an
earthquake, and it was irredeemably hideous. It was late, so
we ate in. The lift to the restaurant floor opened into the
kitchen, so we had to file past the uneaten and unattended
debris of lunch to reach the dining room. Accustomed now
to cheerful Turkish informality we did not find this as strange
as the smiling presence of a female receptionist on the front
desk, a reminder that we were heading into the emancipated
west.

If Aphrodisias was a cluster of gems tarnished by tourism,
Aezani was an unspoiled solitaire diamond. Set on a gentle
square mound lined by ancient timbered farmhouses still
very much in use is the Temple of Zeus, the best preserved
and one of the largest in Turkey. Built in the second century
by Hadrian it is a copy of the earlier Temple of Zeus at Mag-
nesia, in Ionian style no longer fashionable at the time, with
narrow columns and tall elevations. It stands on Phrygian
territory, so that Zeus had to share the temple with the goddess Cybele, revered through orgiastic rites, whose bust
stands beside the elegant ruin. Near the farmhouses local
women were washing clothes at a well. Chickens rummaged

210

for grain round the rusting wreck of what must have been one of the world's earliest combine harvesters. It looked as good a place as any for an orgy.

We were driving north again, towards Bursa on the way back to Istanbul. After Aezani we called in again at Kütahya for the Scholar to have a last look at the castle and then swung north-west towards Bursa. As we reached the winding, hilly stretch which the map accorded a green margin for beauty, the road surface collapsed, night fell and it began to rain. Never expect the expected.

I could not at first put my finger on the odd thing about Bursa. Then as we drove round its smart central precinct looking for a hotel I realised that it was the only town in Turkey we had seen, Istanbul included, where the main streets were properly paved. By day Bursa had the aspect of a rich provincial city with a patrician past, Barcelona, Lyon, or Milan, robbed of capital status by an accident of history. Its well-tended parks, hanging gardens and plane-trees lining the streets bore the hallmarks of civic pride. Bursa It must be the cleanest city in Asia between the Mediterranean and Singapore. Wealth helps. Bursa has Turkey's largest car factory. Before that it did business with German silk merchants.

Though Bursa is an ancient town it was the Ottomans who put it on the map by making it first their capital before the capture of Constantinople, then a centre of religious architecture. It is crowned with mosques, schools and mausoleums. The Green Mosque is by consensus the finest in Turkey, simple in structure, lavish in decoration with a blending of elaborate stone carving and sea-green tiles, sometimes dramatically mixed with deep blue. The visitor is left in no doubt that he is in the presence of a great work of Islam.

The town centre seemed to have resisted concrete and steel. The fine Victorian residences of rich merchants still stood. The souk – rebuilt after a recent fire – still operated, a city within a city. The fine silk market had an idiosyncrasy seemingly not thought odd, except by us: to leave it to return to our hotel by the shortest route we were directed to pass through the public lavatory.

211

We took the motorway to Istanbul, not yet completed and without filling stations. We turned off into a dismal patch of industrial waste trapped between oily shore and motorway. There was no question of petrol, but we had a last and delicious lunch in a transport café that even Turks would consider run down. We found petrol by returning almost empty-tanked in our tracks to a filling station we had passed earlier. It boasted an unusual convenience in the shape of two side-by-side toilets, fully equipped, but with no partition separating them.

We reached Istanbul in time to take Aunt Celeste out to dinner by way of thanks for the party she had given for the Scholar. A mishap revealed a new facet of her character. The restaurant was full, with a small crowd waiting, and owing to a misunderstanding we had no reservation. Aunt Celeste signalled us to wait. Then accosting the head waiter, she achieved a table within minutes.

'*Dans mon métier il faut de l'audace*,' she said with triumph as we sat down. In addition to energy Aunt Celeste had the confidence of a woman accustomed to being courted.

She must also have had confidence in the restaurant. In the light of the long and memorable disquisition on Istanbul's sewage arrangements by Bora, I was impressed by her insistence on trying the local sea bass. It was the best I have ever eaten.

We had picked a hotel to be near the airport for our early-morning departure. We found we were sharing it with carousing callgirls and ravenous mosquitoes; but as I lay awake looking back over our trip I had no regrets for Yeşil Ev, nor for luxury. My single sadness was that we had never met the twentieth-century equivalent of the Turkish sultan who went to war with his library of 50,000 books. We had seen in the Topkapı harem evidence of the scale of Ottoman imperial vision, everywhere else the decay which had replaced it. We had read worldly tales from court, of husbands justifying infidelity ('Better three women of twenty-five than one of seventy-five'), even accepting it in their wives as a price for their good looks ('Better share a good brioche than eat dry bread alone' – adapted into French as 'Better share a good vintage than drink vinegar alone'). Had such sophistication survived? We were in no position to tell; our journey had been a largely unsophisticated one.

What we would be able to attest to, however, was the survival of patrician attitudes at every level of society. At the airport next morning a small boy took my bags. He was clearly keen to practise his English. At the check-in counter he handed me back my tip.

'You can keep the change,' he said.

CHAPTER 6

At Ankara we hired another car and drove south to Haymana, a rapidly expanding city of bleak blocks of flats set on a high point in rolling hills, then on to Polatlı. A military band, wearing bright orange dress uniforms, was performing in the main square in front of the station. Nigel watched them, while I parked and found a room. By the time I came out, bandsmen and bandstand had vanished. Only the presence of military police attested that something out of the ordinary had happened.

Polatlı is distinguished by three things: a surfeit of grand, glittering, gloomy *pasta salonus* and, apparently, only one *lokanta* for 53,000 inhabitants – and that provided small helpings and was by no means full; a station patronised by very few trains (none at all between 9.30 a.m. and 2.30 p.m.) – *çoçuklar* (small boys) were scampering in and out of carriages in a siding when I looked in, with not an official to be seen (Nigel went three times – stations fascinate him); and above the city, a long, tapering line of shaped concrete uprights runs along the crest of the hills which push the Sakarya river to the west, like the stripped spine of an immense dinosaur – commemorating the long-drawn-out battle (24 August–16 September 1921), when an outnumbered Turkish army, brilliantly generaled by Ishmet Pasha, halted the Greek forces advancing on Ankara and threw them back behind the Sakarya river. We saw a lot of the town in a fruitless search for a decent restaurant – apart from *pasta salonus*, the prime sites were occupied by fruit shops and a dealer specialising in

Coca-Cola whose window display consisted of Coca-Cola crates.

We watched Turkish TV news during dinner. There were the following items: (1) a ministerial reception; (2) a Prime Ministerial press conference (Ozal's plump person was occasionally replaced with shots of the assembled press, seen from the front and from the back, of clapping hands, of aides standing to the side, of photographers) (eight minutes); (3) a Prime Ministerial address to officials (six minutes); (4) another press conference; (5) a presentation ceremony; (6) another press conference; (7) a TV control-room (*à propos* of the TV–PTT conflict over cable TV). These items took twenty-one minutes. Foreign news came later, in snippets without pictures.

14 September (Polatlı–Afyon Karahisar)

Nigel had to pay a third and final visit to the empty station before we left. There followed the regular checking of his case. This had several compartments, all done up by zips. The portable processor was concealed in one, and was only noticed once in the course of all airport searches – when it was passed off as another electronic device. Each compartment was specialised: one dealt with 'office matters' and contained a tie, 'hussy' and stapler; the second was devoted to 'documents'; the third had the 'general wardrobe'; the fourth was the 'record department'. Supplementary plastic bags were used for immediate requirements.

We began a new life touring a richer land. Our car was larger, more solid and more powerful. Towns and villages were better built and better kept. Tractors roamed fields and side roads. Vines grew up village houses, many of which were whitewashed.

First, a visit to Gordium, set in a bleached landscape of bare earth and stubble; low *tepes* (artificial mounds) are to be seen everywhere – concentrations of past human life which awe the intruder from the present and remind him that the land has belonged to many, many others; it is not a sombre place, does not remind of death and decay – rather it gives a frisson of excitement to the trespasser, has something of the magical aura of the downs around Avebury.

Two Dutch tourists were leaving as we arrived. Then we had it to ourselves. We walked round the barbed-wire enclosing the deep excavations of houses, palaces, offices, city gate, then returned to Polatlı, in the hope of inspecting the Sakarya memorial at close quarters. We gave a lift to a soldier who was so silent that Nigel forgot he was in the back seat – in spite of the smell of sweat which filled the car. The monument eluded us, but we hit upon the cemetery honouring the remarkably few Turks killed in the battle. White sarcophagi, laid out in lines, are surrounded by low hedges; it is well kept, with trees providing plenty of shade.

On to the next site, Pessinus; past the car-repair sector on the outskirts of Polatlı – the garages cluster around a large, new mosque; up a shallow willow-lined valley, then past low, isolated hills which look like God's *tepes*, to Sivrihisar; then south-east along the edge of the vast plain of the upper Sakarya which runs far away to the south – driving along a recently surfaced road which claimed to be closed. Pessinus stands in an exposed position. It looks as if it must have been rather small and provincial, although it was a metropolitan bishopric. A large, down-at-heel village occupies the centre of the site. The only notable remains are the foundations of a temple (built of Cyclopean blocks), an Odeon and a partially excavated extramural cemetery – plus huge amphorae and *stelai* (carved tombstones) showing weaving and grapes.

At Sivrihisar, the castle perches high above the town on twin jagged peaks and commands a view over the route to Polatlı as well as a full 180° to the south; it must have been an observation and signalling post rather than a base for military action against raiders below. We parked on the outskirts of the town in the bus area, were guided by a boy to a sleazy restaurant, then went in search of the Ulu Camii. From the outside this is a long, low, nondescript building painted a bluey green. It is surrounded on two sides by shops. A stumpy minaret rises from it, with a band of patterned glazed bricks below the parapet. One enters the mosque from the east, through a small courtyard. The floor lies a metre or so below street level. The first impression made by the interior is of space; the second, of a multitude of divisions. A parade of close-packed timber columns (some fifty-five to sixty all told) divide it into five aisles, aligned east–west, with a gallery on the north side. The columns are a mellow, dark brown. Most are surmounted by stalactite capitals, though a minority, in positions of honour (in front of the *mihrab*, and in the row fronting the gallery) have re-used classical capitals, probably brought from Pessinus. The floor is covered with fine old carpets. The *minbar* is elaborately carved. Chandeliers refract the light filtering in through small square windows in the south wall. They gleam red and blue, stained by the hand of God. A group of small boys sat near the *mihrab*, reciting the Koran so rapidly in response to the mullah, that the syllables melted into each other and the sound was a soft drone, as of muted bagpipes. We stood still and immersed ourselves in the place.

The next stop was Amorium, one of the most important cities in the interior of Anatolia in the Byzantine period. Until 1987 it was quite impossible to determine the general state of city life in this heartland of Byzantium between the collapse of the Roman Empire in the mid-seventh century and the arrival of the Seljuk Turks in the late eleventh under whom urban development was rapid and impressive. One scholarly party argued that the existence of a bishopric was a good index of the survival of a functioning city and hence that the network of sees spread over Anatolia (much more closely spaced than in Mediterranean and Continental Europe) attested the wholesale survival of cities, which had been the basic units of Roman economic, social and political life. Another, Gibbonian school was more pessimistic and envisaged a huge number of ragged bishops, scrabbling for a living from sees which, in the Middle Ages, were no more than large, impoverished, mud-brick villages, and engaged in an unending struggle to retain a skeleton labour force to cultivate their lands. Their picture of Byzantium shocked the starry-eyed but delighted the perverse. No Roman urban site in the interior had been surveyed scientifically until 1987, when Martin Harrison, Professor of Roman Archaeology at Oxford, started a survey and selective excavation at Amorium. Using a miracle-working machine which can see the outlines of ancient foundations below a deep coating of later deposits, without the need to excavate, he was able to draw a plan.

To judge by its extent, Roman Amorium was a great city. The site is oval, occupying an area of about 1,400 by 1,100 metres between two streams which converge immediately to the north. There is a small acropolis on a modest eminence in the northern section, which is roughly 300 metres across and forms rather less than a twelfth of the whole site. The city's defences, which include numerous towers, mainly rectangular and pentagonal, were refurbished in the late fifth century. The city declined rapidly after the sixth century, eventually shrinking into what had once been its acropolis. The key piece of evidence for this is provided by deposits of rubbish in the ditch outside the city wall, which ceased around AD 700. Much later, from the eleventh century, there is some evidence of reoccupation of parts of the old city (including the remodeling of a large late Roman church), but it did not revive on anything approaching its ancient scale.

These preliminary conclusions suggest, not unsurprisingly, that both scholarly factions have gone too far. The city did not survive the traumas of the seventh century unscathed, but managed to retain its urban character. It was compressed into a small, more defensible area, the ancient acropolis, where it held its own, except for one disastrous year, in the era of Arab attacks on Anatolia. It became the capital of one of the two main military regions in the interior of Anatolia, as well as the metropolitan see presiding over several dioceses. Its continued existence in an exposed position, in a natural basin on the north side of the Emirdağ, flanked to east and west by low hills, gives the lie to one contention of the Gibbonian school, *viz* that such vulnerable cities either died or migrated at the onset of the Middle Ages. This rooting of the city on its ancient site is all the more remarkable in the case of Amorium, since the Emirdağ massif (the name of which is a typically Turkish deformation of the city's name) formed a large natural fortress immediately to the south in which the people and the administration could have easily found refuge.

The siting of Amorium thus tells us a great deal about the confidence of the Byzantine high command in their ability to hold the open plains of north-west Anatolia and the nodal points formed by the heavily fortified nuclei of a limited number of ancient cities, in the face of the regular raids and occasional full-scale invasions of Arab forces. Some of this confidence may have come from a belief that an array of supernatural forces, chief among them cavalry saints and archangels, would assist the earthly defences and would assure survival, but it must also have been based upon an assessment that available resources, human and material, were capable of maintaining the walls of the reduced cities through the generations and of manning them at times of crisis. In the event, Amorium fell to Arabs only once, in 838 – when forty-one senior officers were captured, taken off to Samarra in Iraq and later, in 845, executed. This earned them the crown of martyrdom (status was almost always required as well as an unpleasant death or extreme asceticism to achieve sainthood).

The Byzantines of the region only lost self-confidence in the late eleventh century, when the Turks overran Armenia and eastern Anatolia and it became obvious that the great plains of the north-west were utterly indefensible. Although individual cities could survive in a state of semi-independence for a generation or so, by manipulating Turco-man groups and doing deals with Seljuk princes, in the long run their fate depended on their position relative to the Seljuk-sponsored network of trade-routes and the degree of security which could be expected. Amorium, located as it was in the frontier zone between Byzantine and Seljuk terri-tory, faded rapidly away in the twelfth century. The Seljuks briefly occupied part of the citadel, but the site was then abandoned until the 1890s when a small mud-brick village recolonised the area south of the citadel. This is now declin-ing in its turn as its inhabitants flock to the rapidly growing cities of the west. What there is of it clusters around the dirt road which cuts through the centre of the site.

We arrived mid-afternoon and were immediately introduced to Martin Harrison's local factotum. He showed us the three main soundings, which have uncovered (1) a small gate into the citadel and two associated rooms, (2) a large public building in the lower city, and (3) a sector of the lower city wall with a complicated building history – not very informative or exciting as yet. Nothing had been found which threw new light on the economic and cultural level of the Byzantine city (which, I suspect, remained very depressed by comparison with its heyday in late Roman times). After a tour in baking heat, during which we felt we ought to take uninteresting photographs to satisfy our guide, we returned to his house. Sheep were being driven into the courtyard, each one, he told us, ready to answer to its name. We waited a little, then were invited into the guest room – separate from the main house, entered from the street, with a large mantlepiece on which the most prestigious possessions were displayed. Our guide greeted us formally with handshakes as we crossed the threshold, summoned his wife who produced *ayran* of which we drank copiously, and suggested killing a 'ship' – an offer which we declined. We stayed a while, communicating by means of my halting Turkish. The professor, to whom immense deference was shown (the bringer of money, employment and status), was the main topic of conversation. We were given a letter to take to him and left.

We were just about on schedule. We drove across the easy pass which runs between the Phrygian highlands to the north-east and the Emirdağ to the south-west, then down a valley, its slopes bespattered with patches of white marble dust, to Iscehisar on the edge of another great plain. Iscehisar occupies the site of ancient Docimium, a city renowned for its marble. The marble industry still flourishes. We counted some sixty marble-cutting (and polishing) factories on the road between Iscehisar and Afyon. All but one were small establishments of roughly the same size – consisting of an enclosure, a frame for lifting and moving marble blocks, cutting equipment and a warehouse. The cut-throat competition of a completely free market has evidently been modified here – as in the case of the goldsmiths of Erzurum – by some collective agreement between the factory bosses and by the maintenance of ties with particular buyers.

Dusk was descending as we came to Afyon Karahisar, ancient Acroenus, a fragrant approach. A huge tip down-wind of the city seemed to be spreading in all directions – with the lighter rubbish scattered far and wide by the strong southerly wind blowing. We found a modern hotel in the centre near a shopping mall, changed rooms after futile attempts by the hotel handyman to put bulbs in the bedside lights which had no sockets, and went in search of dinner. Afyon, like Polatlı, has *pasta salonus* in prime sites, but it also has several restaurants. Ours was a grand one with large mirrors on its walls which are revetted in marble. The chef, fat and unhealthy-looking, stood outside his kitchen, contemplating his customers. There were other tourists dining as well as members of the local élite. Nigel took against the smile on a moustachioed American face. He drank Niz beer. This had an immediate effect. It disconnected appetite from brain – for the first time in Turkey, he just picked at his food.

Outside we went for our customary night stroll round the town. A twin-headed stuffed dog stood in one shop window, catching the eye and presumably luring customers in during shopping hours. A street-cleaner was at work – Nigel commented that he was wearing 'a very smart suit' (this was the beer talking – he was shuffling about in shabby clothes in the ill-lit lane). A young man was operating an excavator with extraordinary virtuosity on a building site – the machine was poised on the edge of a huge hole, scooping up earth and rock, and depositing them on lorries in a succession of rapid, smooth motions. We joined the onlookers and watched until the driver took a break, dismounted, stood with the back of his smart jeans facing us and peed into the dark hole which he had made.

221

Nigel woke but did not stir until nine. He was striving to remain relaxed and emptied of thought until 'the sentries awoke' and could keep anxiety at bay. His chief worry was that he had cancer of the brain. He was having occasional dizzy spells in the morning – for which the rotund, heavy-smoking doctor at Istanbul prescribed some ancient concoction to speed up the circulation. But Nigel *knew* that the cause was cancer.

Breakfast garrulity was the second stage of morning defence. He presented his view of marriage. The wife makes the husband addicted to love; once the addiction has taken hold, her power is assured; she can manage him as she will – all she has to do is withdraw love and apply emotional blackmail.

Afyon Karahisar spreads itself around the foot of an almost sheer rock, on which stands a Seljuk fortress. The few half-accessible points on the south side are guarded by older, ruined walls. The site has not been scientifically investigated. So one can only speculate about the function of these walls and the fate of the ancient city in the early Middle Ages. But it looks as if it shrank much more than Amorium and clung to the steep slope on this side of the acropolis.

We walked through the old quarter of the Turkish town, examining the medieval walls from below. Doorways were thronged with dirty urchins playing or staring contentedly. The mothers vanished at the sight of the camera. The Ulu Camii stands in this quarter, among fine old Turkish houses, many of which are stuccoed and painted in pastel colours. The steps leading up to it were crowded with seated old women. They were there to enjoy each other's company, not to beg. A salesman was unloading brand new carpets from the back of a small pick-up truck. The caretaker of the Ulu Camii was picking and choosing from among those degraded specimens of Turkish weaving, their colours metallic, cold and often clashing. The mosque is an old wooden one, with forty stalactite columns. But it lacks the charm of that at Sivrihisar. It is better lit and taller – there is less sense of

222

entering a separate world, enclosed, divided into innumerable small spaces, suffused with mysterious light.

A large bronze statue of a Turk triumphing over a Greek dominates the garden which forms the only open space in the centre of the city. We gazed at the giant Turk silhouetted against the sky and the prow of the castle, his arms raised with the fingers of the right hand ready to claw at his prostrate opponent. The muscles ripple on his back but the Greek seems to have managed to scoop out much of his stomach and all his reproductive organs before falling to the ground.

We left our visit to the museum to the last. It has evidently been under competent management, which has resisted the forces of the art market over many years. For unlike many other provincial museums, it houses a large and impressive collection. It is a world away from that at Tarsus, which was virtually denuded of exhibits, when I was there in 1974. It includes over thirty pieces of carved marble dating from the tenth and eleventh centuries. There are over twenty elaborately carved beams and a number of rectangular panels with shallow reliefs of crosses, mythical and real creatures. My colleagues, Cyril and Marlia Mango, who have measured and catalogued them, reckon that they come from some twenty separate churches in the general area of Afyon, including probably one or more at Amorium. Those marble pieces provide therefore our first tangible evidence that there was renewed prosperity in such west Anatolian towns as had survived the prolonged crisis between the mid-seventh and mid-ninth centuries. There were patrons who could afford to endow churches with decorated marble sanctuary screens and stone-carvers who were able to execute their commissions competently, albeit in a single style and with a limited repertoire of motifs.

We drove due north over the Afyon plain through the wind-blown rubbish, leaving a sinister, serrated ridge, which looks like a cut-out, to our left, towards the Phrygian highlands. These low rolling hills (the highest is only 1,713 metres) surround a number of interlinked inner basins. They must have been used as a stronghold in the dark age, on the relatively rare occasions when Arab raiding armies penetrated this far into Byzantine territory. The inner basins would provide plenty of grazing for fugitives' livestock while the broad encircling band of hills would deter most raiding horsemen from venturing in. Coming from the south they would have to pick their way through a stony wilderness of hills, covered in extruded bosses and dwarf pine, while from the north they would face bare but higher hills packed tight together.

The rock-cut dwellings around the large village of Ayazını were a disappointment. I had hoped to find traces of defences in their entrances, or a complex on a grand enough scale to have served as a local commander's HQ. All we saw were crude caves cut into the low cliffs on either side of a narrow valley. A group of ten-year-old boys accompanied us. I was apprehensive, remembering (again from 1974) the boys of Diyarbakır and Silvan in the south-east who enjoy stoning tourists. Nigel was friendlier. They were smoking and offered cigarettes to us.

Next stop was Midas Şehir in the heart of the highlands, a massive hill fortress. Huge flat funerary monuments are carved into two isolated, upended rocks. One has been left half-finished. We were guided round a quarter of the circuit, but having no particular interest in the disposition of the defences and being anxious to reach Eskişehir before night-fall, returned to the car and drove on.

It was late afternoon when we reached the shrine of Seyit Battah Gazi above a small run-down town. Pilgrims were drifting off as we walked up the covered way to the walled complex around the shrine. It looks and feels like a small Orthodox monastery, but is built of fine ashlar masonry. Four large buildings stand around an oblong courtyard which is dotted with column drums, capitals, marble panels, Roman tombs. Other pieces of ancient stonework have been built into the walls of the buildings. A large family party was still there. Some of them were tidying up the remains of a feast which they had had in the complex. Others were in the shrine of the Gazi. This is a large chamber attached to the mosque. The Gazi's tomb is twenty-two feet long. It is covered in bright green patterned silk. A huge shiny green ball, like an inflated decoration from a Christmas tree, hangs suspended above the green turban which rests on a post at the head of the tomb. The pilgrims looked shifty when we came in but then continued their devotions. They touched the silk covering of the tomb. They lifted up the turban and held it over their children's heads. A mother made the small child in her arm kiss the frame of the doorway leading into the shrine. The belief in the magical power of relics, conveyed by contact from substance to substance, has not died. Back outside, the head of the family brought us a plate of tepid rice and pieces of mutton. Nigel's appetite died at the sight of it. So I did what justice I could to it. Outside the complex, two severed sheep's horns lay on the ground.

Eskişehir, ancient Dorylaeum, is a large, sprawling, characterless city. Its medieval predecessor, which was Byzantium's main military base on the edge of the Anatolian plateau, has long since been obliterated. It is notable above all for the appalling condition of its main streets. It was as if they were all being resurfaced at the same time. There was no tarmac to be seen. The main hazards for the bumping traffic were protruding manhole covers and potholes. Repulsed from a smart hotel, we found a modest one by the bus station, overlooking the polluted Porsuk river. Restaurants were thin on the ground, and they were all adjuncts to smoke-filled bars in which much heavy drinking was going on. We ate *shish kebabs* in a small, oblong, neon-lit shop unit. The boss was young, hyper-energetic, a Kurd from the east. A friend was drumming up trade by shouting into the darkness outside.

16 September (Eskişehir–Uşak)

First stop was at Kütahya, ancient Cotyaeum, which is connected to Eskişehir by a relatively easy route running between the Phrygian highlands and hills to the west. A huge porcelain factory creates a permanent grey fog on the northern edge of the Kütahya plain. Kütahya didn't seem to

be in the grip of the Islamic revivalists, as the textile manufacturer had claimed at our Istanbul party. An election van was
touring the streets. Full-length posters of the candidate in
white tie and tails were plastered all over it. The men throng-
ing the entrance of the Ulu Camii and sitting in seedy restaurants and cafés paid no attention. The streets were full of
airmen, many of them on their way to the cinema. *Rambo III*
was showing, the soundtrack being relayed by loudspeakers
to the hurrying airmen. Lurid posters, advertising other films
with sensual scenes, framed the broken-down entrance. The
city is full of baths. We counted three men's and one ladies'
in the old quarter around the Ulu Camii. A nauseous sulphur-
ous smell spreads across the town down-wind of the ladies'
bath – which perhaps has to make do on the cheapest
coal.

Afterwards we visited the early medieval fortress which
stands on the sloping top of a steep-sided hill immediately
to the west of the early Turkish town and commands the
plain to the north. It is a powerful complex which seems
to have been built from scratch in the course of the seventh
century. The fortifications have banded brick and stone
masonry which is characteristic for the late Roman period
in western Anatolia. Unusual strength was achieved on
the most vulnerable western section, by the systematic
integration of outer forewall and main inner wall to form
a single deep defensive circuit. This was reinforced by an
array of massive round towers. Further improvements dating from the ninth century, in which the number of towers
was doubled and an extension made to defend a lower
settlement on the north side, suggest that the city was
regarded as a key element in the regional defensive system
and that it had profited from the security provided by its
original endowment of walls and was entering a period of
substantial population growth. It would appear to have
been as large and resilient as Amorium in the dark-age
crisis of Byzantium.

I drove sideseat once too often as we were leaving the
outskirts of Kütahya, Nigel having not noticed a jeep which
had priority. He promptly handed the wheel over to me,

in spite of my protesting that I was tired. We drove south, through a grand country dominated by large, isolated, orange hills – then skirted the Afyon plain and crossed the undulating country which lies to the west of it to meet the railway line at Dumlupınar. It was on this sector of the front that Ataturk launched his counter-offensive in August 1922. He pressed home the initial victory which he won at Afyon, pursuing the Greeks first to Dumlupınar where he outflanked them as they made a stand, then to Uşak where he defeated their second rally, finally as retreat turned into headlong flight to Izmir. Nigel took many photographs of a locomotive which had stopped at Dumlupınar station. Soon we hit the traffic on the main Ankara–Izmir road and I nearly killed us both, by pulling out to pass a truck as soon as a gap appeared in the oncoming traffic – without having looked behind. The car swayed under the air pressure as a yellow car swerved past us at high speed and disappeared into the distance. I drove very slowly the remaining distance to Uşak.

Uşak is a town of 80,000. It stands on the northern edge of a large, not particularly fertile plain, from which the Maeander draws one set of its headwaters. The plain is fissured by some quite impressive canyons towards the south. Like many towns in the west, Uşak is growing fast, as it sucks in population from the surrounding countryside. Three large new housing estates are going up rapidly on the outskirts. A splendid statue of Ataturk, highly recommended to us in England, stands in the main square. The eyes are burning, the fingers splayed as if some burst of energy has just been released through the body and the whole figure is about to leap or fly into action. Yet the long cloak which envelops him hangs absolutely still – in the thrilling moment of suspense before Batman-Ataturk moves.

Every Turkish town has its own particular character. Uşak's is its night life. The streets are full of ten year olds playing games and vendors selling cassettes, wallets, nuts and *köfte* – at a relatively late hour. People hurry home carrying yellow condoms bulging with shopping.

A chandelier shop shimmered at us. In the restaurant, a

large one upstairs, Nigel gave his considered opinion on Turkish TV news – the worst he had ever seen, not even at the level of rushes but of discards. We paid the bill and made to leave.

'Spectacles, testicles, wallet and watch,' said Nigel, patting his person and checking the table for possessions. It was only then that he started back at the sight of a huge marital double bed standing in a position of honour in the middle of the restaurant on the marble floor (black, white and green with flecks of the local condom-yellow). I had seen the bed as we came in but somehow, in this land of peculiarities, it had not seemed at all odd.

17 September (Uşak-Nazilli)

We spent most of the day among the headwaters of the Maeander, which drain the plain of Uşak and a wide, waterlogged valley between Dinar and Çivril to the south-east. These converge beyond the south-west edge of the Uşak plain and provide easy access to the broad valley of the Maeander which runs west to the Aegean. There is another open route to the sea a little further south which runs down a gentle slope from Dinar south-west to the evaporated Acigöl, then into the adjoining broad valley of the Lycus, a tributary of the Maeander. There can be no doubt that once an adversary gains control of the western edge of the Anatolian plateau, as the Turks did in the 1070s, the whole of the rich Maeander region is impossible to defend, with these huge breaches in its natural defences. The same weakness was ruthlessly exploited by the armies of Ataturk in late summer 1922 when they broke through and overran the whole of the seaboard in a fortnight.

It was another day of car-seat research which is only a little better than armchair scholarship. We did, however, get out to examine two middle-Byzantine basilicas at Sebaste, which stand side by side within an enclosure (not a defensive wall – it is thin and has no towers). Their internal marble fittings

228

are now displayed in the Uşak museum. There are no flat, stylised reliefs of fantastic creatures like those at Afyon. The carving is deeper, and the motifs are Christian and geometrical, the most impressive being two carved marble beams (one from each church) with busts of saints, belonging to the sanctuary screens. Sebaste is now a large, decayed village. Girls carrying huge loads looked curiously at us. The stroll around the churches was our most strenuous activity of the day.

We looked from a distance at the steep-sided hill on which stands medieval Eumeneia or a late medieval castle replacing the ancient town. We drove through Gümüşsu, a village set in a small oasis of trees between Çivril and Dinar. Byzantine Choma is thought to be there or nearby (on the ground of the similarity of the names), a place rendered briefly famous because the last notable Anatolian units serving in the late eleventh-century Byzantine army were called after it and made their mark on history, along with a large Turcoman force, when they propelled Nicephorus Botaneiates to power early in 1078. His home town, Lampe, should be in the triangle between Dinar, the Acigöl and Keçiborlu. Our researches there consisted of driving at speed toward the distant Acigöl; its vast surface was transformed by mirage into a sparkling blue, the reality of a mini-Aral sea being signalled by the mini-tornadoes twirling around on its salt crust. There seemed to be no defensible site where a Byzantine magnate, a nascent bourgeoisie and a garrison could conceivably have had the confidence to hold out after the battle of Manzikert, let along manage the Turcoman raiders in the region and turn them into willing auxiliaries. Finally we merely glanced up at Mount Honaz – named after the pilgrimage shrine of the Archangel Michael at Chonae – as we hurried on, determined to reach Aphrodisias before dusk.

Aphrodisias was as artificial and bloated a city as any in Roman Asia Minor. Its agricultural resources were limited. Its position out-of-the-way, far from the coast and hidden from the main valleys of the Lycus and Maeander rivers to the north by a formidable mountain range. We were urged to spend the night in a nearby motel as we arrived, were

229

surrounded by slow-moving gaggles of tourists, waited for rare moments when vistas cleared to take photographs, and were kept out from the monumental centre of the ancient city (and forbidden to photograph it), since the massive project of re-erecting its *disjecta membra* is not yet completed. Nigel aimed for the racetrack and Odeon, both amazingly well-preserved, which he remembered from a past visit. I paused to contemplate the late Roman building work which converted the temple of Aphrodite into the cathedral, and gazed at a standing fragment of the medieval city wall.

We then sped on through the gathering dark and searched for a hotel in Nazilli. This seems to be a brand new town, which has sprung up mushroom-like, with depressing neon-lit streets cutting between tall, homogenised buildings and crisscrossing each other at right angles. At last a neon-lit hotel materialised, carefully paced in a restaurant-less quarter – the Nazilli Commercial Hotel. Only one other table was occupied when we came into the hotel restaurant – discharged by the lift into the kitchen which was far from abuzz with activity. The waiter thought us funny and couldn't stop laughing whenever he left our table. The menu was limited and the food poor. The manager advised the other diners where to stay at their next port of call and offered to make a booking. He then sat down next to Nigel, breathing heavily. He offered to fix us up at Bursa the next night, and then extended his conversational range. He reminisced about his schooldays – his maths teacher had given him four marks for writing 'clean' sums – and about his national service – he spent two years at Doğubayazıt, reading and 'hunting'. Every phrase was prefaced with 'for example'. 'For example', he told us, he had been a journalist writing Hansard reports. 'For example', he said, 'I am a fat man', and then told us wonderingly that a thin Scotsman and his wife had stayed in the hotel on a bicycling holiday. 'For example, what is your profession?' We told him but then he was off again, galvanising his disused English into action and peppering us with short, staccato sentences.

18 September (Nazilli–Bursa)

Nazilli was marginally more inviting by daylight. Solar panels and their associated white canisters festooned all visible roofs. It was the first day of term. From our window high up pupils could be seen making their way down the main streets, smartly turned out. The small ones wore black smocks with white collars, irrespective of sex. The older girls were in white shirts, blue dresses, black stockings, while the older boys sported blazers and grey flannels. They passed below the white corrugated fibreglass awnings above the shops at the cross-roads by our hotel.

We made a long zigzag journey north, stopping for a drink at Alaşehir (ancient Philadelphia), at the north end of the easy pass leading from the Maeander to the Hermus valley, and for lunch at Kula, a bustling market town in the burnt, rolling country which surrounds it (aptly named Katakekaumene in classical times). Our main objectives were the well-preserved temple of Aezani, which stands in one of the several small high plains on the watershed between Gediz and Sakarya rivers, and the Byzantine fortress at Kütahya which I wanted to photograph again, having mistakenly taken slides on our first visit.

Aezani is a magical place. The modern village of beige timber-framed houses straggles along the edge of one side of the temple enclosure. No attempt had been made to encroach on the *temenos*. The temple stands on the highest spot, dominating the other remains of the ancient city (baths, gymnasium, theatre) which keep well clear of the sacred enclosure. There is a huge barrel-vaulted chamber beneath the temple, some forty feet high, into which we descended by a metal ladder. It is awesome. We spoke in whispers.

We sped on, snatching some more photographs at Kütahya, then driving into the setting sun to Tavşanlı. Darkness caught us entering the tough mountains which defend Bithynia against intruders from the open lands of the north-west plateau. We arrived at Bursa at eight, made no attempt to find the hotel into which the manager of the Nazilli Commercial Hotel had booked us, instead grabbing the first room we could find. This was in the rather sumptuous Dikmen Hotel in a sidestreet off the main throroughfare. It pulled rank in its reception area – bulky, upholstered chairs were arranged in four tiers, facing the desk and television. Nigel found himself asking permission of the commissionaire to leave the hotel to look around the town at night.

19 September (Bursa–Istanbul)

We were back in a tourist-inundated world, with monuments tarted up to entice more and more of them to come. Perversely I preferred the Ulu Camii to the more famous, more carefully wrought Green Mosque and Green Tomb. It is a massive, austere building, with the same plan as the mosque at Kütahya (five domes, a pool in the middle inside a marble enclosure); the decoration of its yellow-ochre interior consists of gigantic kufic letters, most but not all framed.

We left Bursa – which announces to its visitors that it is twinned with Darmstadt, Sarajevo, Multan, Oulu, Kairouan, Tiffin, Denizli and Kütahya – on the last leg to Istanbul. We almost ran out of petrol between Izmit and Istanbul, since there appears to be only one garage on the Asian approaches to the great city. We just beat the rush hour. Heavy traffic, belching evil-looking exhaust fumes, moved slowly nose to tail along the bypass. Our windows were tightly shut. We breathed shallowly, as if trapped in a submarine with a diminishing supply of oxygen.

That was just about the end of the second Turkish journey. We gave Celeste dinner in a smart fish restaurant near the airport. Her eyes sparkled. I caught snatches of her and Nigel's animated conversation across the table – something about '*l'audace*' of the Armenian artisans who still live in Istanbul, about a resemblance of turbot to lingerie, about the illiteracy of country folk. The new fishing season had just opened and all Istanbul was feeding on what could be hauled up from the polluted waters of the Marmara.

We spent a short, much-interrupted night in a motel near

232

the airport which serves as a fairly high-class brothel. Taxis congregated around the reception building. Occasionally mysterious cries could be heard. Boys moved stealthily across the garden. A dignified Arab walked at a stately pace, followed by several ladies. The carpet in our room levitated, raised by a ferocious draft. Mosquitoes, bred by the warm, effluent-rich Marmara, divebombed us.

By 5.00 a.m. we were in the air, conveyed by Balkan Airlines in a plane sparsely populated with seats to Plovdiv with middle-aged, thick-set, sour-faced, pin-stripe-besuited stewardesses wordlessly plonking inedible breakfasts in front of us . . .

CHAPTER 7: BULGARIA

I had been there before, for a wedding engineered to give
the Bulgarian bride a foreign passport. It was a cynical, sad
ceremony in Sofia's reproduction cathedral in the depth of a
sixties' winter. The Bulgarian Embassy in London had col-
luded by flying the wedding guests in free in exchange for
the promise of a television film to promote tourism to be
made by the bridegroom, an Australian friend. On my return
a man in a mackintosh called to ask me questions about the
embassy official. Months later, when I next saw the bridegroom, he told me the marriage lasted a month, and the film
was never made. I had never been back.

For the Scholar it was an extension of Byzantium, for me
a curiosity. The curiosity was to see the changes effected
by *perestroika* since my last visit. Officially Bulgaria not only
welcomed the great restructuring; from the propaganda you
might think the regime invented it. 'BULGARIA – QUES-
TIONS AND ANSWERS', handed to me with my visa, said
it sprang from an internal need to meet 'new requirements
of Bulgarian society'. It relegated the Svengali role of Gorbachev's Soviet Union to a single passing reference to 'new
world realities'. Most of the publication dealt with other matters of interest to tourists, including Bulgaria's Esperantist
Union and the biennial Festival of Bulgarian Humour.

The local interpretation of *perestroika*, filtered through
apparatchiks with a stake in the status quo and their jobs
on the line, was couched in subtly different language. The
English-language *Daily News*, published by the official Bul-

234

garian news agency, described *perestroika* as a 'constantly improving dynamic process'; codewords, according to a local diplomat, for 'the mixture as before' being administered by the old guard holding on to power.

At first it certainly looked like the mixture as before. Sofia airport was shut and our old Ilyushin, with the familiar camp-bed seats and khaki covers, was diverted to Plovdiv where unsmiling officials herded us into a Nissen hut. A woman customs officer asked me to give her a new English £5 note in exchange for her torn one. A nervous knitting-machine salesman from Leicester attached himself to us. We were directed into a waiting bus. The knitting-machine sales-man said he had come to sign a contract – not just your routine sale of plant and installation, mind, but a three-year after-sales maintenance clause, which is where you see the profits, personally negotiated with the State Committee at the price he was looking for. No trouble over the money: they had the budget and they needed to spend it.

'That's communism for you,' he whispered into my ear. His self-importance was at odds with the agitation on his face. It was his first trip to Bulgaria. I had the impression his life depended on it.

An hour later a bus decanted us beside a Stalinist war memorial in Sofia. Nobody met us. There was no apparent means of proceeding except on foot. Eventually someone found a taxi. Rejecting the brand new Sheraton we drove to the Hotel Bulgaria on the corner of Sofia's main square with a view of the Central Committee building surmounted by a Red Star, the Bank of Bulgaria and two sentries in dress uniform guarding the tomb of Bulgaria's national hero.

It was where I had stayed before. It had a night club remi-niscent of post-war Hamburg. I had been woken in the night by the sound of metal hitting stone, and looking out of my window saw prisoners replacing cobbles in the square below.

The hotel had changed little in appearance. The lobby was still heavy Cold War beige in colour. With something like nostalgia I recognised the crumbling paint on the pillars, the dated music and defeated air of people waiting for service. More modern hotels built in the intervening years accentu-

235

ated its air of decay, but the Bulgaria remained the traditional place where the government entertained its special guests. Behind the lobby I recognised the entrance to the night club. The knitting-machine salesman was checking in as we arrived. I saw him later in one of the dining rooms with some men who looked like prize fighters in business suits. He seemed more relaxed. Presumably the deal had gone through.

In the streets of the capital sunlight replaced the grim penitential look I remembered. Bright, cheap clothes, heavy-set bodies and peasant faces lent it an easy, provincial air. We sat at a café where I spoke my first Bulgarian word to the waitress. This was 'Havana', the name of a cream bun being eaten by two large ladies at the next table.

The first evening in Sofia did not go entirely smoothly. I had intended to have a haircut in Turkey, a ceremonial ritual with roots in Ottoman grandeur, but had not found the time. I decided to try again in Sofia. The hotel barber was ill and I had made an appointment in a backstreet. On the way I was accosted by a frightened-looking man in a baggy suit offering to change my currency at four times the official rate. We had been warned against touts: the penalty for tourists caught trafficking was serious, for Bulgarians unthinkable. Just then I realised that I had forgotten to bring any Bulgarian money with me; all I had was a German fifty-mark note, no use to a Sofia hairdresser. When I produced it, I thought the man would faint from fear. Moments later I was sitting on a park bench beside him while he counted notes from a wad resembling compost pulled from a back pocket. I quickly became aware that he was counting the same notes twice. But so real was his fear and so violent the trembling of his fingers that I pretended not to notice. I was also quite anxious on my own account to get the transaction over.

The trouble with the haircut was that I knew the Bulgarian for 'Yes' but had forgotten 'No'. When asked by gesture, if I would like more off, I could only say 'Da'. The result was a near crew-cut.

It was a half-hour taxi ride to the Ivan Dujčev Centre – the Institute for Byzantine Studies. Heading away from the town centre was like watching make-up coming off. The clean cheer of shops gave way to drab apartment buildings, not radically different from a cheap capitalist suburban development, except that in the West uniformity derives from economy rather than ideology. At the city's outer ring road the street smartened up for a stretch, becoming smoother and broader. The driver pointed at the square concrete shoulder of building in a gap in some trees. We were approaching the entrance to one of President Zhivkov's residences.

The Institute for Byzantine Studies was a converted private house in a little muddy street. On the doorstep to greet us was a startlingly beautiful girl who introduced herself as Elena. She was tall, with dark eyes and fine cheek bones, and was dressed in jeans and a sweater. She greeted us with a smile and a little bow that charmed me, before leading us into an office where a journal lay open on the desk at an article in English headed: 'BILATERAL TRADE: ALBANIA AND BULGARIA: 1968 . . .' I wondered if we had met Ninotchka.

But it wasn't her desk. Elena was a student of ninth- and tenth-century Byzantine manuscripts, and specialised in handwriting. Her English was near perfect, although her only experience of the West was a trip to Salonika and a brief stay in Rome. She was to be our guide during our brief stay.

Elena showed us round the little centre, a peaceful academic island that could have been anywhere in the world, before taking us back to town by bus, quicker than the taxi ride out. She spent the rest of the afternoon negotiating for a car to take us into the countryside the next day, while the Scholar and I visited Sofia's museums. The one I most wanted to see, the Museum of the Revolutionary Movement in Bulgaria, was closed for development. I ventured a joke.

'For restructuring, you mean?' The official laughed politely. I suppose he had heard it before.

We dined at an Italian restaurant reputed to be the best in town. At least it had an Italian name. We were given a table next to one bearing a plastic sign, Maître D'. While we waited we studied the occupant's working method. His duties apparently did not include showing customers to their table. Nor did he move once from his position, standing propped against an upright piano. He appeared to receive no tips. He spoke to acquaintances entering and leaving. He had evidently reached a socialist utopia of his own, a post in which he had delegated all the work in a country in which he could not be dismissed. There were no Italian dishes on the menu. We ordered a meal blindly. When it came we tried hard, but the food was not eatable.

Hungry but relieved to be outside, we wondered where to go. A young man appeared and offered to take us to the Palace of Culture. We came upon it on one side of a vast square dominated by an immense abstract group of figures locked in the struggle for socialism from which several concrete slabs were missing. Most of the palace, a six-storey building modelled on the lines of an air terminal, was closed. We found a table in a basement café where a friend of our guide's joined us for a round of vodka. Our guide was a steward on the Bulgarian airline's domestic routes whose ambition was to be transferred to the coveted international route so that he could travel abroad. He had just ended two years of national service, famously brutal in Bulgaria, which he refused to talk about. His experience had been bad enough to persuade his slighter younger friend to take the option of five years' factory work.

We had an inside room at the Bulgaria looking on the domed glass roof of the night club, so I was well placed to monitor advances in its musical repertoire since my last visit. It was a hot night and the windows were open. The orchestra went home at two.

Next morning while we were waiting for the car to arrive we had our first telling insight into *perestroika*. On the pavement near the hotel entrance people were queuing at a stand where a fast dwindling pile of newspapers was being sold in an atmosphere of clandestine haste. Assuming it to be *samizdat*, the Scholar strolled over to take a closer look. It was *Pravda*. When we asked for a copy at the main newsagent, we were told it was not on sale.

Our day in the country took us south off the beaten tourist track to Kjustendil. It was the site of Roman sulphur baths and there were still late Roman traces for the Scholar to see. Grand nineteenth-century houses were evidence that until recently it had been a prosperous spa resort. Modern Kjustendil had not been so fortunate, as it had not been selected as a target for tourist development. Food grown in the surrounding fertile fields was diverted by central planning to strategic national showpiece areas, leaving what was once a prosperous town deprived of livelihood. All that was left today was the whiff of sulphur hanging over a ravaged, neglected ruin. Bare-shelved government stores with controlled prices stood next to hardly better stocked private-enterprise shops where prices were beyond the reach of ordinary citizens. Unable to settle elsewhere without permission, its inhabitants wandered the streets empty handed, empty faced. Kjustendil was suffering from collective depression. On the most simplistic level of thinking, it could not be right to make so many people unhappy.

Rila was a different story. It was a showpiece. The charming medieval monastery set in a bowl of mountains had been rebuilt and clinically restored to a standard that would have made its founding monks ill at ease. But it was an admirable tourist attraction, even better propaganda, telling visitors a story of cultural integrity, artistic awareness and religious tolerance.

Back in Sofia, we ordered sandwiches for supper at the hotel. We were about to begin eating when I discovered that I had left my passport and travellers' cheques in the taxi taking us to Kjustendil. We were due to leave early next morning and I lamentably failed the ensuing test of nerve. While I tried in vain to call Elena I switched from sandwiches to the Scholar's Scotch. Then I got through. She had my documents. I went to recover them from the three-roomed flat where she lived with her parents. It was much as I expected, small, neither beautiful nor ugly, tidily arranged. Elena said things had improved of late. Until she was twelve years old the three of them had shared a single room.

A Western ambassador the Scholar and I called on had painted a picture of Bulgaria blacker that we had seen for ourselves. According to him its economic plight ranked with Poland's: a national debt of $10 billion, equivalent to $1,000 a head; economic dependence on a gift of Soviet crude oil refined locally and sold on for hard currency, now about to be cut back; a falling population and falling output. Once a net exporter of food, Bulgaria was now importing it. The only solutions open were a massive rescheduling of loans from Western banks on conditions which might unseat the regime, or else savage economies only enforceable by a return to Stalinist repression. The diplomat told us that his best-informed sources were fellow diplomats from Iron Curtain embassies who delighted in adding to President Zhivkov's problems by leaking vital statistics (classified as state secrets in Bulgaria). They even had a joke: Zhivkov, turned pious in his old age, praying to God each night for the collapse of *perestroika*.

It was this notion that gave me an idea on the flight home for a film script. Owing to a bureaucratic error I had been placed in a first-class seat. Vodka was free. During the long wait on the runway I had two glasses. As we climbed through the cloud over Plovdiv the alcohol took hold. Looking back over our journey I felt a sudden heady urge to sketch out the plot of a spy thriller based on our experiences, perhaps as a way to keep them alive. I ordered another vodka, took out my notebook and began writing, with no idea of how the story would end.

The result must serve as a postscript to my travels with the Scholar.

20 September

The uneaten breakfasts were collected up. The plane had no sooner reached its cruising height than it descended. Thirty-five minutes after leaving Istanbul we were at Plovdiv. The passengers left the plane in a silent rush. The first glimmer

240

of humanity was a smile from the dour woman examining our passports. Were we coming for 'business'? A look of suspicion when we answered no. Had we a hotel reservation? Suspicion deepened at a second no. But then she saw my daughter Eugenie's name on my passport and fleetingly a mother's feelings showed through the mask of her face. A conveyor belt sprang into action in the small airport hall. Suitcases came zipping along and fell off the end. Outside a bus waited to convey us to Sofia: many seats were broken, fixed in an uncomfortable reclining position; they were all covered in crumbs. We dozed on the journey which didn't last long. Bulgaria has acquired a network of fancy motorways since my last visit in 1979.

We were deposited in the middle of a park in Sofia, about half an hour earlier than scheduled. We had gone by the time my friend Dmitri Obolensky, who had been fêted by the Bulgarian academic establishment and had spent a month in Sofia, arrived unexpectedly to meet us – we did not see him before he flew off to Belgrade in the afternoon. Nor did we succeed in meeting a nuclear scientist with whom I had made friends at Oxford and his mother, a distinguished medieval archeologist. We had not heard from them, hence had no idea that they were waiting in vain for us at the station.

We found a room in the Grand Hotel Bulgaria. It was built in the 1930s on an impressive scale. The predominant colours are those of the steppes, brown-beige-ochre (for which part of the spectrum the Turkish languages have an abundance of words). Two ranges of grand public rooms, on the ground and first floors, look out over the main street. In the evening surly thugs serve 'Balkan' steaks upstairs while in the bar below the only food available is sliced tinned ham.

These once-magnificent rooms still impress the Soviet tourists who form most of the hotel's clientèle. Westerners now patronise the Sofia Hotel, an inferior product dating from the 1960s, or the ludicrously plush Balkan Sheraton Hotel in front of which a row of parked Mercedes-Benz advertise themselves for sale at astronomical prices. The hotel impressed us too – Nigel's imagination was stirred and he began concocting a plot for a novel to be set in Zhivkov's Bulgaria. At lunchtime, dazed from lack of sleep, we made our way through the downstairs suite and suddenly came out into a huge, oval, airy room. A small band was playing. The violin whined in a melancholy way. A few couples moved about on the dancefloor. Every table on the ground floor was occupied by a large wedding party. We made our way up a curving flight of broad stairs to a gallery and found a table free. A great flattened glass dome flooded the arena below with light. It seemed to have some sort of movable protective canopy which could be closed at night or in storms.

Outside the sun shone and Sofia looked clean and prosperous. The streets bustled with life. The women were smartly dressed. There was nothing drab or uniform about their clothes. Their eyes sparkled in their well made-up faces as they sat chattering in cafés in the central, monumental area of the city. Glances into shops revealed no shortage of goods behind the plate-glass windows. The economic upsurge which had been very evident between 1965 and 1979 appeared to have continued. The inhabitants of Sofia were well-off and animated. Occasionally a non-conformist figure passed by – an oldish man with a white goatee, a pale young man with thinning hair and the look of an intellectual – suggesting that prosperity was encouraging diversity of inner life as well as dress. At the other end of the spectrum were the youths who crowded into cramped arcades and played space-invader machines.

The half-underground church of St Petka was stiflingly hot, from the throngs of votive candles lit by the faithful who came in a steady stream. The Bulgarian Chamber of Commerce's entrance next door was sadly deserted by comparison. The marble mausoleum of Georgi Dmitrov gleamed, guarded by smartly turned-out sentries in their red ceremonial uniform. Diagonally across the main square rose the National History Museum. The finest portable monuments from all over Bulgaria – funerary reliefs, Roman busts, large torsos, well-carved feet from a lost giant statue, a helmet and armour of moulded bronze, a small stumpy column commemorating one of the victories of Khan Krum . . . – were carefully displayed. Spotlights picked them out. The whole vast interior space of the building – which has been taken over recently from the law courts – seemed to have been treated like a formal garden. The statuary and other items have been arranged so as to please the wandering beholder's eye, within pools of light, the interior analogue to leafy arbours.

Why had we come to Bulgaria? Apart from a natural desire to introduce as much variety as possible into our travels, there were two scholarly purposes. The first was to see the collection of Roman and medieval antiquities in the Archeological Museum, which includes numerous items from the provinces. It had been closed for renovation during my visit in 1979. It had been most frustrating to explore a site, scrutinise the contents of the local museum but then be unable to see the finest artefacts discovered there because they had been spirited away to Sofia. The second was to be given a guided tour of the excavations of the medieval town above modern Şumen in the north-east by the excavator, the nuclear scientist's mother. Neither purpose was achieved. The Archeological Museum was either closed or closing when we turned up – and we only managed one rushed and superficial scan in the course of our stay. And we never made contact with the archeologist. So we found other ways of occupying ourselves.

Nigel sank into a deep sleep immediately after lunch. I sped hollow-eyed to the National History Museum where an exhibition of material from the Hermitage was opening that day. Bright lights, whirring sounds, a face mouthing words and gleaming unnaturally, a huddle of figures around one of the show cases distracted attention from the objects displayed. Bulgarian television was making something of this exhibition of what was advertised as the 'Treasure of Khan Kubrat'. There was a certain irony in this: here were the Bulgarians celebrating the loan of material which they proudly claimed had belonged long ago to one of their earliest rulers; their old ally and protector, the Soviet Union, had supplied it; yet the large collection of gold and silver objects

243

on display had been dug up in the steppe zone of southern Russia and dated from the period when the Bulgars were a purely *Turkish people* and were competing for prestige with numerous rival Turkish peoples in the huge arena of nomad politics which stretched from the Hindu Kush to the Danube. The Bulgarians were glorying in their *Turkishness*. The lavishly produced catalogue included several maps illustrating the triumphant westward advance of a succession of Turkish nomad federations in late antiquity. Yet this was the people who were insisting on their own Slavic character, who had been trying for five years forcibly to assimilate their Turkish minority, who had gone so far as to Slavicise the names of the Turkish dead on their tombstones and had just watched the exodus to Turkey of 320,000 or one third of their Turkish citizens.

The filming stopped. The hubbub died down. I stared at the objects on display, kneeling to get as close as possible. The treasure had indeed belonged to Kubrat – this was the name deciphered on a pair of rings with incised monograms. But Kubrat *was not a Bulgar* – an item of information which I kept to myself. He was the ruler of the Unugundurs, a rival Turkish people, who became a staunch ally of the East Roman Emperor Heraclius in the 630s and helped him destabilise the empire's chief enemy in Europe, the Turkish Avars. Kubrat cemented the alliance by converting to Christianity, a fact attested by his ownership of a large silver plate with a huge *chi-ro* inlaid in gold.

The treasure includes a few rather impressive pieces: a sword with a gold hilt and scabbard, both once inlaid with jewels or cut glass; a massive gold jar with two handles in the form of open-mouthed fish – the body of the jar is decorated by three narrow bands of restrained, mainly vegetal decoration; a silver ribbed jug and scalloped bowl which belong together (for washing at table), both made in Byzantium in the reign of Maurice (582–602) – the handle of the jug consists of a long, sinuous, dragon-like creature, with a markedly Oriental look; and the large silver plate with the *chi-ro*, also made in Byzantium but at a slightly later date (in

244

the last decade or so of the reign (610–41) of Heraclius, Kubrat's ally).

There are some twenty other items, but most look rather tawdry by comparison. Their fabric is flimsy, the decoration plain, the workmanship slipshod. Two gold cups have ridiculously small handles. A gold sceptre ends in a perfectly plain bald pate. A drinking horn is decorated with thin beading. Khan Kubrat seems to have struggled to amass a decent collection of plate. It is poor stuff compared to the fine pieces which percolated into remote recesses of the empire of the Turks, the great eastern neighbour of Unugundurs and the Bulgars which was imploding and disintegrating at this time (the 630s) – these pieces are preserved in various Soviet museums; poor too compared to the Sevso Treasure, which I suspect *was* Bulgar, belonging perhaps to the leader of the first great Bulgar uprising against the Avars which took place around 630. The Sevso Treasure consists of fourteen older Roman silver objects, of impressive dimensions and weight, produced by several workshops to the highest standard of craftsmanship. It was, on my wild surmise, put together by a Bulgar tribal chief who loyally served the Hun cause in eastern Europe in the first half of the fifth century and buried by a distant descendant in the mid-seventh-century crisis of the nomad world. The worn appearance of the objects shows that they were handled over a long period. If I am right and it is a Bulgar treasure, there was a huge disparity in wealth and, probably, in standing between the Bulgar and Unugundur leaderships in the early seventh century. In which case it should cause no surprise that the former prevailed and established two states at either end of the Unugundur territory in the South Russian steppes, on the middle Volga and in north-east Bulgaria, and that these states both survived as great regional powers for several centuries, while the Unugundurs vanished from the historical record, so much so that scholars now deny their separate existence and conflate them with their victorious rivals, the Bulgars.

Back in the hotel room I found Nigel sorting through his possessions. He had woken earlier from his deep sleep and had made a foray into the city. There he encountered a black-

245

market currency dealer. The dealer offered him four times the official rate for fifty marks; he was very nervous and trembled as he counted out 400 lev in Bulgarian notes. Nigel politely refrained from looking closely at the notes, until the dealer was gone – only to discover that he had been swindled and that the denomination of the notes was a quarter of what he had supposed and that he had his lev at the official rate of 1:1 mark.

He had also found a hairdresser and was now off to keep the appointment which he had made. He returned transformed. He had become a high-ranking *apparatchik*. He had had the *nomenklatura* tonsure – hair cut quite short, and then carefully arranged in a barber's equivalent of the planned economy. The force of gravity was defied – all the strands ran *horizontally* back from the temples; the natural exuberance of hair, its disorderliness and untidiness, had been ruthlessly repressed by the application of *fixer* in large quantities; this fixer also gave it a new steel–silvery glow; at the back – and this was the barber's chef d'oeuvre – the two horizontal swathes dovetailed into a single neat vertical seam. It was a perfect socialistic head. Awe at the new Bulgarian *arkadaş* overcame me – but did not prevent me from seizing a camera, brushing all objections aside and taking some photographs, before Nigel himself set about vainly trying to dishevel his head.

21 September (Sofia)

We had no sooner woken up than we were hurrying to call on a diplomat. He was going to be occupied for the rest of our stay with important visitors. So Nigel, the TV mogul, and his academic sidekick could only be fitted in first thing that morning. The diplomat was extraordinarily courteous to the self-invited callers. He was taking a close interest in the state of the Bulgarian economy, which, he said, his new allies among the East European diplomats in Sofia claimed was worse off than Poland's. The foreign debt at $10 billion was as high *per capita* as Poland's but had been amassed in a shorter period (since 1984) and would take far longer to pay off . . .

We bade him goodbye and walked back to the centre to find breakfast. Everyone still looked smart and cheerful. But there was something false about the smartness. The women looked as if they had dressed up in their finest for their venture into the centre of the city. The young men's jeans on closer inspection were inferior East European imitations. The animation was slightly artificial. There were beggars wandering about – four padded quietly among the tables of our café asking for money while Nigel ate a cream cake and I drank coffee. The sentries guarding Georgi Dmitrov's mausoleum were as smart as ever when we passed by, but they were fidgeting. The shop windows were full but now we saw a film of dust covering the gramophones, radios, television sets on display – and a certain sameness in the design of items offered for sale. The most popular shops were Soviet bookshops. The young men were crowding in to get hold of the latest products of *glasnost* (not much of that in Bulgaria) or to buy *Moscow News*. The old ally and patron was now pumping dissident ideas into Bulgaria through all these official outlets. We felt a momentary pang for old Todor Zhivkov, the longest-serving Communist leader, who must have viewed all of this as a nightmare, hoping to wake up before too long and find that once again the mainstay of Bulgaria had returned to orthodox repressive policies . . . Nigel began elaborating the plot of his thriller set in Istanbul and the Hotel Bulgaria, which would revolve around Zhivkov's plot to assassinate Gorbachev . . .

I telephoned Dmitri Obolensky's new Bulgarian friend, Elena Velkovska. She offered to show us round the Ivan Dujčev Centre, a medieval historical institute on the outskirts of Sofia. The taxidriver had difficulty finding it. It is in the middle of a residential district just inside the bypass. The houses are quite substantial, set in their own gardens, but the streets are not made up. The centre is tacked onto Dujčev's house. Dujčev, who died a few years ago, was a distinguished medievalist. He never kowtowed to the regime

247

and lived under a cloud much of his life. Posthumously he has been taken up by the authorities. A brand new, purpose-built institute has been grafted on to his house. It is remarkably gloomy inside. There is not enough light in the rooms to lift the pall cast by the really serious, almost antiquarian scholarship practised there, which is disconnected from teaching. Each room has a large black table, with books piled up around old-fashioned VDUs. Elena took us from room to room, introduced us to a few solemn characters who were at work during the lunch hour, showed us some manuscripts and explained the phenomenon of the institute. The director was the daughter of the Minister of Defence. So she had the influence to get the funding, including a fair amount in hard currency, which the institute needed. This was topped up by donations from abroad which had enabled them to buy a few decent computers and to increase book purchases.

My spirits lifted as we left the building. We walked to the nearest bus stop, at the end of the route. Two or three silent, expressionless people were waiting. A bus appeared and for the sum of 0.06 lev (approximately 1½p) conveyed each of us to a seedy bus junction halfway back to the city centre. We took a taxi for the remainder of the journey. We asked the driver whether he knew of a place where we could hire a car for a day (to make a trip south of Sofia). He took us to a run-down yard in a rural part of Sofia. Oldish cars were dotted about. A man came out of a hut. No, he said, he could only rent out cars to Bulgarians. We drove off and asked our driver whether he would take us. He was keen but already booked for the following day. So an alternative was found over the radio – a reliable character presumably who would watch the foreigners.

It was three. We were famished. We ate thick slices of tinned ham with bread and mustard in the cavernous bar of the Grand Hotel Bulgaria. Large glasses of beer were downed. Elena talked freely. No communist believes *with his mind*, she said, but she saw no prospect of change and no point in dissident activity. She was depressed and resigned to the status quo, and simply wanted to get out herself.

Back to the National History Museum. At Nigel's insist-

248

ence, we searched for the section displaying the glories of Communism in Bulgaria. Nowhere was it to be found. It was explained to us that the lawyers, who had resisted bitterly the plan to take over their building for the museum, were still hanging onto the second floor where the History of Capitalism and Socialism was scheduled to go. So 'it did not exist'. Back downstairs we went, to the main antique and medieval collection. That is exactly what it was – a *collection* of choice pieces, torn away from their sites and indeed the company of other artefacts from the same site (which have been left in the Archeological Museum) and arranged without regard either to chronology or geography. It was dementing to anyone with a serious interest in Bulgaria's history – it represented an ignorant, barbarous attitude to the past, the same attitude as underlay the order to reconstruct two of the great monuments of early medieval Bulgaria ten years earlier – the throne palace at Pliska, which was about to be rebuilt out of huge ancient grey blocks and startlingly white modern ones when I was there in 1979, and the spanking new concrete version of the round church which was rising then at Preslav.

After booking us into a popular Italian restaurant for the unearthly hour of seven, Elena left us. In the main ceremonial square in front of Georgi Dmitrov's mausoleum, a youth parade of some sort was being rehearsed. The children shuffled about out of step. Large ladies tried in vain to direct things better. There was a general air of listlessness. No one wore uniform. There were piles of clothes on the edge of the parade area.

Soon it was time for dinner at the Red Flag Restaurant. There was a table for us. It was the first Italian restaurant we had seen without any Italians working in it. The food was glutinous. The tables, far from huddling together, were separated by large empty spaces as in the most expensive restaurants of the West. The head waiter fascinated Nigel. He stood on the edge of the larger eating area, with nothing to do. He had worked his way up to the top. He had status. He had power. Now he leaned against an upright piano with his eyes half shut and a thin half-smile on his face. He had nothing to do and he was bored out of his mind, save for one moment when he suddenly rushed eagerly to pick up a dropped napkin. Nigel imagined his life. When we gave him a handshake as we left, after one of the worst meals in our travels, a broad smile momentarily lit up his face.

It was dark outside. A figure materialised out of the shadows. You were on the bus this morning, he said. The faintest of recognition came to me – and deep suspicion. He offered to show us round Sofia. Nigel, showing considerably more enthusiasm than I, asked what would he recommend. The Palace of Culture, said he. So off we went with Edward Krustev and a silent friend who spoke no English and little Bulgarian.

It was a kilometre or so to the Palace of Culture – a massive, modern conference hall which stands in the middle of a large, formal park. To our right as we approached it we saw a huge monument commemorating the thirteenth centenary of the founding of the Bulgarian state. 681–1944–1981 were the key dates, their huge digits impressed on the bronze panels affixed to its sides. Socialist realist figures in deep relief and short political slogans form the main decoration. But some of the panels had fallen off, exposing blank rectangular spaces of concrete – *and no one had done anything about putting them back*. That suggested extraordinary sloppiness in the apparatus or a loss of interest in two of the great achievements of communism – the seizure of power over the present in 1944 and its exercise over the past in 1981.

Lights were on inside the Palace of Culture. But there was no possibility of visiting it. It was reserved for conferences, concerts and so forth. Krustev took us to the concourse below. He and his friends, in their late teens or very early twenties, were drawn there at least twice a week. They spent huge sums by Bulgarian standards at the smart café or discotheque. In Krustev's case, the money was supplied by his father who earned five or six times as much from driving a minibus-taxi as he could from his profession as a mechanical engineer. The soft piped music, low lighting, marble paving and wall revetment, glinting dark water in the basin – all these seemed to be pieces of an unimaginably remote West transposed to the heart of Sofia. Krustev wanted to leave and work in Germany. Most of the young, he told us, were apathetic. Was he an *agent provocateur*? I wondered. Surely he was now going rather too far? A second friend of his joined us. Yes, said Krustev, they all saw a gloomy future ahead. Bulgaria was in decline. They knew that but they were trapped, far from the West and without the knowledge of languages to work in the West. My suspicions were gradually being allayed but I remained non-committal. Krustev was a large, strapping young man. He spoke earnestly, a serious smile occasionally breaking out. He obviously did retain hopes for himself. *He* knew English. *He* was determined to get out. His silent friend though, who was several years younger, still had to do his military service. What was that like? we asked. Krustev replied 'horrible' and would not go into detail. His friend had opted to spend five years working in an engine factory twenty kilometres from Sofia rather than do two years in the army.

They accompanied us back to the central area, outside the Balkan Sheraton Hotel. Next door, a red star glowed on a tall spike high above the Central Committee building. Nigel shuddered as he remembered his days of National Service in the Brigade of Guards – his had been the only face without a moustache. We walked back. Sentries armed to the teeth were guarding all government buildings. Strange. Was Zhivkov losing confidence, in spite of his grip over the whole apparatus?

22 *September (Sofia–Kjustendil)*

The taxi picked us up outside the Sofia Hotel. The driver had a long narrow face, the skin pitted, the eyes small and uncommunicative. A suppressed emotion – was it impatience, resentment of the foreigners, suspicion or merely boredom? – seemed to lurk behind his occasional clipped replies.

As we drove south over the pass which squeezes through between Mount Vitoşa and the ranges to the west, I held myself very still and upright – to control a turbulence in the stomach caused by the Red Flag Restaurant. Elena and Nigel chatted away in the back, heedless of bugs. The countryside opened out into a fertile valley. The geometrical shapes of factory buildings, storage tanks, angled conveyor belts and chimneys stood out sharply against the luminous green – a Lowryesque scene, but without the pervading greyness and drabness of a northern land.

Then we came down into the huge, enclosed plain of Kjustendil. This is some fifty kilometres or so south west of Sofia. At a lower elevation and sheltered on all sides by encircling hills, it is one of the richest of all the upland basins of the Balkan interior. Under the Turks it produced grain and fruit in abundance. Its plums were famed throughout the Mediterranean. Its other great resource was the hot springs at Kjustendil itself, which was developed into a small, neat spa town. Once only, in the very distant past, was Kjustendil headline news. The year was 479. The Ostrogoths, at that stage one of two rival Gothic groupings in the Balkans, were retreating west along the main east–west road and had reached Macedonia (south-west of Kjustendil). They had antagonised their rivals, the Thracian Goths in the north-east, by collaborating with the Romans, then alienated the Romans by changing sides just before the start of a planned joint attack on their rivals. A tempting offer came from the Roman authorities – Pautalia, ancient Kjustendil, and its rich plain would be theirs for settlement and cultivation, if they would submit and agree to a long-term military deal (to supply contingents to serve with the Roman armies). It did not take long for Theoderic, their commander, to recognise the trap and break off negotiations. Pautalia and its plain might look like a miniature paradise, where the Goths, travelling now with a huge wagon train (one column alone numbered 2,000 vehicles and carried over 5,000 people, when it fell into Roman hands later), could lead a relaxed life in the midst of plenty, defended on all sides by a natural highland rampart. But Roman roads, the railway tracks of late antiquity, punctured that rampart on three sides. Concerted thrusts along them would be hard to counter, and, in the long run, isolated

and vulnerable, the Ostrogoths would become pliant creatures of the Romans. Theoderic opted for a very different,
though riskier future. He continued the march to the west,
holed up for a number of years in Epirus (modern Albania)
which he turned into a Gothic redoubt, manoeuvred success-
fully against both Romans and Thracian Goths, restored his
prestige, enlarged his following, and finally, late in 488, set
off to establish a kingdom in Italy.

Kjustendil was a shabby, derelict place. The general
impression was that of a shanty town, loosely gathered
around a few more imposing buildings. An administrative
building was fronted by a large square. Preparations were
being made for a parade. Hoses played upon the tarmac. A
few flags hung limply from poles placed around it. A large
concrete store presented a meagre display of children's toys
and cushions behind one huge plate-glass window. Another
department had thrown in the towel and drawn down a
series of vertical slats behind their window. Tough-looking
women were working with a will, washing and wiping the
windows. Ill-dressed people, many of the men unshaven,
moved about lethargically. A few stalls were selling wizened
vegetables.

We made our way to the main thermal spring. A large
Roman bath complex once occupied the site. The water which
issues out at a temperature of 75°F circulated round a system
of vaulted channels under the floor – some of which have
been excavated. A mosque, now converted into a small
museum, attests Turkish interest in the waters. So too does
a low, yellow-stuccoed building with large windows, dating
from the nineteenth century. It it no longer in use. The
garden in which it stands is unkempt. The hot water, foul-
smelling with its rich mineral cocktail, bubbles up inside a
concrete hut. The steam billows out of a small square
window, between rusting iron bars. There is another smaller
outlet on the far side of the town, stopped up by a concrete
slab. The steam forces its way out around the edges. A single
tap nearby is used by locals to fill buckets with the water.
Otherwise no use whatsoever is made of it. Except for two
mosques (the second was disused but in quite good con-

dition) and a few out-of-place nineteenth-century buildings with gay stucco exteriors, Kjustendil was a depressed and depressing place. The inhabitants could not leave. As in the Soviet Union, there was a system of internal passports. All those born in Kjustendil were tied to it except for daytrips and holidays, unless they had skills required elsewhere (or influence). They had become the prisoners of local party bosses who were clearly incompetent or geriatric and had failed to fight for a fair share of commodities for them. Only wood seemed in plentiful supply. It was being delivered by horse-drawn carts, in preparation for the winter ahead.

It was with relief that we left to visit the remains of a late Roman fortress standing on a hillside above the town. A pine forest has grown up around it. There is no modern building in sight. A notice gives a plan of the site – which only a moment's glance at the remains shows is wildly inaccurate. I scrambled about, making a rough sketch, taking photographs. Nigel and Elena talked and waited for me.

We then cut south-east back to the main Strymon valley, had tough *shish kebabs* in a transport café, and drove up a long narrow valley to Rila monastery, under towering mountains. Three tiers of light, airy cloisters look inward over a large, irregularly-shaped courtyard. Two churches, with garish frescoes, stand in the courtyard. The Orthodox Church, Nigel remarked later, like Hollywood, cannot bear to leave any space ungarnished. The treasures of the monastery include a giant votive candle presented by the Sultan Mehmet II, a chocolate-brown wooden cross with the most intricate fretwork imaginable, elaborate Russian silver crosses with inset brown or ochre plaques of biblical or hagiographical scenes, and a three-dimensional Easter cloth with painted soft toys representing St John of Rila and Christ.

Back in Sofia, the driver, who had thawed a bit in the course of the day, dropped us in the main square. We paid him off and told him to take Elena home. We rushed to the Archeological Museum which was closing in half an hour. Back in the hotel and feeling famished, I suggested that we find some food. So we went to the bar for more sliced ham, mustard and bread. Nigel's appetite deserted him. After a while a look of horror suddenly spread over his face. Where was his wallet? Where was his passport? He who spent so much time checking and rechecking his possessions must have left them in the taxi. My advice to remain calm and think fell on deaf ears. He ran back to the room frantic. He had to catch the plane the next day, if he was to make the board meeting he was supposed to chair in London. His attendance was vital. Then there was the thought of several more days' enforced stay in Bulgaria, in the sham brightness of Sofia. Large slugs of whisky had no noticeable calming effect, until he telephoned Elena and she told him that she had rescued the Turkish condom-bag containing his missing essentials from the taxi.

He went off for a drink with Elena in the flat which she shared with her parents. Pleading a still disturbed stomach, I downed my last ever whisky nightcap and went to sleep. And dreamed about a Roman arena, an underground space where I saw black coffin-like boxes, a cricket pitch watched by seated figures and Roman busts . . .

23 September (Sofia–London)

Nigel packed and repacked three times, paled when our taxi did not appear on time, but then cheered himself up with slugs of whisky. The plot of his Bulgarian thriller thickened minute by minute. A beautiful, hyper-intelligent Bulgarian girl now joined an American evangelist in the cast of characters. Scenes would be set at the Yeşil Ev, in Erzurum and in Kjustendil, as well as the grand old hotels we had visited. We drove down the motorway to Plovdiv in a rather superior bus. Tomato-pickers with plastic buckets (the latter adding impressionistic primary colours to the scene) were at work in the fields. Nigel reminisced about the days when he translated Simenon, Auguste le Breton and Guides Bleus (on Turkey and Spain) to keep body and soul together when he was starving as a Reuters trainee in London. His fingers were itching to get at the portable processor once it had slipped through customs and on to the plane. We parted on board, Nigel's ticket being first class. He had kept hold of the whisky bottle and drained it, saying the two As – ALCOHOL and ALTITUDE – enabled an author really to 'harpoon his script'. My neighbour, a manufacturer of knitting machines which make glittery patterned jerseys and cardigans, told me about his successful negotiations and showed me the contract he had won.

We could scarcely move. No airline has ever packed so many seats into so small a space as Balkan Airlines on its flights to London. First-class passengers, though, wallowed in space. Nigel's fingers raced over the keyboard. Page after page went in. He returned to report on progress every now and again. By the time we reached London, he had joined the cast of his characters. I was dazed from the cramped flight and immersed in my latest *arkadaş'* life as a salesman, in search of customers for his machines, travelling across the one-time territory of Byzantium and its commonwealth. Neither Nigel nor I took in the fact that we were home nor that we had already gone off on our separate ways.

POSTSCRIPT: THE GREAT
BULGARIAN PLOT

Bulgarian hardliners are plotting to assassinate President Gorbachev during a visit to Sofia so as to sabotage *perestroika* and bring back the old guard in the Kremlin. By chance a brilliant young Oxford historian, Doctor John Howard-Jameson, has arranged to be in Bulgaria at the same time to study Byzantine cryptography.

A knitting-machine salesman, who turns out to be an MI6 computer expert, gets wind of the plot when he is called in by the Sofia CIA station chief to investigate a new top-secret communications channel discovered during routine electronic surveillance. The knitting-machine salesman flies to Istanbul to report his findings to the CIA regional chief, a Turkish-American called Bora who speaks with a Brooklyn accent. One of Bora's sources is Madame Celeste – known to her clients as Aunt Celeste – who operates a network of high-class brothels and Turkish baths as a cover for intelligence gathering. The agents have a rendezvous at the Yeşil Ev, one of the Madame's more exotic houses. But before the knitting-machine salesman can hand over the evidence he is strangled by the black-bearded pianist who turns out to be a Bulgarian Secret Service assassin.

Meanwhile in a Sofia hotel bedroom a born-again preacher from the US Bible Belt is being led astray. Through the window we can see the Red Star surmounting the Parliament building, and the two sentries in dress uniform in the square below guarding the tomb of Bulgaria's national hero. The heavy Cold War decor has the unmistakable hallmark of the Hotel Bulgaria. Hidden cameras record the preacher's clumsy attempts to make a pass at a raven-haired beauty called Irina who has been promised a passport to study Byzantine history at Oxford in exchange for acting as his interpreter. Both think he has been invited to Bulgaria as a gesture of religious freedom in the name of *perestroika*. In reality he is being framed. The plan is to blackmail him into carrying certain documents which will point the finger at the born-again movement, backed by forty million Americans and known to oppose all dealings with the Anti-Christ, whether Lenin or Gorbachev. Following the assassination, by the time the world's intelligence agencies have unravelled the truth hardliners will have re-established themselves irreversibly in the Kremlin.

In the Turkish baths at Erzurum in Eastern Turkey a fanatical group of right-wing army officers, known as Kemal Ataturk Patriots, hold a clandestine meeting. Outside the building is a statue of the Father of the Nation in visionary posture. The KAP has formed an unholy alliance with the Bulgarian hardliners. They, too, want the destruction of *perestroika*, believing it will cause millions of Soviet Moslems to rise up and unite with Iranian and Turkish Moslems in a movement to create a Moslem Greater Turkestan. This would put paid to the Ataturk dream of a secular westernised state: a death blow by fez against flatcap. Their part in the plot will be to arrest the preacher in Turkey and plant clues leading to shadowy right-wing American pressure groups. This will cause an immediate resumption of the Cold War and stop the Moslem threat in its tracks. One of the group is a banker called Kemal Ozkent, who reports that he already has massive financial support from the US arms lobby which has a stake in perpetuating the arms race.

Eavesdropping on their talk is a muscular masseur. He relays everything back to Aunt Celeste.

On his way to Sofia John Howard-Jameson is stopping off for two nights in Istanbul. He is staying with a former undergraduate friend, Kemal Ozkent. Kemal is at the airport to meet him. His English education has left its mark in the shape of a blue blazer with brass buttons and a set of stock Anglophile responses that make the Scholar feel uncomfortable. Kemal explains that he is a grass widow, as his wife is away with the children, so he has plans to paint the town red with his old chum. Grinning hugely he sweeps the shrinking Scholar off to have a drink at the Yeşil Ev hotel. He orders Scotch. The Scholar drinks water from a bottle he has brought with him from London. Kemal tells the Scholar he knows someone who can lay on a really good time. He asks a waiter if Madame Celeste has been in this evening. At that moment she appears.

Madame Celeste knows more about Kemal than he does about her. His activities in Erzurum have been reported to her. He knows her for her skills in providing professional services. She knows him for his weaknesses: sex – and a loud mouth when drunk. She orders a box of After Eight chocolates for herself, more whisky for him. She encourages him to talk.

The Scholar is surprised at how right-wing his former fellow undergraduate has become. Kemal explains that he has seen the light, that western nations must remain strong, the old school must fight and not surrender to chaos. The West is better off in a Cold War world it knows and largely controls than in a freer world with a sudden change in the balance of power, new destabilising forces unleashed by the break-up of the Soviet Empire, the risk of a fundamentalist Islam annexing millions of restless Soviet Moslems, the danger of a reunited Germany – all with unpredictable repercussions not under American control. He boasts that he has played his part for the Cause, bringing to bear powerful interests he is not at liberty to disclose – people he met recently in Washington and whom he is meeting next day. He drops heavy hints about Gorbachev's days being numbered and plans to change the course of history, sooner than you think . . .

259

Kemal is tight. It is too late to paint the town. The Scholar's virtue is unscathed. Madame Celeste has information to pass to Bora – the American arms lobby has arrived in town.

Howard-Jameson arrives at the Bulgaria to find his appointed research assistant and guide, the beautiful Irina, in a distracted state. During a visit to the medieval monastery at Rila she pours out her heart to him. Having rejected the advances of the preacher her passport is to be withheld unless she complies with new demands. While she thought she was helping restore religious freedom she now finds she has been a party to a plot to do something terrible to President Gorbachev, due next day. While she was being interviewed she saw a document on which was a list of names – all known hardliners with a stake in destroying *perestroika*. She has it with her. Suddenly Ozkent's drunken indiscretions take on a new and sinister meaning. The dreadful truth dawns. A heavy summons lies upon him. His choice is between Byzantine cryptography and the fate of the western world. The struggle lasts only a moment. His duty is clear. Moreover, at any moment the girl may be arrested. Meanwhile, an emotion new to him has dawned.

Irina's inquisitors have assured her there is no future in appealing to the Americans. Apart from the certainty of arrest, there is a new and more understanding CIA chief, who won't believe her. The Scholar senses the shadowy presence of unseen powers, the arms lobby, hardliners of the CIA as well as the KGB. The only chance to avert catastrophe and save the girl is to get to the West where he is confident of being listened to and where the plot can be blown. He must throw caution to the winds.

Train and air travel are out of the question. The pair find a tourist bus about to leave the monastery heading south, towards the frontier with Turkey. Mingling with a crowd of trippers, they smuggle themselves aboard. The Scholar is embarrassed by a small man who has been to Birmingham and wants to talk to him in English. Night falls. Becoming drowsy, the driver slows up. Fearing secret police cars are on their tracks, the Scholar steps forward to urge the driver on. In vain: the driver stops. Everyone gets out to stretch their legs. Only the Scholar and the girl stay behind. Inside the coach an intercom radio crackles. In a split-second decision the Scholar seizes the wheel and drives off, leaving the other passengers standing.

In Sofia frantic orders are being given to all police units to arrest the pair. The last known position of the bus is broadcast on the public radio with an appeal to anyone spotting it to tell the police. The girl translates. The broadcast is being picked up elsewhere as well. In his office Bora is handed a transcript. He calls for a map. After a moment's thought he asks to be put through urgently to Madame Celeste.

Short of the frontier, the Scholar and the girl abandon the coach and walk. They have no plan. But they have no choice either.

As they approach the forbidding barrier, an astonishing spectacle meets their eyes. A coach load of girls, scantily dressed and apparently drunk, are shrieking and teasing the night shift of bewildered frontier guards. Deafening pop music blasting from loudspeakers on board the coach drowns the angry and confused orders of an officer in charge. As the pair gape incredulously in the darkness strong hands seize them and pull them to a gap in the wire. An urgent voice says: 'Diversionary tactics. Move it!' A moment later they are sprinting across no-man's-land.

They reach a road. Waiting for them is a man. Speaking with a Brooklyn accent, he says:

'Welcome to Turkey'. For once in his life the Scholar is lost for words.

'Well, thank you . . .'

Bora's voice replies: 'Don't thank me. Thank Aunt Celeste.' As he is talking the coach draws up. On one side is painted in large letters:

AUNT CELESTE'S ALL–GIRLS DANCING TROUPE

On the other:

THE DAUGHTERS OF CELESTIAL LIGHT

261

As I finished writing London's roofs had begun to appear through the clouds like a hangover breaking into sleep. I went into the economy class to see how the hero of my drama was coping with real life. I found the Scholar folded like a penknife into his narrow seat, reprimanding the passenger in front of him for smoking after the no-smoking sign had been put on.

'Reckless risk to human life . . .'

He might have been addressing John Howard-Jameson. Even so, it had been heady stuff.

The date was 23 September 1989. I put the Great Bulgarian Plot in a drawer at home and forgot about it. Meanwhile I dined out on the confident prediction, based on observation, that some Eastern European regimes might well not last out the century. Not Bulgaria, perhaps, but maybe Poland or Hungary . . .

By Christmas the face of Europe was transformed.